GUNSHIP PILOT

An Attack Helicopter Warrior
Remembers Vietnam

ROBERT F. HARTLEY

LifeRich Publishing is a registered trademark of The Reader's Digest Association, Inc.

LifeRich Publishing books may be ordered through booksellers or by contacting:

LifeRich Publishing
1663 Liberty Drive
Bloomington, IN 47403
www.liferichpublishing.com
1 (888) 238-8637

Because of the dynamic nature of the Internet, any web addresses or links contained in this book may have changed since publication and may no longer be valid. The views expressed in this work are solely those of the author and do not necessarily reflect the views of the publisher, and the publisher hereby disclaims any responsibility for them.

Any people depicted in stock imagery provided by Thinkstock are models, and such images are being used for illustrative purposes only. Certain stock imagery © Thinkstock.

ISBN: 978-1-4897-0394-1 (sc)
ISBN: 978-1-4897-0393-4 (hc)
ISBN: 978-1-4897-0395-8 (e)

Library of Congress Control Number: 2015900427

Print information available on the last page.

LifeRich Publishing rev. date: 2/24/2015

CONTENTS

DEDICATION

To my grandchildren Christian, Rachael, Ethan and Kaitlyn

FOREWORD

Of the 11,827 helicopters shipped to Vietnam, more than 5,086 were destroyed in that beautiful but hostile countryside. Likely most of the more than seven million hours of flight time, was accrued by transportation type helicopters hauling food, water, ammunition, mail, soldiers and medical supplies. Not so for a Gunship pilot. Always on strip alert! Always in the fight when called, diverted to an even more dire fight as a blanket call for gunships meant soldiers (usually small unit Special Forces Teams) were outnumbered and fighting for their lives! They were just a voice on the radio, but a helicopter gunship pilot would give everything to save them. The successes were sweet, the failures are haunting!

Like Bob, I was a young Warrant Officer flying UH-1C "Charlie" Model Helicopter Gunships and then AH-1G Cobras. Unlike Bob, I was in the Air Cavalry. The mission was different but many of the memories are the same. Camp Evans, the A Shau Valley, the lush mountain valleys, clear blue South China Sea, the "craters of the moon" and the "enemies safe haven" beyond. Strip Alert; hours of boredom, feelings of dread when called to venture, vastly outnumbered, into a known enemy stronghold, the moments of terror as enemy gunfire shredded your aircraft and the uncertainty of nursing a wounded bird and crew to where the "good guys" lived.

I've known Bob Hartley for close to forty years, in and out of the Army and all after his tours in Vietnam. Over the years we shared a few war stories, but mostly talked of family, hunting and fishing. As I read Bob's book, I was in Vietnam, in the cockpit with him. You'll be there too! Bob's memories and writing style will take you there.

So, climb aboard, strap in and prepare yourself for an exhilarating ride through the not so friendly skies of Vietnam with Bob Hartley as your guide!

Warning: A Helicopter Gunship Flight can be frightening, humorous, depressing and most certainly exciting, but on this trip neither lethal nor fatal.

Robert (Bob) Mitchell   October 2014
Colonel, US Army (Retired)
AH-1S Cobra Platoon Leader C 7/17 Cav - CPT
AH-1S Cobra Troop Commander B 7/17 Cav - MAJ
AH-64A Apache Squadron Commander 3/6 Cav - LTC
AH-64D Apache Longbow TRADOC Systems Manager - COL

PREFACE

This book is about my life as an attack helicopter pilot during two tours of duty during the Vietnam war. While many combat veterans do not like to talk about what they did during wartime, I felt that I needed to pass along what I learned so that others following in my footsteps could avoid some of the dangers and mistakes that I encountered. As an instructor pilot in the Cobra, I would often use a "War Story" to illustrate a teaching point to my students. After the war, I had several of my former students tell me that my "War Stories" had helped them during their combat tours and may have even saved their lives. Endorsements like that only encouraged me to keep telling my stories.

All the stories contained herein are from my memory. I did not keep a journal of any kind but did refer to copies of my military records to confirm certain dates, flight hours and other assorted data. While many of you may be skeptical that I can remember details from 46 years ago, let me assure you that the facts of these stories are chiseled into my memory like the names on a tombstone. My wife, Nancy, finds it difficult to believe that I can remember these events from so long ago but that I can't remember to take out the trash. Many psychologists call life changing experiences "Significant Emotional Events" and say that these events in our lives help define who we are and that they are "hard wired" into our memory and will stay there until the day we die. While most people only have a few of these events in their lives, I have had many and am sharing them with you in this book. By the way, taking out the trash is usually not considered a "Significant Emotional Event."

Now for the big caveat. While these are MY memories, others that were present for some of the events described herein, may remember things slightly differently. This is perfectly normal and, in fact, expected. During my time in the Army, I attended an aircraft accident investigation course. One of the first things they tell you is that "eye witnesses" are totally unreliable sources of information on what happened. This is not because they are purposely trying to mislead the investigators but simply because they are human and each has their own biases, prejudices, a need to logically order things when there is no order, and simply, a lack of knowledge to understand what they have just observed. In an experiment to prove this, investigators staged an "accident" and asked each of the 30 "eyewitnesses" individually, "What happened?" They got 30 different answers. And so, I ask my fellow warriors who may have been present during some of these stories to keep this in mind if you remember things differently from your point of view.

I think it is important for you, the reader, to know that my main motivation for the things I did was to save as many American lives as possible by effectively using the tools and training I was given. I have no regrets. I must also state that I have no remaining animosity toward and do, in fact, respect the enemy soldiers I faced during the war. Most of them were professionals trying to do their job and acted accordingly but those that perpetrated terrorism on the local civilian populous and captured soldiers should rot in Hell for eternity.

I think you will find my stories interesting, enlightening and sometimes amusing. I have tried to limit the graphic descriptions of blood and gore as much as possible but this is a book about war and some verbal pictures were necessary to tell the story.

Over the years, many people that I've told my stories to would often comment that, "You should write a book!" So, here it is.

ACKNOWLEDGMENTS

First and foremost I wish to thank my wife, Nancy. Without her patience, understanding and encouragement, this project would never have happened. She has been my traveling companion down the road of life and has been by my side as we have survived the many bumps and potholes in that road. She has endured my repeated retelling of most of these stories with tolerance, serenity and a great sense of humor. Thank you, dear!

I would also like to thank my friend and former crew chief, Russ Warriner, for being a pathfinder and showing me the way. When he published his book, "Empty Tubes and Backseat Memories" he encouraged me to write this book by saying, "If I can do it, you can do it." Thanks, Russ.

I met Jerry Guerrein at my local gym a few years ago. It was just before the Kentucky Derby and several other guys were discussing what type of liquor was used to make a Mint Julep. I chimed in and said, "It's bourbon." Jerry immediately backed me up saying, "Yeah! It's bourbon." As I turned to him to thank him for his support, I noticed he had on an "ARMY" T-shirt. He confirmed he had been in the Army when I asked about his shirt, so, I asked what he had done in the Army. He told me he was a helicopter pilot and flew CH-47 Chinooks. Recovering from my surprise, I told him I flew gunships and at that point he said, "We probably know some of the same people." I thought the chances were pretty remote but he persisted by mentioning a name. I told him I did not know that person but he went on. "How about Fred Santoro?" he asked and I just about fell off the bench I was on. Fred is one of my best friends from the Army. After recovering from my shock, Jerry and I continued to compare notes and have been good friends ever since. This coincidence, coupled with the one I detail in the chapter, "Figure the Odds", makes the whole story even stranger.

Over the years, Jerry has encouraged, cajoled, prodded and inspired me to move forward with this book. I am indebted to him for his persistence and friendship. Thanks, Jerry.

I must thank the following friends and family members for the encouragement, enthusiasm and excitement they shared with me while I labored on this project. These include, my children, Rob, Kim and Kris; my sister-in-law, Dr. Joyce Romano; my friends Bob and Marilyn Mitchell, Margie Black, Beth and Catherine Carpenter, Terri and Steve Ballard, Gary Lampe and Renee Green. Thanks to you all!

I must also express my gratitude to Robert S. Maxham, Director, United States Army Aviation Museum, Fort Rucker, Alabama for providing some of the photos presented herein.

I owe a profound debt of gratitude to Dr. David Romano, my brother-in-law, and Dr. William L. Mills, my family physician for their advice and council on dealing with PTSD. Both recommended and encouraged me to write this book as a way to exorcise the ghosts that stomped around in my brain every night bumping into things and waking me up. So far, it has been working well and I have been sleeping better. Thank you, gentlemen.

And finally, I would like to thank you, the reader, for taking my assembled ghosts home with you and giving them a new residence on your bookshelf. Thank you all very much.

CHAPTER 1

How Did I Get Here?

They were just little puffy white clouds. They looked innocent enough, but I had to wonder why they were suddenly appearing at our altitude and directly in front of our aircraft. I was in the right pilot's seat of a UH-1B model Huey helicopter gunship. I was on my first combat mission in Vietnam and we were flying over the A Shau Valley, a place that would soon be known as The Valley of the Shadow of Death. In the left seat, flying the aircraft, was my platoon leader, Captain Dave Whitling. We were looking down into the valley, trying to locate a flight of ten Hueys that were carrying troops to be inserted into a nearby landing zone (LZ). We were to join up on their flight and provide gun cover for them as they landed their troops in the LZ. Captain Whitling and I were both trying to find those lift ships, when I noticed something out of the corner of my eye, towards the front of the aircraft. As I looked up I saw a white puffy cloud, just out in front of our aircraft. I thought, "That's odd, that wasn't there a minute ago."

While I was still looking at the cloud that we were about to pass, I saw a bright orange flash surrounded by black smoke directly in front us and it quickly turned into a white puffy cloud. I could barely contain myself as I fumbled with the button to active my microphone to tell

1

Captain Whitling what I had seen and to assert that we were taking flak. He was somewhat incredulous as he listened to me and as we were discussing it, he also saw a black explosion in front of the aircraft that quickly turned into a white puffy cloud. He immediately began making radio calls, advising everyone on the frequency that we were all being shot at by flak guns. It was surprising to both of us that these flak rounds, once they had exploded, would turn white, unlike all the movies we'd seen of World War II bombing missions over Germany where the flak was invariable black and stayed that way.

We immediately lowered our altitude by 500 feet to avoid the exploding flak and continued to look for the lift ships we were to escort. Suddenly, I noticed that just off our right hand side, and just coming into view from behind us, was a Chinook helicopter that was carrying an artillery howitzer. The thing that caught my attention was the extreme nose down attitude of the Chinook. As he came further into view, I noticed that the entire aft half of the Chinook was engulfed in flames. The aft rotor was the only thing sticking up out of the fireball. Apparently he had been hit in the fuel tank by one of the flak rounds and was diving to get the aircraft onto the ground as quickly as possible. As I watched, I saw little black smoking objects coming out of the tail ramp of the aircraft. After a few seconds I realized that these objects were men running out of the aircraft to get away from the flames, knowing full well, that they would be falling to their deaths. I said to Dave, "Oh my God, look at that." He replied, "Yeah, he doesn't have a tailboom." This seriously puzzled me since the Chinook is not made with a tailboom, so, I turned to see what he was talking about and saw that directly out his window, was a Huey that did not, in fact, have a tailboom and was spinning around in a death spiral on his way to the ground. At that point, I remember feeling an overwhelming sense of doom and thought, "How the Hell did I get here?"

The answer to that question starts back with my earliest memories. It must have been around 1950 or 1951 when I was about 4 or 5 years old. My parents had taken us to an airshow and I was totally in awe of the aircraft I saw there. I remember fighters, bombers and even passenger planes. As I grew up, my closest brother, Terry, and I, continued to be fascinated by all aspects of aviation. We built hundreds of plastic and balsa wood models of airplanes. We knew all the designations and nicknames of the various planes, their capabilities, flaws and some of the major battles they had fought in. A strong desire took hold of me at that time and I knew that my ultimate goal in life was to be a pilot. I also knew that to achieve that goal, I would have to do well in school, especially in math and science. I accomplished that part and graduated from Amityville Memorial High School on Long Island with a New York State Regents diploma. Things were going as planned and I was accepted to and attended Hofstra University in Hempstead, New York.

It was during the spring semester of my second year there, that the train began to come off the tracks. Money was tight and even though I worked a part time job (full time during the summers), I knew I would have to take a semester off in the fall of 1966 to accumulate enough cash to pay my way through school. In those days, there was no such thing as "Financial Aid" and I would just have to take my chances with the Draft Board.

During this same time, I was becoming more and more disenchanted with college life. Most of the professors I had did not refrain from showing their distaste for the war in Vietnam, and the current administration in Washington. My fellow students would attend "Peace Marches" and anti-war demonstrations, regularly. The thing I found most disturbing was that most of my "friends" were attending the demonstrations to "meet chicks, drink beer and smoke dope." They really didn't care about whether the war was right or wrong, as long as it didn't affect their ability to have fun. I saw that during most of the demonstrations, there were only a handful of people running the show who were really and truly committed to their message, while all the others were along for the ride and the kicks they got out of civil disobedience and the partying afterward.

One day, as I walked through the student union contemplating my situation, I passed by the unoccupied Armed Forces recruiting booth and noticed a pamphlet there that said, "High School to Flight School!"

I picked it up and learned that the Army was signing up anyone with a high school diploma for training as a helicopter pilot. To get accepted into the program, a candidate would have to pass an aviation physical exam and an aptitude test. The training would last almost a full year and if the candidate flunked out of the course, he would be released from active duty, if he wished, and would return to his previous civilian status to face his draft board's lottery. I decided to hang on to the pamphlet and see what developed over the summer.

That July, I decided to spend some of my money taking flying lessons at Zahn's Airport in Amityville. I wanted to see if, first, I really liked flying and, secondly, to decide if it was something I wanted to pursue. I started out in a Piper J-3 "Cub" and completed my first solo flight after just 8 hours of flight training. I continued the training and was awarded my private pilots license that September. By then, I was not only sure that I liked flying, but that I wanted to pursue it as a career. I contacted the Army recruiters, passed all the tests and was sworn in on January 25th, 1967.

I graduated from flight school and was appointed as a Warrant Officer in the United States Army at the end of January 1968. I had requested and was awarded additional training in the newest aircraft in the Army's inventory, the AH-1G Huey Cobra. In fact, the aircraft was so new that my instructor pilot only had 12 hours of flight time in the aircraft when we climbed in together on my first flight. It proved to be a very exciting time for both the student and the instructor. I still remember my instructor's words of encouragement today. He said, "Don't worry, we'll figure this out." Talk about the blind leading the blind.

It was during that same summer of 1966 that I met my future wife, Nancy. We dated while I was taking my flying lessons and continued to see each other right up until I left for the Army in January. We stayed in touch while I was in flight school and decided to get married in November of 1968. I only made the decision to get married once I was sure I would graduate and be appointed as an officer in the U.S. Army. My commanding officer gave me a weekend pass and told me

I had to be back for roll call first thing Monday morning, or else. We were married Saturday, had a quick reception and started driving back to Ft. Rucker, Alabama that evening. We arrived back at Ft. Rucker early Monday morning and I was present for roll call, as ordered, even though I was not very sharp during my training flight that day.

As expected, my orders, after flight school and Cobra training, were to Vietnam. After getting Nancy settled back in with her folks, I reported to the replacement detachment in Oakland, California to await a flight overseas. While I was there, I watched President Johnson on television give a major speech on the Vietnam war in which he said, "...I shall not seek, and I will not accept, the nomination of my party for another term as your President." This gave me hope that the war would soon be over and I would be back home before long. Silly me! The date was March 31, 1968 and I was scheduled to fly out the next morning, April Fools Day! Was this whole thing some kind of gigantic cosmic joke? It was starting to seem that way.

After a very long and arduous flight that included several refueling stops, we landed at Bien Hoa Air Force Base. It was a very large, sprawling complex, located just to the east of Saigon. As we stood on the ramp waiting for our bags to be unloaded, we heard the tremendous roar of jet fighters taking off and watched them as they struggled into the sky with their huge bomb loads. A few minutes later we would see the fighters returning and watched them glide in for a landing, minus the bombs. You didn't have to be a genius to know that the war wasn't very far away. In fact, as I sorted through the pile of duffel bags that had been unceremoniously dumped on the ramp, I heard a siren sounding from across the airfield. I stopped and looked around only to see all the personnel that were stationed there were running for cover. Other than us "Newbies" the ramp was deserted. As I looked around for a clue as to what to do, I saw one of the local Air Force guys lean out of his hiding place and say, "You guys should take cover, that siren means we're taking incoming." I did not see or hear any explosions nearby, so, I and the other "Newbies" went back to digging for our bags. I was beginning to wonder about these Air Force guys.

When the "all clear" was sounded, the local personnel emerged from their hiding spots and completed processing us. Six Army buses arrived to take us all over to Long Binh Junction (LBJ), about 6 miles away, to complete our in-processing. It was home to the Headquarters of the United States Army, Vietnam along with many other units including the Army's jail. The jail, appropriately enough, was called the Long Binh Jail or LBJ. I was beginning to see a trend here. You don't suppose that the man's ego was so huge that he wanted to name everything after himself, do you? Anyway, Long Binh was also a huge complex, home to about 60,000 troops, and we would be housed and fed there while we waited for our new assignments.

As we lined up to board the buses to Long Binh, I noticed that the windows of each bus were totally covered with a very heavy metal mesh. I couldn't decide if the mesh was there to keep others out or us in, so, I asked the sergeant in charge of the loading process. He explained that the mesh was there so that as we drove through the villages on our way to Long Binh, the villagers wouldn't be able to throw hand grenades in the windows. Oh! Great! I was so glad that I came here to help these people. I guess throwing flowers was out of the question.

The actual ride was quite thrilling. The six buses were escorted by two Military Police jeeps, each with a manned .50 caliber heavy machine gun that was on a mount that had been welded to the floor. Once we left the airbase, the entire convoy raced at nearly 60 miles per hours through the countryside and the small towns along the way. The horns on the buses and jeeps were being blown continuously to warn the drivers of the hundreds of scooters, mopeds and bicycles that clogged the road, that we were coming through and would not stop for them. No wonder that these people wanted to throw hand grenades at us. I got the distinct feeling that we were running some sort of medieval gauntlet and would soon be pummeled by those around us if we slowed down or stopped. "Quite a nice welcoming ceremony," I thought.

After a few days of in-processing at Long Binh we finally had gotten assignments to our units. I was going to C Battery, 2nd Battalion, 20th Artillery at Camp Evans in the I Corps area, just south of the DMZ and North Vietnam. "Artillery?" I thought. "What the Hell?" I was in aviation, not artillery. I wasn't real thrilled about the location of this unit either. It was in an area that I knew had seen significant fighting around Hue during the battle of Tet only two months before. I had no idea what type of unit the 2nd of the 20th Artillery was, so, I started asking some of the second tour guys. They informed me that it was an Aerial Rocket Artillery (ARA) unit and that their primary mission was to provide artillery support in the form of direct fire aerial rockets for units that were in contact with the enemy. Well, that sounded a little better, I thought.

The next day, we ran the gauntlet again and were bussed back out to Bien Hoa airfield and loaded aboard an Air Force C-130 Hercules cargo plane for the flight north towards our new unit. When we climbed aboard the aircraft, it did not have any seats and we were told by the crew chief to sit on the floor and grab hold of one of the straps that we saw lying there. "Damn!" I thought. "The next thing he's going to tell us is that there is no stewardess with drinks on this flight either."

Anyway, we were expecting to fly directly into Camp Evans and were wondering how long of a flight it would be. Just then, two Air Force pilots came up the back loading ramp and were making their way forward stepping over and around us as we sat on the floor. Someone asked them how long the flight to Camp Evans would be. They both looked at each other, then said, "I don't know about you guys but we're going to Cam Rahn Bay." So, we went to Cam Rahn Bay.

When we landed we were told that we had to take another C-130 flight to An Khe in order to in-process the First Calvary Division's unit headquarters which was located at An Khe. (Why? I still don't know.) After a few days of filling out more paperwork and getting issued our jungle fatigues and jungle boots, we were loaded aboard yet another C-130 and flown to Camp Evans. I was met at the airport by our unit commander and he gave me a ride back to the unit area in his Jeep. During our drive he said that he saw in my records that I was Cobra qualified. I told him, yes, I had just gone through class 2 of the official Cobra qualification course back at Hunter Army Airfield in Savannah.

He told me that our unit did not have any Cobras as yet but that they were supposed to start arriving shortly. Most of the Cobra pilots in Vietnam at that time had been trained locally by the NET Team (New Equipment Training Team) since the Cobra had just been bought by the Army. He also told me that I was the first officially "school trained" Cobra qualified pilot that the unit had. That boosted my spirits a bit.

"Home, Sweet Home" Charlie Battery, 2nd Battalion,
20th Artillery, Camp Evans, Vietnam

CHAPTER 2

My Orientation Flight

My first flight with Charlie Battery was on April 14th. It was a local area orientation conducted by CW3 Robert Maxwell. Mr. Maxwell was sort of a legend in our unit since he had redesigned the SS-11 missile system our unit had been issued, to better dovetail with our mission. The SS-11 was a French designed, wire guided missile that the pilot would hand fly with a joystick to hit hardened point type targets like tanks and bunkers. The system had 6 missiles, 3 per side, mounted on a long boom. The problem with this was the weight of the six missiles precluded us from carrying any other armaments on board. Mr. Maxwell's redesign reduced the number of missiles to 2 but also allowed 36-2.75 inch rockets to be carried. This system allowed more flexibility in the scheduling of the couple of aircraft with the system since the 2.75 inch rocket was our unit's main weapon system but it was nice to have the capability to service hard targets when they popped up.

The author and WO1 Russ Juleen in front of Huey with "Maxwell System"

Anyway, Mr. Maxwell's job that day was to familiarize me with the First Cavalry's Area of Operations (AO) and with my unit's standard operating procedures. Initially, we flew southwest and he showed me the river that separated our AO from the 101st Airborne Division's AO. We then flew northwestward along the foothills of the mountains and he explained that our AO continued westward to the Laotian border. Next, we flew up to the DMZ and he showed me several landmarks to use to avoid flying into North Vietnam, since that would be a very bad thing. Then, it was back south over Quang Tri, south along the beach and back into Camp Evans. While we were flying over the countryside, Mr. Maxwell told me about our unit and our mission.

He said that we were a rather unique unit in that there were only two ever formed during the war and ours was the first. When the First Cavalry Division was reorganized into an air mobile division prior to arriving in Vietnam, it was decided that Division Artillery, with its cannons and howitzers, would be supplemented by a battalion of heavily armed helicopter gunships that would provide direct fire artillery support to our troops in contact with the enemy. Our "Fire Missions" were initiated by the troops in the field when they encountered the enemy and radioed for support. Our operations would be tasked by Division Artillery to launch a section of 2 gunships that would proceed to the troops location and then fire at the enemy for them.

The crew of those gunships were on what was called "Hot" status and were required to be airborne within 2 minutes from the time operations notified them of the mission. This "notification" came in the form of a continuous blast on a Jeep horn that was mounted on a pole over the operations tent. Upon hearing the horn, the "Hot" crew would run to their aircraft and launch, usually in a little more than one minute. Additionally, the "Blue" section crew now knew that they had just moved up to "Hot Status" and the "Standby 1" crew was now "Blue" section, etc.,etc. The equipment used to accomplish these missions were B and C model Hueys that had been fitted with a rack of 24-2.75 inch rockets on each side of the helicopter. Each of these rockets had a bursting radius of about 10 meters or 30 feet. Additionally, the crew chief, who rode with us on every mission, had his M-60 machine gun with plenty of 7.62 mm ammo along. Mr. Maxwell explained that our unit was somewhat unique since almost every time we were launched on a mission we would be in contact with the enemy.

The only exceptions to that rule was when we were occasionally tasked to escort troop carrying Hueys during a combat assault. During these combat assaults, the Huey gunships that belonged to the lift ship company would fly ahead of the line of troop carrying Hueys and "prepare" the landing zone by firing rockets along the tree lines to get any enemy troops in the area to keep their heads down while the lift ships touched down to discharge their passengers. Meanwhile, we were "saddled up" on either side of the rear of the troop ships to continue the suppressive fire as they departed the landing zone. More often than not, the landing zones would be "cold" meaning that neither the lift ships nor the troops they dropped off would be shot at during the assault. He also mentioned "Mortar Patrol" as a secondary mission but said someone else would brief me on that.

I asked him about our call sign, "Blue Max" and he explained that just prior to my arrival, many of the units in the division were required to change their call signs because the enemy could derive a lot of information about our operations and battle plans by simply listening to the call signs of the units chattering on the radios. My predecessors chose "Blue Max" as the new call sign not just because of the movie that had just come out starring George Peppard and Ursula Andress but more because of what the "Blue Max" represented. It was a German World War I medal awarded to a select few aviators who demonstrated exceptional skill, expertise and courage while operating those early flying machines. Mr. Maxwell said that it was those traits that we were trying to emulate by using that call sign. Sounded good to me.

The next day, CW3 Maxwell continued my orientation by taking us up to Khe Sahn and landing there. This was only a couple of days after the First Calvary Division had fought its way into Khe Sahn to liberate the Marines who had been surrounded and cut off for two months during a siege by the North Vietnamese Army. We spent about 15 minutes on the ground talking to some Marines and then cranked up and flew back to Camp Evans. My orientation was over and I was released to go fly missions.

As a new pilot I was required to fly with one of the old-timers and just act as a copilot and do as I was told. That was fine by me since I still had no clue what an actual mission looked like. I was assigned to the 2nd platoon and was settling in quite well. I really liked the other pilots in the platoon and we got along very well right from the beginning. They all wanted to know about the new Cobra gunships that we would soon be getting in our unit and since I had just completed the brand new qualification course back at Savannah, Georgia, I was continuously being asked about the aircraft. They were all very excited about the capabilities of the new machine and couldn't wait for them to start arriving.

The new AH-1G Huey Cobra

That night I was introduced to mortar patrol. This mission entailed flying over our camp at night and keeping watch for the enemy launching mortar and rocket attacks on the LZ. If we saw enemy mortar or rocket fire coming in, we would then roll in and fire rockets back at them to suppress any further incoming and hopefully protect our men and equipment. Usually this mission was fairly boring because we would fly a single aircraft over the LZ at about 3000 feet for about 2 hours, then be replaced on station by another of our aircraft. We would continue to switch off every 2 hours throughout the night until sunrise at which time the 1st of the 9th Cav would conduct its "First Light Recon." Our unit did this mission every night all year long unless weather conditions prevented us from flying. Anyway, my first night of mortar patrol was uneventful and we had the next day off to catch up on our sleep.

CHAPTER 3

Operation Delaware

E arly in the morning on 19th of April we were all called into the operations bunker for a briefing on our next mission. I thought, "Oh, this is cool, this is just like the briefings that I've seen on TV on '12 O'clock High' where all the pilots gathered around and the briefing officer told them what their mission for the day would be." But today I looked around and saw that all the old-timers had very serious looks on their faces. Against the wall was a map that measured about 4 feet by 4 feet and was covered by a piece of canvas on which were stickers that said "SECRET."

The Operations Officer flipped back this cover and revealed Operation Delaware. He proceeded to tell us that our mission was a combat assault into the A Shau Valley with the purpose of interdicting the enemies flow of supplies along the Ho Chi Minh Trail which ran down the middle of the valley. This area was about 15 to 20 miles west of Camp Evans and had not seen US forces for at least three years. It was reported to be swarming with NVA and we could expect extensive antiaircraft fire. That day I would be flying with my platoon leader Captain Dave Whitling and our initial mission was to join up with a flight of Huey lift ships and provide cover while they inserted their troops into the area that would be known as LZ Tiger. The Ops officer told us that there would be many aircraft operating in the area and each of the troop lift formations of Hueys would have a different color call sign like Red Flight and Blue Flight. We were assigned to provide cover for the Green Flight on the first assault. The Green Flight was made up of 10 UH 1D models and each was carrying about eight troops besides it's four crew members. We were told that the first and third brigades of the First Cavalry Division would be conducting this operation and that the 101st Airborne would be providing blocking forces on the south end of the valley. This sounded like a very big operation to me and I was surprised that such an operation would be attempted on such short notice after the entire division had just completed its Operation Pegasus which broke the siege of Khe Sahn only a few days before. During the briefing we were told that the weather would be somewhat dicey in that it was the monsoon season and we could expect clouds over the target area.

After the briefing, Captain Whitling told me our aircraft tail number and asked me to go preflight the aircraft. He said we would be taking on some extra fuel because of the weather and the distance to the target area. We would be flying a B model Huey which is somewhat slower and not as powerful as our C models. Because we would be somewhat overweight on takeoff, Captain Whitling had the crew chief run alongside our aircraft as we began our takeoff run and as we got effective translational lift (the extra lift provided by the forward movement) the crew chief jumped into the aircraft. This was done because the aircraft probably would not have been able to hover with the added weight of the extra fuel and ammunition we were carrying plus the weight of the crew chief. This, it turned out, was a somewhat normal maneuver and many of the other aircraft had to do this same thing that day.

Once airborne, we had about a 15 to 20 minute flight to get to the A Shau Valley. We also had to climb to over 9000 feet in order to clear the mountains that ran down either side of the valley. A heavily loaded B model Huey does not fly well at 9000 feet even on a good day. So, as we were clearing the last ridge line before descending into the valley, our airspeed was all the way back to about 60 knots and we were unable to climb anymore. As we crossed that ridge line we began to look for the Green Flight to join up with them. As I was looking around I saw an F4 Phantom fighter bomber pulling off of his bombing run on what was to be LZ Tiger. I noticed a thin black trail of smoke behind the F4 and watched him as he joined up with his wingman and proceeded down the valley towards Da Nang. Apparently, he had been hit by ground fire on his last pass and was in a hurry to try to get back home. While I was watching this situation play out, Dave Whitling said he saw the Green Flight off to our right. He made radio contact with Green One and told the lift leader that we would be joining up on either side of his lift ships.

Captain Whitling assumed a position on the right side of the Green Flight while our wing man took a position on the left side of the flight. This way we can provide cover for them no matter which side they took fire from. Green One, the Green flight leader, told us that he would be passing over the pinnacle of the mountain just behind where LZ Tiger was and would then circle down to land on the LZ. As Green One passed over the tip of the mountain he called, " Taking fire" and broke to his right. Since Green Two was immediately behind Green One he also called taking fire and taking hits. He said that he had lost his engine oil pressure and his transmission oil pressure but that the engine was still running. Captain Whitling told him to set the aircraft down on the Ho Chi Minh Trail and that we would provide cover in the form of rocket fire on either side of the trail as he landed. Green Two replied that he thought he could make the LZ.

We were all thinking of our lessons in flight school where they tell you that without oil pressure, the transmission on a Huey will seize up after about 2 minutes. So, once again, Capt. Whitling told him to go ahead and put it on the ground but Green Two continued toward LZ Tiger. About 200 meters short of the LZ, Green Two called "engine failure" and we watched as his rotor blades came to a stop at about 200 feet in the air. The aircraft went straight down and was enveloped by a fireball as it hit the ground. We later learned that all on board had been killed except for the crew chief. The story was that when the rotor blades stopped, he had unbuckled his seat belt and jumped clear of the aircraft. It was said that he had broken most of his bones but was alive and was rescued later that day. And so started what would be a horrendous day for all involved.

The rest of the Green flight joined back up with each other after scattering like a covey of quail and proceeded to deposit the rest of their troops on LZ Tiger. We provided cover throughout their assault and no further aircraft from their flight were hit by ground fire during that assault. Once that operation was completed, we were directed to provide cover for other lift ships that were in the area.

As we were climbing back up to altitude to join up with other lift ships we came under intense enemy fire from a 23 mm antiaircraft gun. I got to experience the very distinctive "bump, bump, bump" of those antiaircraft rounds passing very close to our aircraft. It's something I'll never forget since just one hit could have destroyed the helicopter and us. Upon hearing the rounds, Captain Whitling put the aircraft into a very steep dive and pulled out just above the trees in order to evade the enemy fire. At one point I thought we had been hit and that we were going to crash into the trees but he pulled out of the dive and we skimmed along the tops of the trees until we were well clear of the area. Our wing man never did see where the fire was coming from, so he did not return suppressive fire and we made note not to go near that area again.

It was later reported that the entire A Shau Valley area was home to two NVA antiaircraft battalions and that they were well-equipped with the entire array of Soviet antiaircraft weaponry. These included 12.7mm, 14.5mm, 23mm, 37mm and 57mm antiaircraft machine guns and flak cannons. At one point during our very long day, Captain Whitling and I saw what looked like a telephone pole go sailing past our aircraft. We both turned and looked at each other with our jaws hanging open and said, "What the hell was that?" Apparently, the enemy also had some sort of missile they were throwing at us.

Since we had expended most of our ammunition and were low on gas we had to return to Camp Evans to rearm and refuel. We could only stay on station in "The Valley" for about 45 minutes before needing to go back to Evans where we would "Hot" rearm and refuel (this meant doing so with the engine running) so we could get back out to "The Valley" as quickly as possible.

On our next sortie into "The Valley", we were told that a cloud layer was forming at about 8000 feet and to be careful when we let down through it since there were so many helicopters and jets flying around that a mid air collision was a real possibility. As we came down into the valley through the clouds, we began looking around for the next lift that we were to escort to their landing zone. There was a lot of talking on the radio about enemy fire and locations of aircraft that had been shot down. This was the point at which the little puffy white clouds began to appear and brings us full circle back to the question of exactly, "How the Hell did I get here?" Now that you know the answer to that question, let's pick up where we left off. If you recall, the Chinook was diving past us, in a ball of flames, on our right side while the troop carrying Huey, with no tailboom, spun down past us on our left.

The CH-47 Chinook carrying a howitzer. Photo courtesy of the Department of Defense.

We tried to monitor both situations as they developed and saw the Chinook headed for the downed aircrew pickup point which was a junction of two rivers in the Valley. In our initial briefing, we were told that if you got shot down, you were to proceed to the pickup point, if at all possible, and a rescue helicopter would come by once an hour to check to see if anyone was there. Obviously, the crew of the Chinook was planning to get as close to the pickup point as possible. They flared the aircraft just above the river and impacted the water with the tail that was on fire. The entire aircraft slammed down into the water with a big spray and the front end of the aircraft broke off, rolled down the river and came to a stop at the pickup point. We found out later that five of the crew had survived the crash and were picked up shortly afterward. Meanwhile, the Huey without a tailboom continued to spin towards the ground and upon impact the aircraft rolled up on its right side. Amazingly, we watched as many of the troops on board climbed out and proceeded to set up a perimeter around the aircraft. We were surprised that the aircraft did not burn on impact and that so many people survived the crash. We later found out that the pilot who had landed the helicopter, removed his chicken plate so that he could get out of the aircraft easier and was shot dead in the chest by a sniper as he exited.

The rest of the day continued much as it had been so far. We continued to escort lift ships into landing zones and provided direct fire at any antiaircraft sites we could locate. But late in the day, we were notified that we were to provide cover for a CH-54 Flying Crane that was going to be delivering a heavy 155 mm howitzer to LZ Tiger.

The CH-54 Flying Crane. Right photo courtesy of
U.S. Army Aviation Museum Collection.

The Flying Crane was the Army's premier heavy lift helicopter that was capable of carrying 20,000 pounds. We saddled up on either side of the Crane as it came over the ridge line and into the valley. All went well until the Crane came to a high hover over LZ Tiger and was lowering the howitzer into place. Suddenly, we saw an explosion that parted the trees and out of it came a huge 57mm tracer round that ended up streaking about a mile across the valley and landed with a bang in the left engine of the Flying Crane. The Crane continued to hover for about 15 seconds while the ground crew began running in all directions. Ever so slowly, the Crane began to roll to the left and the rate of roll continued to accelerate until the blades hit the ground and the aircraft burst into flames. All three crewmen were killed. We immediately turned our attention on the spot in the jungle where the tracer had come from and proceeded to fire all of our rockets into the area. If we didn't kill the crew of that weapon, we certainly made it a bad day for them. At that point, since we were out of ammo, we returned to Camp Evans for the night.

Capt. Whitling was what we called an old-timer, since he had been in country for almost a year and was due to return to the states in a couple of weeks. I asked him, as we walked back to the tent, if what we had experienced that day was normal for a big operation. He kind of chuckled and said, "No, today was rather unusual." Once I'd gotten something to eat, I sat down to write my wife a letter. In the letter I explained that today's operation was pretty bad and that if this was what it was going to be like for the next 11 plus months, that I probably wouldn't be coming home. I really didn't want to tell her that but I was sure that the news of our losses that day would make the evening news back home and that she would draw the same conclusion anyway. What I didn't know was that the Army had classified any news of the operation since the losses were so high because they didn't want the NVA command to know how much damage they had inflicted on us. Later, we were told that a total of 25 aircraft had been shot down that day to include five Chinook helicopters and the one Flying Crane. Of course, I personally saw the Crane and one Chinook get shot down as well as at least 10 Hueys. I did not even try to count the OH-6 scout aircraft that I saw go down since there were so many. I got little sleep that night thinking of the events of the day and that we were scheduled to go back to "The Valley" tomorrow morning.

The next day we got a breather in that the weather was overcast in The Valley and we could not get out there even though we were launched several times. Again the following day, the weather was keeping our aircraft from reaching The Valley early on but it started to break up later in the day. The section that I was on was launched on a fire mission to The Valley just before sunset. We were told that some of our troops out there had seen lights and activity along the Ho Chi Minh trail and wanted us to come shoot at the bad guys. Even though we had to dodge some clouds on our way out, we did manage to get into The Valley and shoot up the area where the activity was reported. As we climbed out of The Valley on our way home, we once again started to run into the clouds but now it was dark. Capt. Whitling, in the lead aircraft, said we would need to do a formation GCA (Ground Controlled Radar Approach) back into Camp Evans since we were both low on fuel and there wouldn't be enough time for each of us to do an approach without somebody running out of fuel. I was flying with Lt. Dick Hawkins and he did a great job of flying very tight formation on Capt. Whitling's aircraft. After all, we needed to keep his aircraft in sight throughout the approach or we'd be the ones running out of fuel at night and in the clouds. As we made contact with the ground radar controller, he informed us that the weather at Camp Evans had also gone down while we were in The Valley. He reported that the ceiling was 100 feet overcast and visibility was one quarter of a mile. Uh, Oh! The minimum weather for an approach was at least 200 feet and one half mile visibility. We were in trouble! Capt. Whitling declared an emergency and the controller started giving us vectors for a "short approach" to the runway. Dick Hawkins kept his eyes glued to Capt. Whitling's aircraft and mimicked his every turn and movement because he knew that if we lost sight of him, we would probably end up crashing. I was really impressed that Dick was able to fly such a tight formation with only one rotor disk separation between us and Capt. Whitling's aircraft.

After what seemed an eternity, the ground controller was saying, "One half mile from touchdown, on course, on glide path. Over the approach lights, on course, on glide path, take over visually, you're cleared to land." We could finally make out the ground and the "approach lights," which were nothing but a bunch of tin cans that had fuel in them and were set afire, but I have to admit, they were the best looking approach lights I had ever seen. We slowly hovered passed the tower and set down at the refueling point with about 10 minutes of fuel left. I congratulated Dick on doing a great job and we decided we needed a drink once we got back to the tent.

The next day the weather was significantly better and we finally got back out to The Valley. We found that the NVA had abandoned their weapons in place and left for the safety of Laos. It was at this point that the First Cav decided to set up a forward operating base at the old airstrip of A Loi and called it LZ Stallion. We then moved out to, and lived at, LZ Stallion for the next two weeks. We slept in or under our aircraft during that time frame and were prepared to launch our aircraft at a moments notice. Most of the operations being conducted in the valley during this time frame were search and destroy missions to find the enemy weapons that had been left behind and destroy them. I remember seeing one such cache of weapons that was some 20 feet high and about 40 feet around at its base. This cache included a lot of different types of ammunition, brand new AK-47 rifles that were still packed in their crates as well as many antiaircraft weapons. We watched as the explosive ordnance disposal teams rigged this entire pile of weapons with explosives to destroy them all. It was quite a big bang when they set it off.

During the entire time we were living in The Valley, I was assigned as copilot for Captain Frank Thornhill. One night, our section was launched because someone saw enemy movement along the Ho Chi Minh trail and we were to go and destroy any enemy we found. When we arrived in the area, we started taking automatic weapons fire and rolled in to attack the enemy position. Frank was in the left seat firing the rockets and I was in the right seat controlling the weapon system on our first rocket attack. Frank had entered a shallow dive and was firing round after round as we closed in on the enemy's location. I knew we were getting very close to the ground and so I started to yell at Frank saying, "break, break, pull-up!!" I finally shut off the weapon system at which point Frank began to pull out of the dive just as we were skimming the tops of the trees. I knew that Frank had gotten target fixation and would've driven us into the ground had I not shut off the rocket system. I'm sure we scared the hell out of the bad guys that were shooting at us because we had gotten so close. Frank apologized for scaring us and we went back around and continued to shoot into the area until we were out of ammunition. Thankfully, we never got that low again.

While most of our missions in The Valley were fire missions, we were tasked a couple of times with providing escort for the lift ship as they moved troops around in the search for enemy weapons caches. The combat assaults were pretty standard and we would shoot rockets around the edges of the LZ just to make sure that the enemy didn't try shooting at the lift ships as they were touching down. On this particular mission, I was flying with Frank Thornhill again and we were fortunate to also have a door gunner along to help out our crew chief, Russ Warriner.

As we pulled up from our rocket run, it was common for the crew chief and door gunner to begin firing their M-60 machines guns at the tree lines to cover our climb out. Each time they began shooting, I couldn't help but notice that the expended brass cartridges were landing all over me and ricocheting off my helmet. On the next run we made, the torrent of expended shells was even more intense and several of these still smoking little beauties went down my collar and were burning my back. I squirmed and arched my back to ease the pain and as I did so, I heard laughing from the back. I turned to see that Russ and door gunner were "High-Fiving" each other and having a good belly laugh at my expense. I looked to Frank for some sympathy and he was chuckling too.

Hey! Wait a minute. This was turning out to be some sort of conspiracy and I wanted in on the joke. Frank explained, "That's one of the little tricks the crew chiefs play on new pilots. You should feel honored, they only do it to guys they like."

I turned around and said "Thanks" very sarcastically, to Russ and the door gunner. On our way back to LZ Stallion, I asked Russ to show me how it was done. Frank found an area where Russ could shoot his M-60 and he started firing. Instead of watching where the bullets were going, he was instead, tilting the gun, as it fired, to direct the stream of ejected brass towards my location. Once again, the brass was bouncing off my helmet as I held my shirt collar closed. Pretty cool! It was nice to know that we had such a multi-talented crew chief on board. Of course, I wondered, where the heck were all those bullets going?

Anyway, I thought my indoctrination was over but I was wrong. As we cruised along back towards LZ Stallion, I was looking out the windshield and, as a new pilot, paying close attention to what Frank was doing, when, suddenly, a hand came in my door's window and tapped me on the shoulder. I about jumped clear out of my seat and was only kept in place by my seat belt and shoulder harness. I turned to look at where this phantom hand was coming from and saw Russ outside the aircraft, grinning and standing on the skid. He was now reaching toward the exterior windshield with a paper towel in his hand, to clean off any dust or dirt, all while we were flying along at 80 knots. Once he finished doing this, he leaned in the window and, shouting over the wind and rotor noise, asked, "Would you like me to check the oil too, Sir?" Very funny! He held up a portion of his "Monkey Strap" and showed me he was attached by it to the aircraft. The monkey strap was used by some of the crew chiefs to allow them to move around in the back of the aircraft without worrying about falling out. Apparently, it also came in handy when trying to scare the crap out of a new pilot. But all is forgiven. Russ and I have remained good friends over the years.

CHAPTER 4

Benny's Story

A couple of days later I was again flying with Frank. We were the wingman for Capt. Whitling and our section had been scrambled to go shoot for some infantry guys that were taking sniper fire up in the mountains on the south side of the Valley. When we arrived on station, Capt. Whitling was talking to the ground commander and trying to determine where all of his troops were since we needed to know this information before we could shoot. He had the ground commander pop smoke on all of his units in the area so that we could identify them. This proved very difficult because of the triple canopy jungle that dispersed the smoke before it could come up. While he was continuing to talk to the ground commander, we were flying along behind him providing cover for him and looking around for any enemy activity.

At this point we were flying right along the Laotian border with South Vietnam. I was overwhelmed by the contrast between the South Vietnamese countryside and the Laotian countryside. While the South Vietnamese side of the border looked like a moonscape with all the bomb craters that covered The Valley, the Laotian side of the border was lush, green and undamaged. It was while I was marveling at this contrast that

I noticed a truck come over the top of the ridge line from Laos and drive down the hill into South Vietnam, producing a lot of dust behind it. I knew that we didn't have any trucks out in The Valley, so, I yelled at Frank, "I've got a truck over here." He rolled the aircraft into a very tight turn and we watched as the truck skidded to a halt under one lone tree in an area that was denude of any other vegetation. His dust trail pointed to his exact location. Frank called Capt. Whitling and told him about the truck. The ground commander heard the call and told us it had to be a bad guy since our forces didn't have any trucks in The Valley and to "Go ahead and blow him up!!" Frank said, "make me hot" (arm the rocket system) and I did. He then rolled into a very steep dive and fired several pairs of rockets at the trucks location. The first pair went kind of wild since we didn't have much airspeed but the second, third and fourth pairs went right into the tree where the truck was hiding. Besides the normal rocket explosions we also saw a secondary explosion that indicated that we had hit the truck and set off something they were carrying.

As we pulled out of our dive, several things began to happen at once. I believe that the truck must have been carrying lunch to a bunch of hungry NVA soldiers that were now very pissed off that they weren't getting any lunch today because of us. As a result, each of them decided to unload their AK-47s at us. As we were pulling up, bullets began flying everywhere. Things at this point started to move in slow motion, kind of like when you're in a serious car accident. I saw a shower of what looked like snow floating down in front of me. It felt like someone had hit the back of my seat with a 5 pound sledge hammer at least twice and I was fascinated while looking at the instrument panel to see gauges just disappear into the panel. This entire sequence took approximately ten seconds but felt like a lifetime.

After all the noise had stopped and time resumed it's normal flow, I realized that we had just been shot to hell. I looked at Frank and asked, "Are you all right??" He looked back at me with eyes as big as saucers and said, "Yeah, I'm okay, are you??" I told him I was and turned to check on our crew chief Benny (SP4 Ben Stevens). Benny's normal station was on the left side behind Frank where he would sit in the cargo door opening and cover us with his M-60 machine gun during breaks after a gun run. I glanced back, expecting Benny to be right where I had last seen him but he wasn't there. Panicked, I then turned in my seat, grabbing my armor plating to see the entire cargo area and discovered Benny IS GONE!! I told Frank, and he too craned his entire body around to look for Benny but he was indeed, GONE. As shocking as that was, we had other things to worry about.

Apparently, since we took the gunfire from behind, several of those rounds hit the back of my armor plated seat, several went over my head and shattered the little plexiglass window there (causing the "snow") and others flew between Frank and I and punched out several of our engine instruments. There were now just very neat holes in the panel where the instruments had been, almost as if someone had unscrewed and removed them. I quickly scanned the remaining instruments and the Caution/Warning panel to assess our situation and noticed that our 20 minute fuel low warning light was on. I thought, "That's strange!!" I remembered that when we rolled into our dive that we had over 600 pounds of fuel or enough for about an hour of flight. I quickly consulted the actual fuel gauge and was shocked to see the quantity rapidly going down through 200 pounds heading toward ZERO!!

I told Frank that we must be leaking a lot of gas and to quickly find someplace to land. He said he had already picked out a place and pointed out a small fire base just ahead of us. The fire base had three 105mm howitzers in it and only about enough room for two helicopters. Frank had called Capt. Whitling in the other aircraft and told him that we'd been pretty well shot up and had to make an emergency landing. Capt. Whitling called to say they were quite a way back but were catching up to us and he said, "It looks like you have a big hunk of junk hanging off your aircraft." We looked at each other and shrugged our shoulders since we had no idea what that could be. As we began to slow down for our approach into the fire base, we suddenly heard a loud whooshing sound and were confuse as to where it was coming from but we were sure it wasn't a good thing.

At this point, Capt. Whitling had caught up with us and called us to say, "That thing we saw hanging from you aircraft is your crew chief." Oh, Crap!! Most of the crew chiefs would take the back plate out of their body armor and sit on it to protect the family jewels but Benny, thankfully, had kept his plate in place since that was where the Army said it was suppose to be. As a result the two rounds that would have killed him, instead knocked him out and threw him out the cargo door. Luckily, Benny had his monkey strap on that day. Though he'd been knocked unconscious by the impact of the bullets and bruised very badly, he was alive and dangling from his strap. Benny regained consciousness as we began our approach to the fire base and wanted to tell us that he was hanging below the aircraft and to not land on him. When he keyed his microphone to talk to us he found that his mic had been blown around behind his helmet. This is what was producing the scary whooshing sound as he was being dragged through the air at about 70 knots.

Meanwhile, back in the cockpit, Frank was increasing his approach angle to avoid dragging Benny through the concertina wire that surrounded the fire base. The fuel gauge was reading nearly zero and the artillerymen in the fire base were all running for cover. As we cleared the wire, I looked back in time to see Benny's hands latch onto the edge of the cargo door and he threw himself into the aircraft. I told Frank, "Benny's IN!!" and he began to lower the aircraft to the ground when the engine quit due to fuel starvation. He did a hovering autorotation from about 5 feet. We landed hard and spread the skids but we all survived. The artillerymen came over to help us out of our somewhat bent and broken aircraft and helped Benny out of his body armor. Benny painfully took off his shirt to reveal two huge bruises on his back that looked like he had been kicked by a mule.

Benny was evacuated back to Camp Evans and spent several days recovering from his wounds before resuming flying. Frank and I got to sit around the fire base for a few hours waiting for the maintenance bird to show up. When the maintenance guys got there, they began inspecting the aircraft to see if they could patch it up enough to fly it out. It didn't take long for them to determine that that was not going to happen. They began preparing the aircraft to be hoisted out on a sling by a Chinook. As they prepped it they said that they found 29 bullet entry holes and they were curious as to how close the rounds passed by my head. They had me sit in my seat and stretched a cord from each of the bullet holes behind my seat to the where the bullets went out the little window over my head and found that the cord bent over my helmet in each case. They said that I should be dead and we all wondered how the bullets could have missed me. It was then that I realized that I had briefly looked down to shut off the rocket system when we pulled out of the dive. Whew, that was close. The maintenance guys also determined that several of the support beams in the airframe had been hit and the aircraft would have to be sent away for a depot level overhaul. I think it is interesting to note that the area where we were shot up would become the site of the infamous battle of "Hamburger Hill" one year later. So, in conclusion, the score was: U.S. Army destroys one beat up, rattletrap NVA truck and the NVA shoots down one U.S. Army helicopter. A draw at best.

The maintenance bird dropped Frank and I off at LZ Stallion as they headed back to Camp Evans. We met up with Capt. Whitling and the others and were given, though reluctantly, another aircraft to fly. We were told that the area where we were shot up proved to be a hot spot of enemy activity and that there were continuing battles there all day long. It had turned into such a major battle that a B-52 strike was scheduled for the area that evening. For those that don't know, a B-52 bombing strike is called an "Arc Light" and consists of 3 bombers carrying a mix of 500, 750, and 2000 pound bombs which are dropped in parallel strings and pretty much obliterate anything in a target area box that typically measures 1000 meters by 1000 meters. It is quite an awesome thing to watch and that night's mission was set to hit an area that was only 2 to 3 kilometers (about 1 to 2 miles) away from us. It was a clear night and even though they were flying at over 30,000 feet, we actually saw the bombers coming up The Valley from the south. While they were still pretty far south of our position, I noticed the lead bomber had started to turn around and head back the way he had come. He was followed in turn by each of the other bombers and someone said, "They've already dropped their bombs and are headed home." It seemed like a very long time elapsed before the first bombs started to hit the target area. As the bombs went off, the night turned to day and we could see everything around us light up. The noise and concussions were absolutely terrifying but the one thing that astounded me was looking down at my feet and watching the ground drop away about a foot and then come slamming back up to my boots with each explosion. A totally awesome and frightening experience.

We continued to operate out of LZ Stallion for the next few weeks but most of the intense fighting had subsided. We would hear explosions at various times during the day but they were usually just the Explosive Ordnance Disposal (EOD) guys blowing up enemy weapons caches. One day we were just sitting around our aircraft at LZ Stallion watching a flight of two F-4s doing bombing runs up near the north end of The Valley. As one of the jets was pulling out of a bomb run we saw him take hits from enemy ground fire. He joined up with his wingman and they headed south towards our location on their way to Da Nang. The F-4 that was hit was trailing a lot of black smoke and as they passed over us it looked like the stricken aircraft stopped moving while his wingman continued south. Very quickly we realized that it looked that way because he was now heading straight down at us. The thought of trying to run may have crossed my mind but it was all over before I could even start to move. We saw one parachute open and almost instantly the aircraft impacted the ground about 200 yards away from us with a huge explosion. Dirt and tiny pieces of metal showered down on us.

The F-4 has a crew of 2 and since there was only one parachute we knew that the other crewman had gone in with the aircraft. We turned our attention back to the lone parachute that was drifting down towards us and were relieved to see a flight of about 8 Hueys that had been working in the area were now circling him and waiting for him to land so they could pick him up. We then walked outside the LZs perimeter to the smoking hole in the ground. Previously, I had been up close to F-4s that were parked on the ramp at various airfields and was impressed with how big they were but currently I was looking down into a hole that was, perhaps, ten feet deep and eight feet across and now contained one of those planes. The area around the hole was covered by small chunks of metal no bigger than the palm of your hand and we searched for any large pieces that might be recognizable but to no avail. I said a prayer for the crewman and walked back to my helicopter. The A Shau Valley had claimed another. I really hated this place.

It was the beginning of May and we had been living in The Valley for two weeks now and were beginning to smell like it. Things were very quiet and we hadn't been scrambled out on very many missions at all but, we were still pulling "strip alert" by sitting in our helicopters. It was late afternoon and Frank was stretched out in his seat, I was asleep on the cargo compartment floor and our crew chief was sleeping in a hammock he had hung under the tail boom. We were all rudely awakened by the sound of artillery shells exploding around us. We scrambled around getting the blades untied and the aircraft started so we could get airborne to go find the bad guys that were shooting at us. After what seemed to be an eternity, we finally took off, even though the crew chief's hammock was still hanging under the tail boom. We were told by operations that the artillery was coming over the border from Laos and that officially, we were not suppose to shoot back but that if we wanted to unload our rockets into a "safe area" we could do so. Ops also told us that once we "unloaded" our rockets we could return to Camp Evans and our mission in The Valley would be over. We had a pretty good idea of where the artillery was coming from so, Frank said, "Put me up hot and select salvo." I did as I was told and Frank raised the nose of the aircraft and salvo-ed all 48 rockets into the suspected enemy position which happened to be in very lush, green jungle just the other side of the moonscape terrain we'd been living in. It gave me some sense of closure as we turned northeast and began our climb over the mountains toward Camp Evans.

Over the next few days the rest of troops and equipment were reposition back to Camp Evans and we completed the withdrawal from The Valley on May 16th. They said that we accomplished the goals of our incursion into the enemy sanctuary known as The A Shau Valley but my sense was that we only temporarily postponed the enemy's march southward.

CHAPTER 5

Tommie

Things were kind of slow for the next few days as we recovered from operation Delaware. We all got to meet our new pilot, Tommie Rolf and I was especially glad to see him since that meant that I was no longer the FNG or "freaking new guy." Tommie would now have to put up with the old guys jokes like "Hey! New Guy, go get me ten yards of flight line." or "Hey! New Guy, get me a bucket of rotorwash and meet me at the aircraft." Tommie had a good sense of humor and I told him to just ignore them and they would stop before too long.

On the morning of May 19th the word quickly spread that today was Ho Chi Minh's birthday and that we could expect a possible ground attack or, at least, incoming rocket or mortar attacks that night. Tommie was excited because he had completed his orientation flights and was scheduled to fly the next day. It was early evening and Tommie had gone out to the flightline to preflight his assigned aircraft for the next day. Several of us had decided to set up out lawn chairs on top of our bunker and watch the area near the foothills to our southwest. This area was known as "Rocket Alley" and we were sure that if the enemy launched a rocket attack that night it would come from there.

We didn't have to wait very long because shortly after the sun dipped behind the mountains to our west, we saw 3 rockets take off from the area we were watching. Knowing that the time of flight of these rockets was about 15 seconds, we calmly got up, folded our chairs and walked down into the bunker.

I was just unfolding my chair as we heard the incoming rounds pass overhead. This was followed by two very close "Karumps" and a third more distant "Karump" as the rounds exploded on impact. I settled into my chair up against the east wall of the bunker expecting several more waves of rockets to come in. After a couple of minutes we started to look at each other with puzzlement since no more rockets were arriving. We peeked out the door of the bunker to discover that there was a small fire burning in the jeep refueling area about 100 meters away but we saw no other damage nor any more incoming rounds. We gathered our chairs and resumed our positions on top of the bunker just in time to see one of our aircraft taking off and proceeding to the "Rocket Alley" area. We later found out that this aircraft was manned by Jim Krull and Tommie Rolf. It seems that Jim was out setting up his aircraft for mortar patrol that night and Tommie was down the flightline preflighting his aircraft for the next day when the rockets arrived. Jim grabbed Tommie and put him in the right seat so that they could get airborne and go shoot up the bad guys that had launched the rockets. It's possible that their arrival over "Rocket Alley" made the enemy rethink their options and choose not to launch any more rounds.

It was now getting pretty dark and we could see that there was another fire burning on the other side of the landing zone. Camp Evans was a pretty big place. It was about one mile in diameter with an airstrip about 5000 feet long bisecting it. It was "Home" to about 7000 troops and 150 helicopters. As we watched this new fire we saw small explosions and a bunch of tracer ammunition get tossed up in the air. We were then told that one of the enemy rockets had landed in the ammo dump and started the fire. As we watched, the fire progressively got larger and was now setting off the pyrotechnics. These were the hand held parachute flares used for illumination and the star clusters used for signaling at night. The star clusters came in different colors and resembled the type of fireworks normally seen on the 4th of July. So, when an entire pallet of these would explode in the fire, the sky would light up and you could hear a muffled cheer from the troops watching the show around the LZ. But, things were about to get very serious. The fire now set off a pallet of 2.75 inch rockets and as we heard the distinctive "Whoosh" of rockets taking off, we immediately started scrambling for the bunker because we knew that when those rockets landed they we going to explode. We were barely inside the bunker when we heard the sound of rockets detonating all around the LZ.

We felt much safer once we were in the bunker because, as bunkers went, ours was the Cadillac of bunkers. The pilots of first and second platoons built this shared bunker by having a bulldozer carve out a hole about 25 feet long by 12 feet wide and 15 feet deep. We lined the walls with empty rocket boxes, had a wood floor and were particularly proud of the roof. The roof, from bottom to top, was made of one set of 4 by 12 wooden beams placed vertically on the side walls of rocket boxes, then another set of 4 by 12s were layered horizontally on top of the first beams to form a "T." We then placed two layers of rocket boxes filled with dirt on top of the beams and covered the whole thing with 2 feet of dirt. The bunker served not only as our refuge during incoming but also as our rec room. We had lighting in the form of several 60 watt bulbs suspended from the ceiling along with several oscillating fans and even a small refrigerator to keep our beer and soda cold. We had made a large table for playing cards and, occasionally, we'd even set up a ping pong table down there. But tonight we were using it for it's primary purpose of safety.

The explosions from the ammo dump continued to get louder and more frequent as the night wore on. The fire was now burning into the artillery ammunition and whole pallets of shells would explode at once creating a huge fireball, not unlike a nuclear explosion. We would take turns peeking out of the bunker to watch the fire. Even though the fire was almost a mile away, the entire landing zone was aglow with its light. Halfway to the fire we could see the control tower at the airfield and about

30 meters away was a slight ridge line that all our aircraft were parked on. Closer in, at about 10 meters, was a rice paddy that was about 15 feet wide with a small foot bridge we would use to run to our aircraft when we got a mission. As I watched the fire, a pallet of ammo would explode and initially it looked like someone had taken a flash picture of me from 6 inches away. The initial flash of light from the explosion was absolutely blinding. As your vision returned you would see the orange fireball and the shock wave rushing at you. Because of our distance, the shock wave and sound of the explosion would take 5 to 6 seconds to arrive. You could actually see it because the blast would condense the very humid air and form a semi opaque cloud that, along with the dust it picked up, came rushing at you at the speed of sound. As it passed the control tower, the tower would sway. As it passed our helicopters, the tied down rotor blades would flap violently. As it crossed the rice paddy, all the 2 foot tall rice would flatten into the water. As it arrived at your location, you would simultaneously hear the deafening "BOOM" and feel the concussion. When I say feel the concussion, I want you to imagine someone slapping you across the face as hard as they can. Now, imagine that slap hitting your entire body at once. The frequency of the blasts seemed to be increasing and there would be a minor blast every one to two minutes and a large blast once every 5 to 10 minutes. Jim Krull and Tommie Rolf had returned from their hastily launched mortar patrol mission and now all the pilots of first and second platoon were sitting around up against the walls of the bunker. Bracing for whatever came next.

Everyone was somewhat dazed, there was little conversation and there certainly would be no card playing tonight. We were all jolted out of our stupor when three pilots from the 229th assault helicopter unit came staggering into or bunker. They looked like each had a severe sunburn and every inch of their exposed skin was bright red with blisters all over. Their eyes, when they opened them, were nothing but small pupils surrounded by blood where the whites of their eyes should be. They laid on the floor and asked for medical assistance. They told us that their bunker was very close to the ammo dump and that a little while ago a blast had ruptured several 55 gallon drums of liquid CS gas and that it had run downhill into their bunker. This gas is the military's much stronger version of tear gas or Mace and had been condensed even more into liquid form so it could be sprayed by helicopters into enemy areas. After a short time of exposure, the men had decided to take a chance with the exploding ammo dump and head as far away from there as possible. Someone went and got our medic and he gave them a shot of some painkiller after he examined them. He then arranged for them to be transported to the aid station.

We were all very grim faced at this point since the frequency of the explosions showed no signs of abating and we all began to wonder as to exactly how much ammo could be left to burn? Jerry, one of the pilots from first platoon, had taken up the position by the door and was watching the ammo dump. We all saw the next flash and braced for the shock wave that was coming. Jerry leaned in the door and said, "That one was huge!!" and was hit by the blast as he turned back. We were all looking at him as he made his announcement and now watched as he flew backwards across the bunker and impacted the far wall. He struggled to his feet, dusted himself off, swore a couple of times then went back to his post by the door. As I looked to my left, I saw Tommie Rolf get out of his chair and start walking towards me. He was headed toward the refrigerator to my right and said to me, "I think I need a Coke after that one. Do you want anything, Bob?" He was now about 4 feet from me and I began to say, "No thanks, Tommie." but never got the words out of my mouth. In the blink of an eye, there was a terrible "CRASH" and I was now covered in dirt up to my chest. I, and the others, had no idea what just happened but knew it wasn't good. The air was thick with dust and smoke, there was now a big pile of dirt in the middle of the bunker that looked like an inverted ice cream cone and was pointing to a 3 foot hole in the ceiling. Observing this took about a quarter of a second while I was busy trying to extricate myself from the dirt pile and get the hell out of there. As I stood up, I promptly smashed my head into a fractured 4 by 12 beam that now pointed down from atop the rocket boxes, to the center of the floor under the dirt pile. As I recovered and was now crawling over the dirt pile, I saw that everyone else was rapidly evacuating the bunker and I followed suit. I ran through the second platoon tent and across to third platoons bunker. As I went I noticed that there was a lot of unexploded ordnance strewn across the ground and tried to avoid stepping on or disturbing any of it since it would now be very unstable and subject to detonation at the slightest touch. Inside third platoons bunker, everyone wanted to know what just happened because they had heard the loud and unusual sound. I told them what I had seen and said I didn't think it was an explosion of any kind but beyond that I had no idea.

As we talked, I noticed something moving along a ledge of dirt just above and behind the heads of the men opposite me in the bunker. We sat facing each other about 3 to 4 feet apart and since the only source of lighting in their bunker was flashlights, I could not make out what it was because of the odd shadows thrown off by the lights. (As I mentioned, not exactly a Cadillac class bunker.) I said, "What's that?" and pointed to the critter. As they turned around and shone their lights on the critter all hell broke loose. The "Critter" turned out to be a Bamboo Viper whose other name was "The Two Step Viper." It was about 15 inches long and about the size of your pinky finger in diameter and it was said that if you were bitten by one you would only get to take two steps before dying. After much jumping around and flailing of various objects at the critter, it now lay dead on the floor of the bunker. We all felt a bit creeped out and some were nursing bumps and bruises that resulted from the melee.

The operations officer stuck his head into the bunker and said he was trying to account for everyone that had vacated our bunker. He saw me and said everyone was accounted for except Tommie Rolf. He asked, "Has anyone seen him?" It was then that I realized that I was talking to Tommie when the "Crash" happened. I said, "I think Tommie is under the dirt pile." We all scrambled out and ran over to the other bunker and started digging in the dirt pile. It wasn't long before his body was discovered and we figured out what had happened. Apparently, the last blast that had hurled Jerry across the bunker also hurled a very large artillery round into the air.

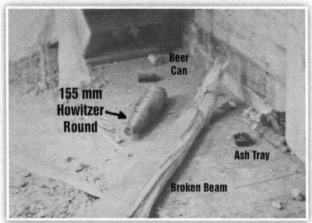

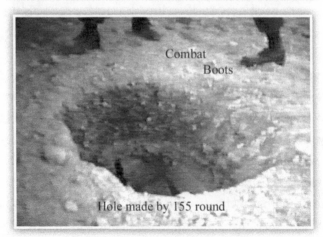

Destruction caused by ammo dump explosion.
Top photos courtesy of Russ Warriner.

When this unfused round, which weighed about 100 pounds, came back to earth, it had covered almost a mile over land and crashed into the roof of our bunker without exploding. After it had penetrated the 2 feet of dirt, the two layers of rocket boxes and snapped the 4 by 12 beams like toothpicks, it hit Tommie in the head and killed him instantly. As it bounced around, it also broke Jim Krull's leg. Jim had been sitting almost directly across the bunker from me before the impact.

Once Tommie's body was recovered, Jim and Tommie were loaded onto the same truck and sent over to the aid station. Jim's leg was pretty well mangled and the medical folks were able to save it but Jim still walks with a limp today. Even though Tommie had died the evening of the 19th of May, his name is on "The Wall" under 20 May 1968 since the aid station did not get around to declaring him dead until after midnight.

The explosions continued through the night but tapered off as dawn was breaking. We ventured out just after sunrise to see the ground completely littered with trash and unexploded ordnance and a large plume of smoke still rising from the ammo dump. Most of the tents had holes ripped in them and a few were totally collapsed. We found that most of our helicopters were inoperable due to the damage they sustained during the night. We later were told that over ten million pounds of explosives had been blown up that night. If you do the math, that is equivalent to between one quarter to one third the size of the atomic bomb dropped on Hiroshima. The amazing part was that while there had been several troops injured, only one had died. Tommie!! He was a good guy and would be sorely missed.

The next few days were a blur of activity trying to restore our areas and helicopters to some sort of normalcy. The EOD guys showed up and very carefully removed all the unexploded ordnance lying around. We were busy patching tents and putting up new ones and the crew chiefs were busy repairing our broken helicopters. You could tell that everyone's nerves were still on edge since we would all jump about 10 feet straight up every time the EOD guys would detonate a pile of the unexploded ordnance at a site about 1000 meters west of Camp.

They would perform this heart stopping exercise at irregular intervals throughout the day. Every time they would do it, and once I'd gotten my heart beating again, I'd look in awe at the mushroom cloud that was produced by the blast. These clouds would often reach up to 6,000 to 8,000 feet and I couldn't help but wonder how high they went the night of the fire. Anyway, I'd wished that they could have warned us of the impending blast by sounding a horn or something which may have prevented me from calling them every unsavory name that I knew and even some that I made up.

We were still in the midst of the northern monsoon season and it would rain at least some each day. At one point, we had a cold front come through and the rain came down in buckets for about 5 days straight, the temperature dropped into the 40s and we were freezing. Our battery area had been set up on a terraced hillside which was now a cascading waterfall and the wooden pallets that we used for flooring were all floating, in a heap, on the downhill side of the tent. Perhaps the oddest situation was the Mexican standoff that happened when a group of about 20 rats, that had been chased out of there hiding areas by the rain, were now atop one of the floating pallets on one side of the tent and we were standing on another pallet on the other side, also trying to stay dry. We had formed a sort of informal pact in that we didn't bother them and they didn't bother us. The tent stakes that kept our tent up had become loose from all the rain and Frank said to me, "Come on, we've got to go pound the stakes back in before the tent collapses." So, we went out in the pouring rain and as Frank hit the stakes with a 10 pound sledgehammer, he had me hold his belt to keep him from slipping around in the mud. After having reset several of the metal stakes, we were both looking at the head of the next stake that Frank was about to hit, when we saw a small lightning bolt jump out of the head of the stake and hit head of the sledgehammer as Frank was in mid swing. A big bolt of lightning had just hit the radio antennae about 20 feet away and a small portion of it wanted to get to the head of Frank's sledgehammer. Anyway, the sledgehammer went flying off in one direction and Frank and I went dancing off in another after the bolt passed through our bodies. We were both shaking our hands in the air trying to get rid of the intense tingling sensation. It probably looked like we were performing some ancient Indian rain dance or had just totally lost our minds as we danced around. We decided that that was enough tent maintenance for one day.

The author, Lt. Jackson and WO1 Steve Woods during monsoons

The rains continued. Now our subterranean bunker, that had just been repaired from the artillery round damage, was totally flooded. While we sat around in the tent trying to stay dry, we were devising a plan on how to drain the water out of the bunker once the rains stopped. We had just about settled on a plan when we heard some strange snapping, crackling and popping noises coming from the bunker. As we approached the doorway to the bunker, we watched in disbelief as the entire roof slowly collapsed into the hole that had once been our refuge. Oh!! Crap!! Back to the drawing board. I was beginning to really hate this place. Just think, in another 35 days we'd get our own chapter in the Bible. But, just like Noah, we eventually saw the sun reappear and got back to work fixing our hole in the ground.

The bunker collapses from monsoon rains

Repair work starts on the bunker

As we resumed flying, we saw that the countryside had not fared very well either. The rivers and streams were all overflowing their banks and we saw many human and animal bodies floating along toward the sea. The First Cavalry Division conducted a number of airlift operations to help local civilians reposition to higher ground until the waters retreated.

Shortly after the floods subsided, we got a mission to escort a combat assault that was being put into an LZ out in the coastal flats just northeast of Camp Evans. This mission was to put several companies of infantry on the ground to conduct a search and clear operation in this region because the local villagers were complaining that, after the floods, the NVA had moved into the area and were seizing rice and other supplies and generally terrorizing the residents. We were briefed that there would be 10 Hueys in the lift and they would make three sorties into the LZ to land all the troops participating in the operation. We were also told that some of the artillery that would be preparing the LZ would be naval gunfire from the U.S.S. New Jersey. Oh! Cool!! We were all excited to be able to work with the WWII battleship that was a piece of history. This old battlewagon had an awesome amount of firepower and we wondered if she was going to be firing her 16 inch guns into the LZ during the prep. The projectiles from these guns each weighed 2000 pounds, as much as a Volkswagen Beetle, and we had heard that it was very impressive when all three guns in one turret fired simultaneously and the rounds landed on the target side by side.

They said, "As per SOP, at one minute before landing on the first sortie, the artillery would shut off and the last rounds would be indicated by a white phosphorus round."

This procedure indicated to the lift ships, that were now on short final approach, that no more artillery rounds would be impacting the LZ and that they were cleared to land. We would begin firing our rockets around the perimeter of the LZ as soon as we saw the white phosphorous rounds impact. This would provide continuous suppressive fire for the lift ships throughout their approach, landing and departure. As if this weren't enough firepower, each of the 10 Hueys had two M-60 machine guns and 8 troops sitting in the cargo door with their guns pointed out at anyone who might decide to take a shot at them.

We took off, rendezvoused with the lift ships and were proceeding toward the LZ. We could see the artillery rounds impacting the LZ but the explosions all seemed to be of "normal" size. Suddenly, right down the long axis of the LZ, three huge blasts detonated in a row sending smoke and debris in every direction and nearly obscuring our view of the site. I quickly turned my attention toward the sea and could just barely make out a very large ship on the horizon. As I was watching it, I saw a big flash emit from its front end. I radioed to everyone that, "The New Jersey just fired again, watch the LZ."

As I was moving my eyes toward the LZ, I actually saw the 3 rounds streaking toward their target. The LZ once again erupted with three huge geysers of dirt and debris and we were now close enough to hear and feel the concussion from the blasts. The lift ships were approaching the one minute out point and we were all watching for the white phosphorous rounds to impact.

Impact they did. A blinding flash went off in the LZ as if someone were taking our picture with the world's largest flashbulb. While temporarily blinded by this flash, the lift ships flew straight into a huge white cloud that was getting larger by the moment. The cloud of white phosphorus smoke was now totally obscuring the LZ and all of the lift ships. Since we had not yet entered the cloud, we broke away from it and headed back the way we had come. The lead Huey's pilot was on the radio ordering the rest of his flight to "execute inadvertent IMC breakup procedures!" This was a plan that had been devised in case a flight of aircraft, flying in close proximity to one another, inadvertently flew into the clouds (Instrument Meteorological Conditions) and lost sight of one another. To prevent mid-air collisions, the lead aircraft, commonly called chalk one, would fly straight ahead, chalk two would turn 30 degrees to the right, chalk three 30 degrees left, chalk four 60 degrees right, etc. Once clear of the clouds, they would join back up visually.

As we watched the cloud, hoping there would be no mid-airs, the Hueys all exited the cloud headed in different directions and looked very much like a covey of quail that had been flushed by a bird dog.

The flight joined back up and headed for the LZ as the cloud there was dissipating. We provided covering fire as they touched down and dropped off their troops and the rest of the mission went off without a hitch. We did note in our after action report that while we appreciated the naval gunfire, in the future, they could keep their white phosphorous rounds to themselves.

The weather slowly improved and our operations got back to normal. Dave Whitling came to me and said we'd be flying together the next day and that our section was scheduled to fly cover for a combat assault of 8 Huey lift ships that would be putting troops into a landing zone in the foothills of the mountains to our southwest. He said that the intell didn't indicate very much enemy activity in the area, so, it should be a milk run. It was a beautiful morning and the sun was shining as we, and our wingman, took off in our B model Hueys and headed to the rendezvous area to join up with the lift ships. As we neared the area, we saw the flight of lift ships orbiting a couple of miles to the south of the LZ. We also noticed an unusual number of Command & Control (C&C) aircraft flying in circles over the proposed LZ. Normally there would be 2 or 3 C&C aircraft overhead for such a mission but today there were at least 7 flying in circles at about 6,000 to 8,000 feet. "How strange," we thought. There was a corresponding large amount of radio traffic going on, too. We also noted that there was not any artillery prep of the area going on and were confused by that. Dave then contacted the "Head Honcho" C&C ship and reported that we were on station and ready to escort the lift ships.

"Head Honcho" then told us that there was a CH-54 Flying Crane approaching the area from the north and that we should "saddle-up" on him and escort him to the LZ. The Crane was flying at about 2,500 feet when we spotted him and we assumed our positions on either side. I thought that maybe the Crane was bringing in an artillery piece that would be put down in the LZ but as we pulled alongside there was no sling load under the Crane. What I did notice was that the Crane's rotor blades were coned up significantly as if the aircraft was carrying a huge load but I saw none.

As we approached the LZ we saw the proposed landing zone was not an open field but a heavily jungled area with trees that were 100 to 150 feet tall. Our confusion was ended abruptly when the Crane pilot's voice came on the radio and said, "Bombs away in 3-2-1" at which point we saw a very large bomb detach from the bottom of the Crane and head earthward trailing a tiny drogue parachute behind it. Simultaneously, the Crane shot straight upward and disappeared from sight and Dave and I looked at each other with eyes the size of saucers. Once again, we found ourselves in the wrong place at the wrong time. Dave cranked the aircraft into a very hard right turn and started to dive away from the LZ. Even with the sun shining, we saw the incredibly bright flash as "The Bomb" exploded behind us. A few seconds later the shock wave caught up with us. Initially, it was like being lifted by a wave in the surf but within a second or so, there was the tremendous "BOOM" and a feeling that the wave had crashed on top of us. Dave quickly regained control of the aircraft and we turned back around to see a burgeoning and angry looking mushroom cloud climbing past the C&C aircraft orbiting above us. Dave asked the "Head Honcho" C&C aircraft, "What the HELL was that?" He replied, "Oh! Didn't anybody tell you that we were experimenting with creating an instant LZ using old 20,000 pound "Blockbuster Bombs" from the mid 1950s and the B-36 bomber days?" Dave replied, "NNNOOO!! I think I would have remembered that. You almost blew us out of the sky!"

"Oh! Sorry about that but you can go 'saddle up' on the lift ships and escort them to the LZ now." Dave was still shouting obscenities that I could hear even though his mic was not on and there was plenty of ambient noise from the engine, rotors and wind. We joined up with the lift ships just as the lead Huey was approaching the smoking hole. Lead said, "Alright, this is going to be a single shipper so, the rest of you hold off to the south until I come out." The other Huey's peeled off and headed south while we set up a racetrack orbit on either side of the LZ to provide cover. The lead Huey disappeared into the smoking hole for about 2 minutes then, slowly, climbed back out after dropping off his troops and told the second lift ship to proceed in but to be careful of all the broken trees. The smoke was beginning to clear and we could see that the LZ was clogged with hundreds of trees that had been splintered and stripped of their bark and looked like a huge game of pick-up stix. Typically, the first aircraft into such an LZ would carry a bunch of engineers with their chainsaws to cut down any snags that might interfere with other helicopters arriving. The engineers that the lead ship had dropped off were now calling for him to come back to extract them because the hole was so steep and so deep that they couldn't crawl up out of it. Hummm! Instant LZ....Good idea BUT....!!

Over the next few weeks we flew quite a lot of missions. The weather had improved significantly and the focus of the Divisions operations had shifted to conducting "Search and Clear" sweeps of large areas of the coastal plain in our area of operations. These missions would start in the morning with several airlifts of troops into areas around some towns and villages that were suspected of harboring NVA and Viet Cong troops. Usually, these would be joint operations that included ARVN (Army of the Republic of South Vietnam) troops. We would fly cover during the airlift ops and then return to Camp Evans to rearm and refuel. Quite often we would be just completing our refueling and rearming and we'd be scrambled by operations to return to the area because a fire fight had started and we were needed to shoot for the friendlies. Many times the mission briefing that we got on the radio on our way back out would say that the unit in trouble was close to being overrun by the enemy. Upon arriving, it would turn out to be that the ARVN unit and the handful of American advisers to the unit, along with several ARVN officers and NCOs were, indeed, surrounded. Typically, it was usually a much larger ARVN unit, like a battalion, that had come up against a smaller enemy force and during the ensuing battle, many of the South Vietnamese soldiers would throw down their guns and run, leaving the others to fend for themselves. The reason for this behavior was that the average ARVN soldier was a conscript that had previously been a fisherman or farmer, been drafted, given brief training and pressed into service. Individually, they did not care who was in charge in Saigon, be they South Vietnamese or North Vietnamese. All they wanted to do was fish or farm and raise their families. I need to make it clear that I did meet many ARVN officers and soldiers that were, indeed, very brave and dedicated individuals but a very large majority of the rank and file had no patriotism or national pride, and truly did not care who won.

After witnessing this situation time after time, I and many of the other pilots in the unit realized that there was no hope that the South was ever going to win the war. Over the years I've thought often about all the lives, both friendly and enemy, that would have been saved had only General Westmoreland and Secretary of Defense Robert McNamara seen and comprehended this behavior. I still find it amazing that I could recognize this situation after only a few weeks in country but the guys in charge of running this war, were blind to it. As a result of my observations, I changed my main motivation from protecting the "Freedom Loving People of South Vietnam," to doing everything I could to ensure that as many American soldiers got home alive, as possible.

Around the same time, I got orders from our battalion headquarters to go to Vung Tau to pick up a Cobra helicopter and fly it back to our battery. Yeah! We were finally starting to get our Cobras. The Cobra would significantly enhance our capabilities since it could carry 28 more rockets than our current B & C model Hueys, was much faster, had air conditioning and a flexible turret with a 7.62mm minigun capable of firing 4000 rounds per minute. The minigun was a six barrel Gatling type machine gun and was very effective against personnel in the open. Having these new aircraft meant that each time we launched a section of two Cobras on a fire mission, we would be arriving on station with 152 rockets and about 3000 rounds of minigun ammo between us. That's a lot of firepower.

As I prepared to board the C-130 for my trip to Vung Tau, I met several other pilots from other First Cavalry Division units who were also going to ferry Cobras back for their units. Since we would be flying back as single pilots in each aircraft, we agreed to stick together and fly back as a group thereby providing mutual support if we ran into any problems. Vung Tau was a small peninsula that jutted out into the South China Sea just southeast of Saigon. After we checked into the Pacific Hotel, we agreed to meet down in the bar. The hotel was centrally located in downtown and served as the BOQ (Bachelor Officers Quarters) and Officers Club. While at the bar we learned from some of the officers stationed there, that Vung Tau was considered a resort city of sorts and that we could feel safe there since the area was not just a spot that US troops could come to for an in-country R&R (Rest & Relaxation) but where the NVA also allowed their troops to R&R. An unofficial truce existed between both parties and no one was suppose to do anything to screw it up. The local guys told us that East Beach was run by the Americans and that we could go there to relax and enjoy the ocean but they said DO NOT go to West Beach since this was where the NVA troops hung out. While the American troops wore their uniforms around town, the NVA troops did not but it was not hard to spot them. Many North Vietnamese were taller and bigger than their South Vietnamese brethren and these large military aged males would stare at you with hatred in their eyes when you encountered them on the street. The whole thing gave me a very creepy feeling and I couldn't wait to get out of there. The next day we went out to the airfield and were taken to our aircraft where we conducted an inventory, a preflight inspection and a run-up of the aircraft. Once we were satisfied that everything was in order, we signed for the helicopter, cranked up and headed north. I must say that, from the air, South Vietnam was a very pretty place. We flew along the beach with it's azure blue waters. To our left was green jungle that periodically dissolved into the geometrically eye pleasing rice paddies and groves of banana trees. At several points along our flight path, the mountain range to our left would encroach on the sea to our right and we could observe a beautiful crystal clear mountain stream cascading down through the lush green jungle vegetation on its way to the sea. We would comment to each other over the radio that this place was so beautiful that it could be a vacation resort destination if there weren't a war going on.

The author climbs into a new Cobra

As we cruised along, one of the other pilots asked if any of us had ever seen anyone do a loop in a Cobra. We all replied "No" to his question whereupon, he said, "Okay, watch this!" We were all cruising at 5000 feet and he then climbed to 8000 feet, pulled the nose of the Cobra up to vertical and the aircraft began to fall backwards into its own rotor system. As we watched, the Cobra wobbled and floundered around inverted and he passed our altitude going down like a rock. Ever so slowly, the nose of the aircraft began to point earthward as he fell toward the ground and he eventually pulled out of the screaming ass dive just 1000 feet above the ground. I was amazed at how stupid and dangerous this maneuver was since the Cobra has a semi-rigid rotor system like the Huey. In this system, the two rotor blades teeter-totter back and forth on a hub mounted to the mast. In normal flight, the aircraft virtually hangs from the rotor and is kept there by gravity and/ or centrifugal force during dives and turns. But in this situation, the aircraft was falling into the rotor, unloading it and allowing it to wildly flop around. It is possible, in this situation, for the rotor to flop into the mast, cutting through the mast and separating the rotor from helicopter with disastrous results. There was no skill involved, only pure luck that this fool did not wind up buried about 20 feet under the jungle. We all told him that it was a dumb thing to do and that he should check over the aircraft since he probably overstressed many components doing his stunt.

CHAPTER 6

Aircraft Commander

Over the next few weeks, I made several trips to Vung Tau to ferry aircraft back to our unit. We were quickly approaching the 50% level of Cobras to Hueys. The unit had received some more Cobra qualified pilots and some of our Huey pilots had been sent off to Cobra Qualification Classes. During this transition, we were a little shorthanded at times and it was decided that I would start training to be checked out as an aircraft commander. This was quite an honor since some pilots went their entire one year tour of duty without ever being qualified as an A/C. I was a little reluctant because of the tremendous responsibility involved but all the old timers assured me that I would do fine. It was about this time that we had a pilot arrive in our unit from our "sister" unit, "A" Battery. WO1 Brown had been transferred to us as a replacement for Tommie Rolf and we could always use more help, so, we welcomed him aboard. It wasn't long after Warrant Officer Brown arrived that he was flying front seat in a Cobra with his platoon leader, Captain Bill Brummer, on a night mission to provide cover for a medevac out in the mountains. During the mission, the weather closed in, they inadvertently flew into the clouds and got vertigo since their attitude indicator had failed. The first generation of attitude indicators in the Cobra were very unreliable and would often roll over and die during a simple turn or upon pulling out of a dive. The end result that night was that they became inverted and fell out of the clouds upside down but managed to right the aircraft and return to Camp Evans. The next morning, we all went out to look over the aircraft to see what damage they had done. We were amazed that the damage was so extensive. The maintenance inspectors had found over 200 Red X conditions on the aircraft. A single Red X was sufficient to ground an aircraft and prevent it from being flown until repaired, but 200? As we looked at the aircraft, we were stunned that they even made it back. All five transmission mounts were broken. These are like shock absorbers that dampen out vibrations from the rotor system to the airframe. The rotor blades were BENT! As I held the end of the blade in my hands and looked along its length, I noticed that about 6 feet from the tip there was a 6 inch drop in the blade before it straightened out and continued toward the mast. The mast had been bumped several times and was now oblong instead of round and the bumped portion had several vertical cracks in it. Then someone showed me the "Lift Link." The Lift Link is a square steel bar about one inch wide and about 8 inches long that is THE connection between rotor system and the airframe. Should this link fail, the rotor and the airframe would separate in flight and each would go its own way, but mostly, straight down. As I looked at this lift link I was shocked to see that it had been stretched about 2 inches and cracked through either end to the point where there was but an eighth of an inch of metal keeping the Cobra in the sky. This incident reminded me of the pilot that had done the "Loop" while we were flying back from Vung Tau only a few weeks ago and I couldn't help but wonder how much damage he had done to his aircraft. Anyway, the maintenance folks had decided that the damage was too extensive and that the aircraft would need to be sent back to the states for a major overhaul. I could see another trip to Vung Tau in my future to pick up a new Cobra.

My training for Aircraft Commander status was progressing nicely and I was being assigned a Cobra almost every day. I would fly the aircraft from the backseat, since this was the pilots station, while one of the current A/Cs would be in my front seat, telling me where and when to fire the rockets while they operated the radios and coordinated the attack. It was during this training period that I found out how tricky the NVA was. We would be scrambled out to shoot for some friendly unit that was in contact with the bad guys and we'd call for the friendlies to "Pop Smoke." The friendlies would then throw out a smoke grenade and we would identify the color of the smoke to verify their position. The Aircraft Commander would say, "We've got your yellow smoke in sight, where are your troops in reference to the smoke?" Whereupon, the ground commander would say something like, "I verify yellow smoke. All of my troops are West of the smoke and the enemy is East of the smoke, about 100 meters." At this point we would have a pretty good idea of where everyone was and we'd and be able to form an attack plan.

That was the way things normally went, but on occasion, we'd called for smoke, and suddenly, there would be 4 or 5 smokes in a rainbow of colors, emanating from everywhere. This was usually the NVA trying to confuse the situation and delay us from starting our rocket runs. Another trick they would pull was that they would see what color grenade the friendlies threw and they would throw out the same color. But the best of all his tricks had to be the "Phony Ground Commander" trick. In this ruse, the NVA had found the frequency that the American forces were using and had someone with an American accent and a more powerful radio, talk to us as if he were the American ground commander. This imposter would even throw out smoke to identify his position and give us directions to fire on the position actually occupied by the Americans. If things seemed screwy, we would ask our "Friendly Guy" to authenticate the message. To authenticate he needed to have a current CEOI (Communications and Electronics Operating Instructions handbook). These were code books that each field commander and each aircrew carried and were only good for 30 days at a time. A new CEOI would immediately be issued if one was missing or compromised in any way.

When the "Phony Ground Commander" was unable to authenticate, we would broadcast that the Real American Commander should come up on his alternate frequency which we knew after consulting the CEOI. When we switched frequencies, the Real Ground Commander would authenticate and tell us that he could hear our conversations with the Phony Guy and he was worried that we were going to fire on his position. Since Phony Guy had already identified his position with smoke, we would just verify it with the Real Ground Commander, then shoot up Phony Guys location. It was kind of scary knowing you had been talking to the enemy.

While I was still in training for Aircraft Commander, I was scrambled out on a fire mission with my platoon leader in the front seat as the actual A/C. As we got airborne, he called Ops to get our mission and we were told to join up with the 1st platoon section that had been launched a few minutes ago. That section, lead by Captain Barloco, determined that additional assets from our unit would be necessary to handle the mission since they had encountered a large enemy force and the friendly forces on the ground were locked in a dynamic fire fight with these bad guys. As we arrived on station, Captain Barloco was briefing us on the situation and said he'd mark the area where the enemy was by shooting some rockets into it. Captain Barloco was flying a B Model Huey that day and had a machine gunner on board, in addition to the crew chief, to provide covering fire when they pulled out of their rocket runs. I had positioned us above and behind Captain Barloco so we could see exactly where he was shooting. As he pulled out of his dive, after marking the enemy location, we saw his gunner continuing to shoot his M-60 machine gun into the enemy position to cover their break. Suddenly, there was a big explosion on the side of Captain Barloco's aircraft. He called and said they were hit but the aircraft was still flyable so they headed back to Camp Evans and the hospital pad.

We followed him back just in case he had to set down and once he landed at Evans, we returned to complete the mission. We were afraid that he'd been hit by an RPG so the rest of our runs were from a slightly higher altitude. That evening we found out that the explosion was actually a "Self Inflicted Wound" in that the gunner had gotten target fixation and walked his stream of bullets right into the rocket tubes causing one of the rocket warheads to explode. Needless to say, we had some remedial training for all of our door gunners after that incident.

Around this time I was checked out as an Aircraft Commander and began flying as a wingman to my section leaders. I continued to learn a lot about tactics and various situations that would develop on our fire missions. One thing that I noticed on several occasions was that when there was a heated fire fight going on and the ground commander was shouting and sounded frightened and we could hear machine guns firing and grenades exploding in the background while trying to talk to us on the radio, he would often give us conflicting information on the location of his troops. I was very impressed by the way our section leaders would be able to detect, by his voice, that he may be confused and the last thing we wanted to do was to fire on our own troops because of his confusion. They would try to calm him down and then orient him by pointing out landmarks that he should be able to see and ask for additional smoke grenades to be thrown out. The problem often came down to the fact that he had confused his cardinal directions, for example he was thinking that north was south and east was west. So, the Section Leaders would have him pop smoke on his location and then throw a different colored smoke towards the enemy. Once we saw the second smoke we knew, for instance, that the enemy was west of his location and not east as he had been claiming.

Our Standard Operating Procedures required us to always start a fire mission by shooting a "Marking Pair" of rockets into the suspected enemy position so that if we had the wrong location we would minimize any injuries to friendlies before unloading on the area. The section leaders would say to the ground commander, "I've identified the enemy position and am rolling in with a marking pair. Adjust my wingman." After the rounds hit the target area, the ground commander would say, "That's perfect, fire for effect" or, "Move your rounds 30 meters further east and fire for effect." Whereupon, I would make the necessary adjustment and fire 5 or 6 pair of rockets into the target. These adjustments would continue throughout the mission as the enemy and friendly forces moved around on the battlefield. The mission would end when the enemy position and threat was eliminated and we were released by the ground commander, however, if we were running out of ammunition and the battle was still on going, we would call operations to have them launch another section to take over while we went back to rearm and refuel.

Often, after a very hot battle, the ground commander would thank us for, "...saving our ass." But what we really appreciated were those ground commanders that had been confused on their position, thanking us for calming them down before they had us fire on their own troops. I made a mental note of making very sure of friendly positions before firing when I became a section leader.

In fact, it wasn't long before I was appointed as a section leader and was having to develop attack plans for my 2 aircraft on fire missions. Some of our "Old Timer" section leaders had completed their tours of duty and been reassigned back to the States, so, someone had to take their positions and many of them had recommended me. While I was honored, I was very nervous assuming that much responsibility. The first missions I went on were kind of run of the mill. Nothing unusual, no requirements to shoot close to the friendly forces, and no others strange situations, so, I was feeling pretty good about the job I was doing. As they say, "Pride goeth before the fall." This applies since my next mission was to help out some Long Range Recon Patrol guys (LRRPS) that had been discovered by the NVA and were trying to evade and escape.

The LRRPS were specially trained infantrymen, normally assembled into teams of five men, that were sent out into the jungle for about 30 days at a time. Their mission was to sneak around, find the enemy, follow the enemy and report back in on the enemy's movements and operations. Above all else, they were NOT to engage the enemy since they were normally, heavily outnumbered. When we arrived on station, I made contact with the LRRP team and they explained that they were running to the west and would mark their position by dropping a smoke grenade. I identified the smoke and rolled in with a marking pair. The LRRPs said, between breaths as they ran, "That's good, shoot 'em up." My wingman rolled in and fired several pair where I had just shot and I came back around and fired again. Suddenly, the LRRPs were yelling on the radio to, "CEASE FIRE! CEASE FIRE! YOU'VE HIT ONE OF OUR GUYS!!"

"Oh, Crap!" I thought, how is that possible? Did he go back for something? Was he bringing up the rear? How the hell could that have happened? The Huey that had been sent out to extract the LRRPs was just arriving on station and he swooped in for a quick pickup. The LRRPs managed to recover the body of their teammate and jumped on board the Huey for a quick getaway. After they were out of the area we unloaded the rest of our ammo on the NVA position and returned to Camp Evans. Upon landing we were met by the Battery Commander and the Operations Officer. They told me that there would be an Article 32 investigation under the Uniformed Code of Military Justice into the "Friendly Fire" incident and that I was grounded until it was completed. As if I didn't already feel like crap.

Two days later the investigators from the CID (Criminal Investigations Division) arrived at our area and took sworn statements from all the crew members involved in the mission. I was envisioning all kinds of consequences and was sure that at the very least, I would never again be a section leader or even an aircraft commander. I was even beginning to wonder what Ft. Leavenworth would be like.

The next day, the Battery Commander called all 4 of us into his tent. I already felt miserable about what had happened and was ready for any punishment deemed necessary. As we all stood at attention in front of his desk, the CO said, "Relax, you guys didn't kill the LRRP!!"

"WHAT??" we all said in unison.

The CO explained that the investigation team found that the LRRP had been shot in the back by an RPG (rocket propelled grenade) launched by the NVA. Since it was a rocket, of sorts, the other LRRPS thought it was one of ours and had called the cease fire. We were still very sad that the LRRP had been killed but very happy to find out that we didn't do it. Talk about mixed emotions!! The CO told us to stop by operations and get our assignments for tomorrow, we were all back on flight status, " ...and, by the way, you guys saved the lives of the other four LRRPs."

CHAPTER 7

Air To Air Combat?

I t was only a few days later that I was assigned mortar patrol again. This time I was flying a B model Huey and we were doing our normal orbits around Camp Evans keeping an eye out for the bad guys launching mortars or rockets at the LZ. Around midnight I got a call from my controller at Division Artillery asking if we could see any other helicopters flying along the beach to our east. We scanned the area but did not see anything unusual and reported that back to the controller. There was silence for a few minutes then the controller called back and said that headquarters wanted us to go fly up the beach and if we encountered any ENEMY helicopters, we should shoot them down. "WHAT?? Are you kidding?"

"NO Sir, we are not kidding!! We have reports from some of our troops on the ground that they have observed helicopters flying southbound from the DMZ and landing on the beach to discharge troops and we have confirmed that no friendly forces are involved in any such operation and that the division does not have any other aircraft airborne at this time other than yours. The division commander requests that you proceed to the area and engage any enemy helicopters you find."

Well, this totally boggled my mind and as I turned to fly towards the beach I had the controller authenticate his message just to make sure this wasn't the enemy screwing with us again. He gave us the proper authentication and said, "The CG (Commanding General) wants continuous updates as you check this out." I said, "Roger that!" and gave them my present position as I proceeded to the beach. I then told my crew chief and door gunner that they were NOT to fire if they saw anything until I authorized them to shoot. I also had the artillery controller prepare to fire illumination flares along the beach in case I did see anything so I could try to ID the aircraft before we engaged them. Since we were reportedly the only friendly aircraft in the area, I shut off my anti-collision light and position lights so the enemy wouldn't see us coming. We were at 3000 feet as we hit the beach and turned north toward the DMZ. There was a partial moon that night and I was hoping we'd be able to spot a flicker from the rotor blades or some other reflection that would reveal the enemy aircraft. As we flew along the beach I slowed down and lowered our altitude so I would be in a better position to engage the enemy. I was in the process of reporting our position to the artillery controller when the UHF radio came to life and interrupted me with the following message that was being broadcast in the blind. "This is Panama Radar on guard frequency with a WARNING for all friendly aircraft operating in the vicinity of the DMZ. Get on the ground IMMEDIATELY!! Hawk missiles are about to be launched at enemy aircraft in the vicinity of the DMZ. Panama Radar, out!"

Oh! Crap!! The Hawk missiles were very large anti-aircraft missiles located near the Hi-Van pass area near Da Nang and had sufficient range to cover all of the I Corps area. I was pretty sure that I was one, if not, the only aircraft they could see on their radar since I was still at about 1500 feet above the ground and the enemy was, reportedly, on the beach or a lot closer to it than I was. While Air Force and Navy aircraft were all equipped with an electronic box called an IFF (Identification, Friend or Foe) few, if any, Army aircraft had this capability. It was considered nonessential since we never engaged in air to air combat, UNTIL TODAY!!

I bottomed the collective pitch and pointed the nose down at a very steep angle and drove the airspeed up past the red-line on the gauge as I tried to loose altitude as quickly as possible. I thought, well, if they fire that Hawk missile at us, we might see the flash but we'll never hear the BOOM!! All the time we were in the dive I was yelling at the artillery controller to stop the Hawk battery from firing since we were probably his only target. I didn't get a response from the controller since we were now too low for radio reception. We continued south along the beach, skimming over the waves, until we were due East of Camp Evans. As we turned inbound, we re-established commo with the artillery controller and told him we were returning to base since we were almost shot down by the Hawk battery. He apologized and said there was some coordination problems that had to be worked out. I'LL SAY!!

I suggested, as calmly as possible, that the next time they have suspected enemy helicopters cross the DMZ, that they call the Air Force or Navy fighters to handle them. I may have made some references to his level of education and the purity of his family lineage at the same time. Anyway, we lived to fight another day and there never was another report of enemy helicopters buzzing around.

CHAPTER 8

New Stuff

One day I was called into operations and told that my section had been given a mission of covering a C-130 Hercules cargo aircraft that would be doing some low level spraying mission and my section of Cobras would be following him on his spraying runs to provide covering fire in case he was shot at while at treetop level. The ops officer told me that the name of the mission was "Operation Ranch Hand" and the C-130 would be spraying a herbicide that would make all the leaves fall off the trees in the jungle so we could detect the enemy better. I asked if we would need to wear our gas masks during the operation like we did when we covered other aircraft spraying liquid CS (riot gas). He said, "No that's not necessary, they told us that this stuff only affects the plants and trees and is safe if humans come in contact with it." That was fine with me since it was always a real pain if you had to fly with your gas mask on since it limited your visibility and often fogged up.

We took off and met up with the C-130 a couple of miles west of Camp Evans. When we established radio contact with him, he told us what area he would be spraying and I told him that we would be flying directly behind him and at the same altitude. I said that if he started to get shot at that he just needed to call, "Taking fire!!" and we would immediately fire rockets into the area under his tail, so, don't be surprised by the BOOMS. I told him that we could stay with him as long as he wasn't going any faster than 140 knots. He replied that that would be okay. As we followed him on his runs, our aircraft were completely soaked by his spray and I was a bit concerned about the chemical getting into our fresh air systems as well as the electronics and other equipment. I tried to fly a bit higher and still be in a position to provide covering fire but this proved to be very difficult and, after all, my primary mission was to keep the C-130 from getting shot down. I would just have to apologize the crew chief when I told him he'd have to wash the aircraft thoroughly and check out the systems for any residue of the chemical. I asked the C-130 pilot what this chemical was so we could use the right cleaning stuff on our aircraft and he replied, "Oh! It's some new stuff they call Agent Orange."

Speaking of new stuff, our headquarters called down to say that there was a class that was being given by the ordnance Branch folks on some new rockets that we would soon start getting and they needed a few pilots from our battery to attend. I was among the group selected to go and soon was sitting in a class on the new 17 pound warhead rocket, the new proximity fuse for our regular 10 pound warhead rockets and a totally new rocket called the Flechette.

Author with 10 and 17 pound warhead rockets

The 17 pounders were virtually the same as our 10 pounders, they explained, but with almost double the bang, so, we would have to be careful shooting them near friendly troops. We all agreed that more bang would be nice and looked forward to getting some of the new warheads to try out.

Next, they told us about rockets we'd be getting with a proximity fuse. They explained that these rockets were designed to detonated just above the ground so that most of the blast was not absorbed by the dirt or mud and would prove more lethal than the impact fuses we were currently using. They told us it worked by emitting a radio wave and it would detonate when it detected the wave being reflected back by the ground, a tree or something else. We told them that these rockets may work well when we were shooting out near the beach or coastal flats, but they might be a problem when we were shooting out in the triple canopy jungles in the mountains to our west. At least, with the regular fuses, we had a good chance of our rockets getting down through the trees in the mountains but with these proximity fuses, we'd only be killing birds and monkeys in the treetops. Their answer was that we would have to decide when it would be most advantageous to use them. Okay then!!

Finally, they brought out the new Flechette rocket. They explained that each rocket warhead contained 2,200 nails with tiny fins where the head of the nail would normally be. When the rocket was fired, it would accelerate to almost the speed of sound before the rocket motor burned out. At rocket motor burnout and maximum velocity, the fuse would fire and all 2,200 of these one inch long darts would be blown out the front of the warhead, much like a shotgun blast. They told us that when a pair of these rockets were fired at the optimum angle and range, that it would result in lethal coverage of an area the size of a football field. They did qualify the lethality of the Flechette by saying that it was not effective against people that had any kind of overhead cover like a tree or bunker. One of the pilots said, "So, you're telling us that these will be good whenever we find about 100 enemy soldiers marching in formation down Highway 1. Is that right?"

"Exactly!!" said the ordnance Branch instructor, not knowing he had just been ridiculed since that kind of scenario never happens. The instructor went on to say that because of it's wide area of coverage, we were not allowed to fire these rockets within 1,000 meters of friendly forces just in case there was a rocket motor malfunction that sent the rocket astray. The instructor had no comment when we explained that our primary mission was close air support for troops in contact and that 1,000 meters wasn't really CLOSE!!

As we rode back to the battery area, we discussed our mixed feelings about what we had learned. It was agreed that while there were some "Pros" about the new equipment, there certainly were a lot of "Cons" to contend with. We'd just have to wait until we received the new stuff and check it out in the free fire areas before we gave it a thumbs up or down.

In just over a week we received a load of the new 17 pound warheads and promptly loaded them up and headed for the free fire zone to check them out. A free fire zone was an area that had been cleared of any civilians or friendly troops so that we could test fire weapons without endangering anyone, except, perhaps, any enemy troops that might be transiting the area and that was just their tough luck.

Upon arriving at the free fire zone, we picked out a tree that stood alone in a field and agreed that it would be our target. I volunteered to go first and rolled into a dive at the lone tree. I fired a pair of the 17 pounders and they headed straight toward the tree. I continued the dive, keeping the tree in my cross hairs. The rocket motors burned out at about 1,000 meters, as expected, and I waited for the twin blasts of the new warheads to demolish the tree. And I waited... and I waited... but I finally had to pull out of the dive because I was going way too fast. As I pulled up, the guys in the other aircraft came on the radio laughing and saying, "You didn't even come close. That was terrible!!" As I turned my aircraft back towards them, I looked down and saw that the smoke from my 2 rockets was rising from a spot at least 100 meters short of the tree. I was not able to see the rockets explode because they had dropped precipitously after rocket motor burnout and impacted well below my line of sight. Uh-Oh! That was not good.

I told the other guys what had happened but they remained unconvinced. Each of them, in turn, fired at the tree with similar results. We all agreed, this wasn't good, indeed!

We continued to try different attack scenarios and found that if we fired within 1,000 meters, we could easily hit the target but further out than that, the rockets fell like a Simonized brick and would impact well below the line of sight to the target. We finally found that by putting the cross hairs on the target, then raising the nose and applying some "Super Elevation" we could hit the target at ranges beyond 1,000 meters but it was a guessing game at best. We agreed that the other pilots in the unit would need to come out and practice firing these rockets before we could use them near any friendlies and we certainly could not fire them over the heads of any friendlies.

NEXT!! The next innovation we received were the rockets with the proximity fuses, so, several of us loaded up a bunch of these and headed for the free fire zone again. That poor tree was once again in for it, we hoped. We were all surprised and happy to see that these rockets operated as advertised. We found that they had the same flight characteristics of our regular 10 pound warhead rockets and they did explode just above the ground producing a very pronounced shrapnel pattern around our tree. Okay! We could use these whenever we were operating out along the beach or the coastal flats area. We also tried them in a jungle area in the free fire zone that had trees about 60 feet tall. Just as we suspected. The rockets exploded in the treetops, sending a shower of shredded leaves, coconuts and dead birds down on anyone who might be standing under the trees. The only affect this may have on an enemy soldier on the ground under a tree would be to scare the hell out of him while covering him with dead monkeys and bird feces or, maybe, just make him die laughing. Either way!

The next time we were covering lift ships on a combat assault out near the beach, we had decided to use these rounds to shoot along the tree lines on either side of the landing zone. When it was my turn to shoot, I rolled in and fired several pair of rockets and they started exploding right in front of my aircraft. WHOA! What the Hell!! I pulled up abruptly to avoid the cloud of self induced flak but we still had a bunch of shrapnel scrape over our canopy and damage our rotor blades. I immediately switched over to the inboard rocket pods, since we had loaded regular 10 pound rockets there, and completed the mission.

On arrival back at Camp Evans, I told the ops officer about what had happened and he said that there had been reports from other units about the same thing happening to them. It turned out that the proximity fuses were too sensitive and were detecting the other rocket that was flying along side it as the pair was launched. Once the rockets got about 30 to 40 meters in front of the launcher, they detected each other and detonated. Quite exciting but not something I wanted to repeat, so, we chose not to use the prox fuses until this problem had been totally resolved.

And last but not least, the Flechette rockets arrived. Needless to say, we were once again on our way back out to the free fire zone to check out the "Nails." That poor tree was in for it again. We would roll in and fire these, as we'd been told, very lethal rockets and watch for the devastation. NOTHING!! Again, NOTHING!! We were firing from the correct altitudes and dive angles but saw no effects on the target area. The only thing we did observe, on occasion, was a spent rocket tube impact the ground and tumbling end over end until it came to rest. Very disappointing!! After all, we were gunship pilots and liked to blow things up. These things were shaping up to be total DUDS.

A single Flechette "nail" next to a penny and quarter

At this point, one of the guys spied a small stream running through the corner of our free fire zone and decided to shoot at it. We watched as he shot and saw a 75 meter stretch of the stream erupt into a geyser of water shooting up to about 20 feet in the air. ALL RIGHT!! Now we knew we were doing something. We all joined in the fray, firing rocket after rocket into the stream and getting quite comfortable with this weapon. By the time we ran out of ammo and headed back to Evans, I was sure there wasn't a fish, frog or even tadpole left alive in that stream. We were quite impressed and readily accepted this new weapon into our inventory.

While that pretty much sums up all the new innovations in rockets, there was an additional "Innovation" in the rocket system that the research and development folks failed to inform us about. Allow me to apologize for getting "technical" in the following story but I believe it will help you understand how this situation developed.

We often had several rockets that would not fire when we hit the launch button. This sometimes occurred because, in the heat of battle, the pilot firing the rockets would punch the button too fast. The electronic firing system, called the intervelometer, would sequence the rockets so that two rockets from the same pod would not fire simultaneously. They designed it this way so that the rockets would not "bump" into each other during launch, otherwise the "bump" might send the rockets careening out of control. To accomplish this, the intervelometer required at least one tenth of a second between each button push so it could sequence to the next rocket to be fired. If the pilot hit the button too fast, the intervelometer would skip the next rocket in sequence, leaving it in the tube. This "hung rocket" situation would also occur sometimes because the electrical contacts on the back of the rocket had become dirty. The "why" didn't matter much to us. We could see that we still had rockets in the pod by looking out at them. This was frustrating since, very often, the troops on the ground still needed more fire support and a replacement section of gunships had not arrived yet. When we were flying Huey gunships, the crew chief, with his monkey strap on, would be able to climb out on the rocket pod and re-seat the electrical contacts so that we might be able to fire that rocket on the next pass. But, in the Cobra, this was not possible. The only option we had to salvage the stuck rockets was to pull the "ROCKETS" circuit breaker, wait ten seconds then push it back in. This action allowed the intervelometer to reset to tube #1, which would allow it to send an electrical charge to each rocket tube, in sequence, again. Usually, resetting the circuit breaker would allow us to get an additional 2 or 3 rockets per pod to fire, thus, helping out the troops on the ground.

It seems that the maintenance folks did not like the idea of us constantly pulling and resetting the "ROCKETS" circuit breaker and were afraid we'd start breaking them with this repeated action. They had complained about it to their superiors, who, in turn, complained to the research and development folks, who had a bright idea on how to fix the problem. Rather than just sending a bunch more 25 cent circuit breakers out to our units, the R&D guys redesigned the intervelometers. They called their creation the "B" model intervelometer and promptly sent them out to the field to replace our current "A" models. They "Fixed" the problem with the "A" models by having the "B" model apply a firing charge to not just the current rocket being fired but ALSO to each of the previously fired tubes. That way, they reasoned, any "hung rockets" would repeatedly try to fire, each time the button was pushed. Good idea, right? Does anyone see a potential problem here?

Well, yours truly got to experience the problem first hand. My section was launched to go shoot for a unit that was in contact with some NVA out in the foothills of the mountains. We identified all the friendlies and proceeded to shoot up the enemy's location. We had just finished firing all of our outboard rockets and switched over to the inboards when the ground commander called and said he wanted to reposition some of his troops. He said it would take about 15 to 20 minutes to do that and asked if we had enough fuel to stay on station that long. I told him that since we had already fired half of our rockets, it would be better for us to go rearm and refuel and that we could be back in that amount of time to continue. He agreed and released us. We hurried back to Camp Evans where we rearmed and refueled without shutting down. This was a normal thing to do especially when a battle was ongoing.

As we had promised, we arrived back on station in about 15 minutes and again checked in with the ground commander. He told us that his troops now had the NVA backed up against a mountain and he was ready for us to shoot them up. I surveyed the area as his troops marked their new positions and I noticed a resupply Huey about 1000 meters off to my right, up a draw, sideways to me with both cargo doors open. He was lowering supplies by rope to some other unit in that area. He was far enough away that he would not be a factor, so, I elected not to try to raise him on guard frequency, besides, he'd probably be done shortly. I told the ground commander that I was rolling in with a marking pair and to adjust my wingman. He rogered my transmission and I lowered my nose, lined up on the bad guys and punched the rocket button one time. BOOM!! We came to a complete stop in the air as all 38 rockets in my outboard rocket pods fired simultaneously. OH! MY GOD!! All the rockets were colliding with each other and shooting off in all different directions. I watched in horror as one rocket, in particular, made a sharp right turn and headed straight for the Huey hovering up the draw to my right. I couldn't help but watch as that rocket streaked in and was going to hit the Huey dead center. But miracles do happen! The rocket went in one cargo door and out the other and impacted further up the draw. I saw the crew chief kick all the other supplies out the door as the pilot lowered the nose and got the hell out of there as quickly as possible. I'm sure they all required a change of underwear when they got home. They were, and probably still are, trying to figure out what the hell that thing was that just zoomed through their cargo compartment. If you are reading this and were one of the crew on that aircraft, let me take this opportunity to apologize for that. I'm really sorry.

Meanwhile, back at the ranch, I watched as all the other rockets impacted all over the place, including some of the friendlies positions. As I was about to call the ground commander and apologize for the malfunction, he beat me to it. He called and said, "That was great Max, do that again!!"

NO! NO! NO! I was not doing anything AGAIN. I asked him to check with each of his elements to make sure no one was injured since we had just had a malfunction and fired more than one pair of rockets. (An understatement, to say the least.) He assured me that everyone was okay and that the rockets really put a hurting on the enemy. I told him that I was going to have to return to Evans because of the malfunction and that we would send out another section to complete the mission.

Now for the postmortem. After landing, we got together with the ops officer, the maintenance officer and the commander to discuss what had happened. After I filled them in on the "malfunction", the maintenance officer spoke up and said "It wasn't a malfunction, that's the way the B model intervelometer is supposed to work." We all stared at him like he had two heads and simultaneously said, "What?" He explained that the "new" model intervelometer was designed to apply a firing voltage to not only the pair of rockets currently being fired but also to all previously fired tubes in an attempt to fire any hung rockets. He said my problem came about because I didn't totally shut down my aircraft before reloading. "That's the only way to reset the intervelometers to zero." he explained. We all looked at him with stunned expressions on our faces and our jaws hung open like we were trying to catch flies. Even though I wanted to strangle this rear echelon asshole, who had never seen combat, I deferred to the unit commander who told the maintenance officer, in no uncertain terms, to remove ALL the "New" intervelometers from our aircraft and put the old ones back in. The commander then told the maintenance officer that, if he EVER again changed a piece of equipment on our aircraft without briefing him and the pilots on those changes, he would be out of a job permanently!! The commander said, "Do you even realize that we could have KILLED a bunch of American soldiers today, and it would have been your fault?" The maintenance officer looked like a balloon that someone was letting the air out of. The CO dismissed him and he scurried out to go change intervelometers. The CO then said, "Do those jackasses in R&D think we are fighting a gentleman's war here? Do they think we sit down to have TEA between missions? I've got to fire off a letter up the chain of command telling them to stop sending us these 'improvements' without checking with the guys on the front lines first."

We never had an issue with intervelometers again.

CHAPTER 9

Life Around Camp

I think it's time to change gears and tell you about some of our every day living stories around camp. While we did live in tents and slept on cots, we certainly weren't complaining because we knew how our troops out in the field lived and by comparison, we had it pretty good. Our unit had a cook assigned to it and he did an excellent job considering the raw materials he had to work with. After all, what could you do with powdered eggs to make them like the real thing? Answer: NOTHING!! Many of the guys developed a life long addition to Louisiana hot sauce just to make some of the canned and reconstituted stuff palatable. Our cook also managed to wheel and deal some things and trade some favors to occasionally get us fresh stuff like hamburgers and even steaks. What a treat!

We were usually able to get a warm/hot shower once a day in the evening. The shower "room" was nothing but a wooden framework that supported an old decommissioned Air Force drop tank that had an immersion heater mounted in it to heat the water. About dinnertime each day, one of our truck drivers would fill the tank with water and light the diesel fueled heater. That way, by the time we finished dinner and had gathered our towels and soap, the water was reasonably warm.

Timing was of the essence because if you started too early, the water was still cold, and if you were late, the water was either very hot or not there at all. If you were on "Hot" status, you would ask one of the other pilots to sit in for you while you got a quick shower in case a mission came down and you had to launch.

This brings us to our accommodations for the restroom. Since the First Cavalry was technically "in the field," we had no indoor plumbing and had to rely on outhouses for relief, if you will. It was up to each unit to construct their own facility but the basic design was the same. Instead of a hole in the ground under the outhouse, the design required that the end of a 55 gallon steel drum, about a foot tall, be situated under the toilet seat to collect the "deposits." There was a door on the back of the outhouse that provided access to these collection drums, and once a day, usually first thing in the morning, they would be removed to a safe distance, jet fuel would be poured over the contents and they would be set afire. The resulting fire would produce large columns of very thick, black smoke that would hang in the air until dissipated by helicopter rotor wash or a breeze. This smoke had a very distinctive odor to it, as you can imagine, and it was not pleasant at all. Once the fire went out and all the "deposits" had been turned to ash, the drums would be returned to their collection locations to receive new "deposits." In the Vietnam classic movie "Apocalypse, Now," Robert Duvall's character, Colonel Kilgore, famously says, "I love the smell of Napalm in the morning." as a black cloud of smoke drifts behind him. If you are ever watching this film with a Vietnam veteran and notice a smile cross his face as that line is said, it's because the veteran knows that, chances are, the black cloud and pungent odor is NOT from Napalm.

The job of removing the drums, dousing the contents with fuel and setting them ablaze was accomplished by Vietnamese civilians that were hired by the Division as day laborers. These day laborers were usually elderly men and women. Quite often they would put a small amount of fuel into the drums, after they cooled, to counter the smell of the new "deposits." You might consider it a form of "Air Freshener," of sorts and I must admit, it did help, somewhat. As military protocol required, we had two separate facilities. One for the enlisted ranks and one for the officers. At this point, I hope some of you smokers can see where I'm going with this. Anyway, just after sunset, a large hue and cry went up and we all ran outside to see what it was about. As we exited the tent, we saw flames leaping into the air off our left. The officer's outhouse was totally engulfed in flames. We ran down to it to make sure it was unoccupied and having determine it was vacant, we backed off to watch it burn. As I got to a comfortable distance from it, I suddenly saw Steve Woods run past me toward the fire. "What the hell was he doing?", I thought. Certainly, he hadn't left anything in there that he wanted to retrieve. As I watched, he ran up to a 55 gallon steel drum standing next to the outhouse that was full of jet fuel used to burn the "deposits." He grabbed the drum and started to roll it away from the flames to prevent it from exploding. Once I realized what he was doing, I started running towards him to help. As I did so, I noticed one of our new lieutenants was already half way to Steve. As he came up behind Steve, who was, I'm sure, wondering if the drum would explode before he could get it out of the way, I saw the LT raise an aircraft fire extinguisher, aim it at the fire while holding it next to Steve's ear, and pulled the trigger. To this day, I have never seen a man jump higher than Steve did that night. When he came back to earth, he saw the LT with the extinguisher in his hand and realized that the exploding, screeching sound that he heard was produced by this dumb ass, using an extinguisher that would barely put out a match. Steve simply lost it. He grabbed the extinguisher out of the lieutenant's hands and was last seen chasing him down the flight line, intent on putting that fire extinguisher firmly up the area that the LT uses to make "deposits."

The next day was spent tearing apart rocket boxes for new lumber to built a replacement outhouse. We were also looking for an officer that smoked and was having a hard time sitting down due to a singed posterior. We finally noticed who it was and approached him with our suspicions. He admitted to throwing a cigarette between his legs just prior to wiping and was forced to vacate the premises when there was a sudden flash, bang, under his butt. He was, and rightly so, the subject of many jokes and ridicule during the following weeks.

Most Americans believe in the philosophy that bigger is better and who were we to argue? The new outhouse was bigger and better than our previous model. We built it with 5 holes instead of the normal 3 and immediately started taking, you'll pardon the expression but, crap from the enlisted men who still had a 3 hole model. They loved to tell us that we needed a 5 hole model since the officers were so full of crap. It was all in good humor and we really liked our new 5 hole model (and were sure that the enlisted men were just jealous).

The new outhouse was built in the same area that the old one had occupied. As I mentioned, our battery area was located on a terraced hillside and the new building was at the bottom of the hill and slightly west of the row of tents. Stretching off to the east from our new building was a small runway that had been scraped out of the dirt and provided a spot for our neighboring unit, the 1st of the 9th Cav, to marshal its lift helicopters while loading up its troops for a combat assault. The runway could also be used by any helicopter that had an emergency and needed to make a running landing. By using this small runway, the emergency aircraft would prevent shutting down the main runway to the larger fixed wing aircraft like C-130s. Since the end of the makeshift runway was adjacent to our tents, we decided to use a portion, just in front of our new outhouse, to set up a volleyball court complete with a net. Someone manufactured poles for the net by welding a 3 inch diameter steel pole to a decommissioned two and a half ton truck wheel. Each of these weighed about 75 pounds and did a great job of keeping the net tight even if someone ran into it during a game.

One morning, several of us were sitting on our lawn chairs on top of our bunker drinking coffee and waiting for a mission. I looked off to the west and saw a flight of five Huey lift ships heading our way from the mountains. I noticed that they all had "Men on Strings" under them. This term meant that a soldier was dangling on a rope about 50 to 70 feet below the aircraft. This situation would normally develop because a group of soldiers, commonly a LRRP team of 5 men, needed immediate extraction from a heavily treed area where the lift ships couldn't land. The lift ships would hover over the treetops and throw down a 5 pound bar with a rope attached. The LRRP would sit on the bar and clip himself to the rope and the Huey would climb straight up, extracting the LRRP from the jungle. Since most lift ships did not have a winch on board to haul the LRRPs in, the LRRPs had to endure their ride to safety while being battered by 60 to 80 knot winds. To lessen the abuse by the wind, they would get out their poncho and wrap themselves in it. Even though they could no longer see where they were going, they said it was better than the wind.

Huey with soldier on a "string." Photo courtesy of
the United States Army Aviation Museum.

I watched as the Hueys descended toward us and realized that they were headed for the small, makeshift runway adjacent to our area. The lead aircraft kept getting lower and lower and I realized that things were about to go bad. We all jumped up and began running toward the runway, waving our arms over our heads to get the pilot's attention since he was about to run his passenger on the string through our newly constructed outhouse. Too late!! The poor soul impacted our lavish, new facility and boards and drums went flying in all directions. Oh!! Crap!! (Literally.)

Since the victim's progress had been slowed by the facility, the Huey's nose pitched down and to compensate, the dumb ass pilot pulled the nose up and added more power. This maneuver suddenly extracted the wayward traveler from the wreckage of our revered facility and catapulted him down the runway and straight into our volleyball net. It was at this point that the crew chief on the Huey was screaming at the pilot so loudly, that we could hear him on the ground. The pilot finally figured out the error of his ways and decided to pull the Huey up to a high hover to get his passenger off the ground. And, once again, cause and effect and physics came into play. The LRRP, who was now totally entangled in the volleyball net and being beaten by the poles and wheels, was now fired like a slingshot up and out in front of the Huey, stopping his climb just in front of the cockpit windshield. He slowly began to drop back and soon looked like the pendulum on a grandfather clock gradually coming to rest. We ran over to him, lowered him to the ground and freed him from the volleyball net and ropes. He said he was OK but he was covered by numerous cuts, bruises and welts.

Men from the 1st of the 9th Cav came running up and took control of the poor bastard and we walked back to our area. It was time to start collecting boards and to get the hammers out again. We were becoming experts at constructing outhouses and I wondered if there was some sort of college credit I could get toward a degree.

The NVA really hated the 1st Cavalry Division. And, as if to prove this point, they would rocket or fire mortars into Camp Evans about every other night or so. This was why we had a mortar patrol mission when many other compounds around the country felt no need for such protection since they rarely or infrequently were attacked in this way. We were quite used to being awaken by the sound of incoming rounds impacting somewhere on the LZ. I had developed a sixth sense where I could actually hear the rockets taking off or the thump of the mortars being fired. Even though I was sound asleep, my mind would hear the sounds of a launch and, very often, I would awaken as I was already halfway to the bunker and the incoming rounds were just starting to explode. In fact, many of my tent mates would say, "If you see Hartley jump up and start running, don't ask any questions, just follow him!"

Anyway, one night, I heard the sound of incoming and was running toward the bunker and as I passed Frank Thornhill's bunk, I grabbed his feet and yelled "Incoming!" since I knew that Frank was a heavy sleeper. The rest of the guys in the platoon came pouring into the bunker just as the first rounds started to impact. I looked around. No Frank! We all gathered at the doorway and started yelling, "Frank, wake up!"

Frank finally came to and took off running through the tent...the wrong way! We all watched as he ran head long into the tent pole at the far end of the tent. We heard a somewhat moist sounding "Ba-Whap" as he hit the pole face first, followed by a groan. He slowly slid down the pole and into a heap on the floor. We were all yelling at him again saying, "This way, Frank! Come this way!"

As if to motivate him, another round impacted very close to our tent. Frank was up and running again and this time he was running toward the bunker and us. Yeah!

Unfortunately, Frank forgot that the tent had two poles. "Ba-Whap!" again.

Once again, Frank sank to the floor with a groan. We continued to yell at him saying, "Come on Frank, get up!" Frank slowly stood up, looked at us with blood running down his face and said, "AW, SCREW IT!!" and went back to bed.

Just then we heard the distinctive noise of the mortar patrol aircraft firing his rockets at the enemy position and knew that the incoming was over.

We tried not to laugh the next morning when we saw Frank nursing his fat lip, swollen nose and a goose egg on his forehead. He said, "Ha! Ha! Very funny! Next time, just let me sleep! Okay?"

Much of our supplies came overland from the port of Da Nang and were trucked up Highway 1 in convoys. I'm not sure why, but the Division was having problems with the shipments, and essential items, like ammo and food, were now the only supplies being trucked in. We heard rumors of ground attacks on the convoys and road work problems but the end result was that non-essential items like beer and sodas were not getting through. (How could they say that beer was "Non-essential"?) Anyway, whenever this happened, our CO would authorize a couple of our Hueys to fly down to Da Nang and pick up what we needed. Normally, 2 Hueys could easily carry back a full pallet of beer and soda. But now, since we had turned in half of our Hueys for Cobras, and several of the others were down for maintenance, we were starting to get thirsty. Some of us got together and figured out that we could carry a full pallet of soda and beer back in 2 Cobras. We could accomplish this by pulling out the 2 ammo drums in the turret ammo bay and loading it with cases and then pulling apart the remaining cases and sliding the cans down the empty rocket tubes. We had checked it out and found that the cans fit perfectly in the tubes. Once we did the weight and balance computations and determined that it was safe and that we wouldn't overstress any part of the aircraft, we presented the plan to the CO. Even though he was a bit hesitant, he went ahead and approved our plan and gave us a requisition order for the beer and soda.

Bright and early the next morning, we took off for Da Nang on our resupply mission. We landed at the supply depot and presented our requisition to the officer in charge. We asked if he could have his forklift operator set the pallet down between our parked helicopters and that we'd handle it from there. He agreed and walked over to the door to see where we were parked. The double take that he did was like something out of a comedy movie. He turned back to us with his mouth agape and said, "Are you guys pulling my leg?"

"Uh, no sir!" was our response.

He just shook his head and said, "This, I've got to see."

As I recall, it took all four of us about 2 hours to break down the pallet and load the cans into the rocket tubes and ammo bay but we did it!

The officer in charge and a bunch of his men came out to watch us take off. After all, they were witnessing history. As we climbed out of the Da Nang area we decided to fly home over the Hai Van Pass since it was a shorter route than flying out over the ocean. Besides, we wanted to see what the problem was with the convoys that used the pass to deliver our supplies. As we cruised over the pass at about 1500 feet above the ground, I was looking down out of the side of my canopy at the trucks slowly climbing the steep hill up to the pass. As I watched them, suddenly, I saw something tumble away from my aircraft. "What the hell was that?" I turned further in my seat and saw that almost every rocket tube now had a soda or beer can hanging out the front of it. Oh! Crap!!

I slowed the aircraft down and pointed the nose up at a pretty good angle while shaking the stick fore and aft. While this maneuver managed to make most of the cans fall back into their tubes, my copilot was wondering if I was having some sort of seizure. I told him what I was doing and he quickly looked back at the rocket pods just in time to see another beer can launch itself on a bombing run. I called my wingman and told him what was going on and, after a quick check, he said he was having the same problem. We found that by flying at about 40 knots, the cans would vibrate toward the rear of the rocket pod instead of out the front. Our basic error was that we assumed that the 80 to 100 knots of airspeed would create enough air pressure to hold the cans in place. Yes! Yes! We all know what "assume" means.

Even though our flight home was now taking twice as long at 40 knots and we were a couple of cases short of a full load, we were still greeted by our thirsty comrades as conquering heroes when we arrived. In our after action report we strongly recommended that anyone attempting to duplicate our feat, bring along a roll of duct tape to cover the front of the rocket pods. We also heard a rumor that some of the convoy truck drivers reported being "Bombed" with soda and beer cans while they were driving up Highway 1 through the Hai Van Pass. They said these soda and beer cans would just fall out of the sky and explode when they hit the ground. I said, "You can't believe anything those guys say, they were probably smoking some of the local weed. Far out, Dude!!"

CHAPTER 10

RATS

RATS! Why did it have to be RATS? I hate RATS! Rats were an ever present problem with our living conditions. Rarely did we see them during the day but at night we could hear them scurrying about our tent looking for anything to eat. When the engineers constructed the frame that our tent was draped over, they very kindly built a shelf about a foot wide at eye level, running down either side of the tent. This was a very nice addition that allowed us to store some of our personal items up off the floor to keep the rats from chewing them up. I guess it was silly of us to assume that the rats wouldn't be able to get up on the shelf.

Our cots were typically arranged on either side of the center aisle with our feet near the aisle and our heads near the outer wall and, coincidentally, under the shelf. One of the items we all kept on the shelf was our shaving kit that would contain our razors, shaving cream, shampoo and a bar of soap in one of those plastic soap dishes. Who knew that rats liked to eat SOAP? Well, if someone did, they didn't tell us. Very often, on our way to the shower, we'd find that our soap dishes had been gnawed open and our bar of soap was half eaten. Yuck!

We all slept under mosquito netting that was draped over a T-bar attached to the foot and head of our cot. When we retired for the night, we would tuck the netting in under our air mattress to seal out the mosquitoes and the RATS.

One night, as I was drifting off to sleep, I heard a rat scurry overhead on the shelf. He was joined a few seconds later by a second rat and they began to screech and fight over my soap. They were locked in mortal combat as they fell off the shelf, along with my shaving kit, and the whole mess landed in the middle of my chest. I immediately screamed like a little girl, jumped straight up while flailing my arms around like a windmill. As I went up, the rats fell off my chest and were now fighting by my feet. This commotion did not go unnoticed by my roommates. All of them were now wide awake, grabbing flashlights and saying, "What the hell is going on?"

I was now illuminated by at least 6 flashlights as I stood in the center of my cot, draped from head to foot in mosquito netting and doing my best impression of a Highland Jig, all the while screaming like a banshee. At first, my audience was as frightened as I was but once they figured out what was going on, they all dissolved into hysterical laughter. Some were pointing and laughing so hard that they couldn't even speak as tears rolled down their faces. "Ha! Ha! Very funny, but your time is coming," I thought.

I was sure that someone else would soon have a close encounter of the rat kind and I would be pointing and laughing at them. In fact a few weeks later, I was sound asleep and was having a dream of someone massaging my feet. As I slowly awakened, I realized that something was, in fact, nibbling on my toes. Almost simultaneously, I became fully awake just as the rat bit down on my big toe. Here we go again. Instead of screaming like a little girl this time, I yelled out in pain along with a few well chosen profanities and was again standing draped in mosquito netting while clutching my foot and hopping about like I was in some sort of one legged race. Once again, the flashlights came out and I was illuminated like King Kong climbing the Empire State building. This time the laughter subsided quickly as the other guys realized that I had been bitten. We looked at the bite under the flashlights and determined that the rat didn't break the skin. Even so, my toe was still very sore for the next few days. Did I mention that I HATE RATS!!

Even though the following story is out of sequence and actually took place about 6 months later in Quan Loi, I think it would be appropriate to tell it now since we are discussing (or disgusted by) RATS. Anyway, early one evening we were all sitting around the tent reviewing the events of the day and some of the guys from first platoon were over, telling jokes and tall tales about their exploits. I was trying to write a letter to my wife, Nancy, but the din was too loud for me to concentrate. Finally, the group said, "Let's go over to the Officers Club and get a drink." They tried to drag me with them but I said I had to finish my letter and then I'd be over. The boisterous crowd finally left and I went back to writing, now that I was alone. I was in mid tent, sitting in my lawn chair facing the front door with my cot behind me and my table/desk to my right.

All was finally quiet and I was staring out the door while I mentally composed my next line. Suddenly, in through the front door strode an exceptionally large rat. With a very brazen attitude, he strolled down the center aisle as if he owned the place. He would look left into someone's area, take a couple of sniffs of the air and then move further up the aisle towards me then look right and sniff once again. I knew he could see me but, apparently, he was not disturbed by my presence. As he got closer, I slowly reached over with my right hand and pulled my .45 pistol out of the holster that was hanging by my bed.

The rat was now at the foot of Steve Woods' bed, directly across the aisle from me. I slowly pulled the slide back on my pistol to put a round in the chamber as the rat started walking away from me and under Steve's bunk. I got up and walked across the aisle as the rat emerged from under the bed and promptly walked under a metal gym type locker that Steve used to store some of his clothes. It was a bit of a tight spot with Steve's bunk and mosquito netting touching my right elbow and the metal locker a few inches to my left but I could see the rat under the locker, so, I took aim and fired. The rat was killed immediately and the sound of the gunshot reverberated off the metal locker with a very loud "Ba-Wangggg." I also noticed that Steve's mosquito netting went flying up from the muzzle blast or, perhaps, from the ejected cartridge. Anyway, I was surprised at how loud the .45 was in an enclosed area. Oh! Well, time to collect and dispose of the carcass.

As I was getting a flight glove to pick up the dead rat, two of the guys that had gone to the club came in and said, "Where's Steve going?" I said,"What?"

They said, "He just went running out of here like he was on fire. Looked like he was headed for the bunker and he seemed pretty scared."

Suddenly, it was all clear. Steve had been sleeping in his bunk the whole time, that is, until I fired my pistol about 6 inches from his head! He thought we were taking incoming and left so fast that I never even saw him, just the flapping of his mosquito netting. He was headed to the safety of the bunker as fast as his naked feet would carry him. Needless to say, I was not his favorite person for the next few days. I kept trying to tell him that the rat probably would have eaten him if I didn't shoot it first. He wasn't buying it. Eventually, he forgave me but when the CO got wind of what had happened, he issued an order prohibiting any more rat shootings. I still hate RATS!!

CHAPTER 11

Working with the Marines

W e continued to get fire missions called down and had to scramble to be off the ground within our allotted 2 minutes. Most of the time they were carbon copy type missions in that we would arrive on station, make contact with the friendly forces, identify their position and the enemies location, fire on the enemy until our ammo was expended, then return to base. I say this because this was our typical day. I don't want you to think that we only had the exceptional type missions I've mentioned up to this point but that those exceptional mission kind of punctuated our "normal" existence and are remembered in detail because, in one way or another, they were "Significant Emotional Events" to us.

Another of those exceptional type missions came down the chain of command and tasked our unit to send four of our aircraft and crews down to the Da Nang area to support the Marines. The mission had come down from General Westmoreland's office in Saigon. In the briefing we got, we were told that the Marines had been engaged in a battle just west of Da Nang for three days now and were suffering heavy casualties while trying to take a hill that was occupied on top by dug in NVA forces. Since General Westmoreland was in charge of all U.S.

Forces in Vietnam, he decided to reinforce the Marines with a lot more firepower so they could be victorious in this battle.

We saluted smartly, packed a bag and took off headed for Da Nang. We would be staging out of the U.S. Army airfield at Marble Mountain and would be working directly for the Colonel in charge of the Marines that were trying to take the hill.

When we landed at Marble Mountain, we were told by the Black Cats Ops Officer that we could bunk in their Officers Club for as long as we needed. The Black Cats were the 282nd Assault Helicopter Company stationed at Marble Mountain and they gave us great support. Once we had unloaded our bedrolls and other stuff, we fueled up and headed for the battle area.

The hill that was causing all the commotion was one that was situated overlooking the river that came out of the Elephant Valley area which was a renown NVA hot spot. It was also an area that the enemy used to launch 122 mm and 140 mm rockets at the airfield called Da Nang Main.

Da Nang Main was a huge complex and had twin 10,000 foot runways and was home to the Vietnamese Air Force as well as units of the U.S. Army, Navy, Air Force and Marines. Additionally, there were contracted U.S. airline flights bringing in and taking out troops for the war. So, as you can see, it was a very busy place and in need of protection. The Marine unit attacking the hill was doing it's best to eliminate the threat and we were more than willing to assist them.

When we arrived on station, we checked in by radio with the Marine Colonel and told him who we were and what we could do for him. He rogered our transmission and then told us to hold off to the north and out of the way. While we were holding, we saw other units arrive on station and be told the same thing. One such unit was our next door neighbors at Evans, the 1st of the 9th Cav. They had also been sent down from Camp Evans to help out. Once they had checked in with the Colonel, they too were told to hold off to the north and out of the way. About this time an Air Force Forward Air Controller (FAC) arrived in his small Cessna spotter airplane and, also, checked in with the Marine Colonel. The FAC told the Colonel that he had 4 F-4 fighter bombers on station ready to bomb that hill and eliminate the bad guys. The Colonel also told him to hold. The FAC explained that the jets only had about 15 minutes of fuel before they would need to head for home. The Colonel rogered that but made no further comment. After the 15 minutes expired, the FAC told the Colonel he needed to use the F-4s or lose them. The Colonel said, "Send them home." Unbelievable, we thought.

While all of this was going on, we kept seeing medevac helicopters arriving, loading wounded Marines and leaving. We also noted that there was little or no artillery impacting the hill. The rounds we did see hit the hill were, apparently, coming from the mortars that the Marines had with them. I knew there were plenty of Army fire bases nearby that could provided enough shells to totally cover the top of that hill but that wasn't happening either. We contacted the 1st of the 9th on our air to air frequency to discuss this perplexing situation and asked, "WHAT THE HELL IS GOING ON HERE???"

As we talked about it, we came to the conclusion that the Marine Colonel didn't want to "share" any of the glory of a victory with any of the other services, so, he just continued to tell his men to, "Fix bayonets and charge!!" Their Guts and his Glory, "Semper Fi" and "Gung Ho" and all that crap.

As if to confirm our assessment, a flight of 2 Marine Huey gunships arrived on station and checked in with the Colonel. Each of these aircraft carried two 7 shot rocket pods for a grand total of 28 rockets while we had been boring holes in the sky with our 4 aircraft and 304 rockets on board.

The Colonel immediately gave the Marine gunships a target to shoot at and thanked them profusely when they were done. The Marine gunship commander said that they had to leave right away since they were "Bingo" on fuel and had a long flight back to the aircraft carrier. He told the Colonel he didn't think they could get back here today to help since it was already 1 PM and the turn around time for rearming and refueling on the aircraft carrier was pretty long.

I couldn't help but marvel at how crazy that all sounded since Da Nang Main was only a few miles away with plenty of fuel and rockets. What were they thinking?

We held in our designated area for as long as we could then told the Colonel that we had to go get fuel too. We asked if he wanted us to dump our rockets on any particular target before we left but he said no. He also told us, "Don't hurry back, we've got this thing pretty well in hand."

We made the round trip to Marble Mountain 3 times that day and didn't fire one rocket at the enemy. We continued to see Medevac helicopters arriving to pick up the dead and wounded Marines throughout the day. It was the most frustrating experience I ever had.

After a restless night trying to sleep at the Officers Club, we were up early to head back out to the battle area. Once again we were assigned to our holding area and we resigned ourselves to another day of boring holes in the sky while burning copious amounts of fuel.

OH-6A Light Observation Helicopter also called a Loach or scout.
Photo courtesy of the United States Army Aviation Museum Collection.

About mid morning, I noticed that one of the 1st of the 9th's scout helicopter or Loaches (LOH or Light Observation Helicopters) was flying around down low just north of the hill. I was sure this activity had not been approved by the Marine Colonel. I called the 1st of the 9th commander on our air to air frequency and asked what the LOH was up to. Since the Marine Colonel couldn't hear us on our air to air freq, the 1st of the 9th commander said his story was that the LOH was scouting around to make sure the NVA wasn't infiltrating reinforcements into the area but that he was really trying to develop something on his own so that we could get involved and do something here. I told him that I agreed with him and we were ready to help out with whatever developed. We didn't have to wait very long. The Loach flew low over the north end of the hill and promptly called, "TAKING FIRE, TAKING HITS, GOING DOWN!!" This call was made on the FM frequency that the Marine Colonel was monitoring, so, he was immediately aware of what was happening. As I watched, the Loach made a perfect landing about one third of the way up the hill just behind a mound of dirt that protected it from fire from the hilltop. I must admit that I don't know to this day whether this whole thing was staged or if they really got shot down.

Anyway, we watched as the crew of 2 got out of the LOH and took up defensive positions in a nearby crater. The 1st of the 9th commander told the Colonel that he was launching a rescue operation to retrieve his aircraft and crew. The Colonel said he would send some of his men over to help but the commander said, "No, we can handle it but we need all your units to mark their locations and take cover because we are coming in with a full combat assault."

The Colonel began to protest but the commander cut him short saying, "It's my men and my aircraft and we are coming in for them, get ready!"

Very quickly, marking panels and smoke grenades started to appear around the base of the hill showing where all the Marines were. None of them were more than a third of the way up the hill, so, we'd be clear to shoot up the top of the hill. The 1st of the 9th commander called me and said, "Max, I've got a load of artillery coming in on the hilltop and I need you to shoot up any areas they miss as my lift ships are landing near the downed aircraft. Can you do that for me?" I replied, "You betcha! We've got your guys covered."

On board his lift ships was a platoon of about 20 of his own U.S. Army infantry troopers that would secure the area around the downed aircraft and make sure the crew was on board one of the Hueys as it left.

As the flight of Huey lift ships headed toward the hill, the artillery began impacting the hilltop and we began firing rockets at any spot that a round had not recently hit. I had arranged for us to set up a "Daisy Chain" so that as I pulled out of my rocket run, my wingman was rolling in to be followed by the third and fourth Cobra, in sequence, until I was in position to roll in again. This kept a continuous rain of rockets, along with the artillery, impacting the hilltop throughout the time that the Hueys made their approach, landing and departure. During this time, the top of the hill was totally obscured by smoke and dust from the exploding munitions and it was doubtful that the enemy could have seen anything, even if they did stick their heads up. We were happy to hear that the Hueys never took any fire during the assault and that the downed crew had made it out safely.

As the dust settled, the Blues (U.S. Army infantry guys) set up a perimeter around the downed Loach. The 1st of the 9th commander told them they would have to expand the perimeter so that they'd have a secure enough area to bring in a recovery helicopter to sling load out the downed aircraft. The Blues platoon leader said that was fine and they would move out shortly towards the top of the hill. I informed the commander that we were low on ammo and fuel so I'd like to go rearm and refuel before the Blues started their move. He agreed and off we went.

When we returned we saw a couple of F-4s pulling out of a dive right over the hill and several bombs exploding on the hilltop. I thought, "All Right! We've finally gotten the Air Force involved in this thing."

With us back on station, the 1st of the 9th commander gave the OK to the Blues platoon leader to move out towards the top of the hill to "Secure a larger perimeter."

Almost as soon as the Blues started to move up the hill, they started taking fire. The 1st of the 9th Cobras fired up the area first, then we added a few rounds for good measure. Once again, the Blues moved out toward the top of the hill and once again, they started taking fire and once again, we shot up the area.

This process continued for the next 45 minutes or so until the Blues were on top of the hill on the north end. From this advantageous position, the Blues platoon leader could effectively direct artillery fire and air strikes on the enemy positions further down the ridge line. The bad guys were paying a heavy price for allowing the Blues to advance this far. We refueled and rearmed a couple of more times and were there to cover the Blues as they made their way down the ridge line. By late afternoon, they had secured the entire hilltop and the Marines were now able to walk up the hill and relieve them. The Loach was recovered, the Blues were picked up by their Hueys and we were released to go back home to Camp Evans.

I think the moral of this story is that a combined arms team is much more effective at winning a battle than bravado and foolish pride.

Let me make it perfectly clear that I have nothing but the utmost respect for the Marines who were trying to take that hill. It was the Colonel that I despised. He refused any help from the other services and continually sacrificed the lives and limbs of the men he was suppose to shepherd for nothing more than his own personal glory. The true heroes here were the individual Marines, who fought for a bad leader and the Blues platoon leader and his men. While it is probably true that the Marines' repeated attacks had worn down the enemy's defenses, I can assure you that the Blues did not have a cake walk taking that hill. I am very thankful that I did not run across too many other incompetent and egotistical leaders, like the Colonel, during my 2 years at war.

Things back at Camp Evans were pretty normal when we returned. We continued to get missions down but the frequency and intensity had abated significantly. Most fire missions were to shoot for troops taking sniper fire or that had become involved in a skirmish with a small enemy force. My section was launched to go help a company of infantry that had been conducting a "search and clear" operation when they were pinned down by sniper fire. When we arrived on station, we had them pop smoke and identified their position. It was relatively easy to spot the friendly troops because they were in the coastal flats area east of Camp Evans and had taken cover behind the sand dunes in the area. We could see each of the soldiers laying prone behind the dunes that had small tufts of grass growing on top. They all had their weapons oriented toward the one structure in the area, a small Roman Catholic church with a belfry.

The ground commander told me that the bad guys were holed up in the church and had snipers in the belfry that were able to keep his men pinned down. I asked him what he wanted me to do and he said, "Blow up the church!!"

"Whoa!! Really?" I said. Then I told him that I would have to check with headquarters to see if such a thing could or would be approved. The ground commander said, " Take your time, we're not going anywhere!"

I called back to our operations and explained my situation and asked for guidance in this delicate situation. Our RTO (radio/telephone operator at our operations office) told me to standby since he couldn't make that decision and said he'd get the Commanding Officer and Operations Officer on line to decide. The CO came on the radio and said he would have to check with Division Operations for guidance and to standby.

The CO called back and said Division Headquarters was going to have to check with the local province chief and possibly the church hierarchy to prevent an unpleasant political situation from developing. I informed my boss that we were starting to get low on fuel, so, could they hurry up the decision makers a bit?

I continued to keep the ground commander informed of what was going on back at the head-shed and said that if any of his men were threatened or hit by the sniper, that I would immediately take out the church. He thanked me and said that all his men were currently under cover and safe but that they couldn't move at all.

Finally, my CO called back and said that it had been approved by Division HQ to blow up the church. I told the CO that I would need him to authenticate that message and I would need the initials of all the people in the chain of command that approved the destruction of the church. (Just to cover my ass.)

The CO authenticated the message with the proper response from the CEOI and passed along the five sets of initials including the province chief's. As I wrote the initials down on my canopy with a grease pencil, I couldn't help but feel that there was one set of initials missing. Oh! Well. I guess I'll just have to try to explain to "The Big Guy" after I leave this earth.

I told my wingman to just cover me and that I would do the deed myself. He rogered my call and said that was fine with him.

I dropped down to about 100 feet over the sand and lined up with the front door of the church. No need for a marking pair here, so, I fired 4 times and 8 rockets flew in the front door and down the aisle of the church before exploding and totally destroying the structure. As I banked away I saw the belfry tumble to the ground and the rest of the church collapse into the sandy soil.

I climbed back to altitude and noticed that the troops were already up and moving towards the ruins. After a few minutes, the ground commander released us to return home but not before telling us we had killed 5 bad guys occupying the church. I guess I'll just have to live a long time because when I pass, I'm sure Saint Peter is going to give me hell when I show up at the Pearly Gates.

CHAPTER 12

The Secret War

As many people now know, there was a Secret War being conducted alongside our overt military involvement in South Vietnam. Much of this involved the CIA conducting classified missions in Laos and Cambodia to report on and thwart efforts by the North Vietnamese to build up supply depots and troops concentrations just over the border. They did this because they knew that the U.S. Military was not supposed to cross the border and attack them or the U.S. would be accused of invading a sovereign nation by the world community and much saber rattling would ensue, lead by the USSR and China.

Nevertheless, we did conduct small, clandestine operations in these countries. Most of these operations involved small groups of Rangers or Special Forces that would be dropped off by helicopters across the border, where they would then spy on the enemy's movements and activities. They would report back directly to Washington, D.C. via special communications links and, we were told, that the National Security Council and Henry Kissinger himself were monitoring the missions as they progressed.

I know all this because I participated in several of these missions. Most of these missions were pretty straight forward and not much different than our normal combat assault missions where we would escort and protect the lift ships while they landed in an LZ to drop off troops. These Missions were called CCN or Command and Control North. There was also a CCC for the Central portion of the country and a CCS for down South.

One day our Operations Officer came to me and said that my name had come up on an unofficial duty roster, and that I had "Volunteered" to be the Cobra section leader on tomorrow's mission. I wasn't sure if this was an endorsement of their trust in me or if I had just been screwed but I copied down the info on the mission and went to brief the other pilots in my section.

Early the next morning, my wingman and I took off and headed for the Da Nang area, once again. We arrived overhead the Special Forces compound just as the 5 Huey lift ships were landing. The compound was rather unusual since it was enclosed by a 12 foot tall cyclone fence topped with several rolls of concertina wire and looked very much like a present day penitentiary. We circled while the Hueys tied down their blades, then, landed next to them. It was a very tight squeeze with all 7 helicopters sharing an area half the size of a football field and containing several mess hall type buildings to boot. Once we had tied down our rotor blades, we headed to the briefing building to find out the details of our mission.

As we entered, we were stopped by a very serious looking Special Forces Sergeant who asked for our ID cards. We handed them over and he studied them very carefully then compared them to a roster he had on a clipboard. Once he was satisfied with who we were, I put out my hand to retrieve my ID card. He glared at me while holding our IDs even closer. He then said," Sir, I'll be keeping these during today's mission and I also need all of you to surrender your dog tags and jungle fatigue shirts. You'll be going in 'Sterile' today." As we complied, he handed us new fatigue shirts that were devoid of any name tags, rank insignia, unit patches or even the U.S. Army tag. This was not a good sign. It meant that they were expecting significant resistance from the enemy today and that they were afraid someone would get shot down on the other side of the border.

The official briefing confirmed this and the briefing officer actually used the phrase that "The Secretary will disavow any knowledge..." In other words, if you're shot down, you're on your own IF you survive. Oh! Great!! I sure am glad I "Volunteered" for this mission. As we were walking out of the briefing room towards our aircraft, I couldn't help but think, "While 'The Secretary' may be able to disavow us, how was he going to pretend that the huge piece of machinery I was walking to, with U.S. ARMY painted down its side, didn't exist?" Military Intelligence truly is a contradiction in terms.

The mission was to drop off five Special Forces team members across the border in Laos by hovering over the trees in the desired location and having them repel down ropes through the trees. These men all boarded the lead Huey while the other four aircraft were loaded with devices called "Nightingales." They were nothing more than a 4 by 6 foot section of chicken wire on a wooden frame onto which a series of fireworks had been attached. Once the fuse on this device was lit, it sounded like a real firefight was in progress complete with rat-a-tat-tats and hand grenade like explosions. When we arrived in the target area, the other four Hueys would spread out and simulate putting the troops into areas away from where the actual insertion was taking place. They would also light the fuse to a Nightingale and throw it out. The resulting chaos would serve to confuse the enemy and divert attention away from the actual insertion point. Meanwhile, my wingman and I would provide covering fire but only if one of the lift ships began taking enemy fire.

Today's mission went off without a hitch. As I watched, the four decoy Hueys simulate putting in troops, I saw the lead Huey come to a hover over the trees, 5 ropes, each with a metal bar on the end were tossed out the cargo doors on either side, followed very quickly by 5 men sliding down those ropes and disappearing into the jungle. As the ropes were being pull back up, the lead Huey lowered his nose and climbed away from the insertion site. The whole process had taken about 15 seconds from when the Huey came to a hover until he was climbing back out of the area. Very professional, I thought. None of the Hueys had taken any enemy fire and we all climbed to altitude and joined back up for our flight back to Da Nang.

We all began to relax as we crossed back into South Vietnam and were looking forward to going home after our debriefing. Da Nang was just coming into view as we heard, "Prairie Fire, Prairie Fire, Prairie Fire." broadcast on our operations frequency. This was a code that meant that we had to return immediately to extract the team we had just put in because they were under attack and about to be overrun. In an instant, all 7 of us turned around and headed back.

I called the lead Huey and said we would sprint ahead since the Cobra could go faster than the Hueys. I pulled in max power right up to the redline and we were now doing 150 knots trying to get to those guys as fast as possible. I checked my fuel status and saw that we only had about 40 minutes left until we would flame out and go down. There was no choice. We had to go help those guys. We wouldn't make it back to Da Nang on this fuel load!

As we cleared the mountains and could talk to the Special Forces team again, we asked for a situation report (SITREP). As soon as the team leader keyed his mike, I knew it was bad because I could hear a bunch of yelling and screaming in the background along with a lot of close machine gun fire and explosions. The team leader said they were surrounded by about 100 NVA and had one severely wounded man. He told me that they were exactly where we had dropped them off and that we could shoot anywhere around them since the enemy had them surrounded. I rogered his transmission and told him to get their heads down, I would be firing very close. He said, "Believe me, our heads are down."

I fired a marking pair and asked the team leader, "Is that a good area?" He replied, "Excellent, shoot 'em up!! They are all looking and shooting at you now!! Be careful!" Great!! And me without an ID card!

My wingman and I were still firing all around the edges of the Special Forces team's location as the Hueys arrived. The lead Huey told the team leader to get ready for extraction and that he would be overhead in about one minute. The team leader assured him that they were ready to get the hell out of there.

As the lead Huey came to a hover over the team, the ropes with bars attached were again thrown down into the jungle. Almost immediately, the Huey began taking fire from below and I could see hunks of metal being blown off the aircraft. I have to give that pilot a lot of credit because he maintained a rock steady hover even though bullets were piercing his aircraft from every direction. By following the ropes down, we knew exactly where the team was and could now shoot much closer to their position. I slowed to just above a hover and told my front seat gunner to shoot his minigun around the hovering Huey to suppress the enemy ground fire. I could see by his tracers he was doing an excellent job. Very quickly, the team leader said they were all hooked up and ready to come out. The lead Huey started a very slow climb straight up so as to give the men on the ropes time to push their way around tree branches and limbs. As the men cleared the treetops, we could see that four of them were firing their guns back at the area they had just vacated. Sadly, the fifth man just hung limply on his rope but we had all five.

The lead Huey slowly accelerated and began a turned back towards Da Nang. The other Hueys joined up with him as my wingman and I turned our attention back to the extraction site. I told him, "Let's dump the rest of these rockets on these assholes and get the hell out of here. Selecting Salvo."

I rolled in and held the fire button down as the rest of my rockets roared out of my tubes and into the extraction site. My wingman followed suit and soon an area about 70 meters in diameter was covered with smoke from exploding warheads.

We quickly caught up with the flight of Hueys since we were now much lighter having expended all of our rockets and almost all of our fuel. The lead Huey asked me our fuel status and I said we had about 10 minutes of fuel left till burnout. He solemnly rogered my transmission. For those that don't know, there is no "Bailing Out" of a helicopter and that's probably a good thing since you'd likely end up as sliced baloney. The helicopter option is to land. Somewhere, anywhere but, land. Unfortunately, there was nothing but triple canopy jungle for as far as the eye could see. Luckily, the Huey flights normal area of operations was around the Da Nang area and lead called me up to say they wouldn't be able to get all the way back to Da Nang either but he knew a place in Elephant Valley where we all could set down. Did we think we could make it that far? I replied, "We'll just have to see." I said.

As I was watching the fuel gauge drop below 100 lbs we turned a corner around a mountain and Elephant Valley came into view.

While a piece of flat terrain was a very welcome sight, I knew that Elephant Valley was a hang out for the NVA, so, our problems weren't over yet.

The 5 Hueys set down in trail formation on a dirt trail running though a clearing. I told my wingman to land in front of the lead Huey and I'd land in the rear and turn around and, together, we would protect the formation with our turret weapons for as long as our fuel held out. The Special Forces were now off their ropes and helping to set up a perimeter around the aircraft and the wounded man was being tended to by a medic. I couldn't help but feel like there were a thousand NVA eyes watching us.

I was the last one to see it but within only a few minutes, two CH-47 Chinook helicopters appeared over our location and set down up front. Apparently, they had been notified by the people (read Kissinger) monitoring our mission and been dispatched about the time we had turned around to go get the Special Forces guys. They were carrying blivets of jet fuel and soon we were all refueled and on our way home. I love it when a plan comes together.

We completed our debrief at the Special Forces compound and headed back to Camp Evans. We were looking forward to "Home" and some more "Normal" missions.

CHAPTER 13

The Kool-Aid

It was the middle of summer now and the temperatures soared to near 100 degrees every day and the humidity was in the mid 90% range. Very uncomfortable, to say the least. Since the Cobra had an air conditioning system, we actually looked forward to getting a fire mission because that meant we could cool off a bit.

It was during this time that things were about to get even more "Uncomfortable." Most of the guys didn't have much of an appetite because of the hot weather but we would still go to our mess tent and get a little something to eat. But the main draw there was that our cook always had a huge bowl of Kool-Aid made up with chunks of ice floating in it. It was one of the main things we liked to drink since the milk we got through the military was what they called "Filled Milk." I'm not sure what it's processing involved but they said it wouldn't spoil at our higher temperatures and lack of refrigeration. While that may have been true, it was also not very palatable. It kind of tasted like cardboard and was very slimy going down your throat. While we did have beer and sodas, we couldn't drink the beer while on duty and we had to pay for each can of soda.

Each day our cook would send a couple of enlisted men over to the water point with a truck to pick up our allotment of ice for the day. The potable ice was made by the Corps of Engineers and was very safe to consume.

On one particular day, the two Einsteins that went to the water point saw that the line for ice was about 2 hours long, so, they decided to go to the local Vietnamese village to buy the ice. That way, they reasoned, they could also spend some time in the local brothel without being missed. What they didn't know was that the ice they bought was made out of river water and was for cooling only, not drinking. Do you remember the phrase, "Don't drink the Kool-Aid."? Well, "DON'T DRINK THE KOOL-AID!!!"

Unfortunately, nobody knew. Not even our two Einsteins. And so, we drank the Kool-Aid at lunch. It didn't take long. We all started having stomach cramps and the lines outside our outhouses were growing by the hour.

While there were a few guys that didn't drink the Kool-Aid, about 80% of the unit did and we were all sick. It turned out to be amoebic dysentery and the medical folks said there was little they could do to help us. They said the most important thing was to avoid becoming dehydrated. That was kind of hard to do since everything we drank came out the other end, it seemed, within 30 minutes of going in. Our unit medic was giving us anti-diarrhea medication in the form of a little white pill but it was having no effect at all. In fact, I'm pretty sure I heard it go "Klink" into the can about 30 minutes after taking it and it looked pretty much like it did when I swallowed it.

We all felt pretty weak and drained, if you'll pardon the expression, but the missions kept coming down and we kept flying them. The crew chiefs said to not worry about it if we had an "accident" while flying since, they too, were in the same boat. We all took to sitting on towels while flying just to make the clean up easier when we landed. When the fire mission horn was sounded, we previously would run full tilt to our aircraft to get airborne as quickly as possible, but now, the best anyone could do was a modest trot.

I clearly remember the following incident and think it sums up how we were handling our situation. Several of us were lounging in our lawn chairs outside the tent so that we had a clear path to the outhouse about ten yards away. The fire mission horn went off and the crew members of the hot section began to run/trot out to the flight line. One of those crew members was a lieutenant who was wearing an old one piece gray flight suit. We all watched him as he started across the little metal bridge that crossed our rice paddy. As he reached mid-span he stopped and stood very still with his hands clenched at his side. Suddenly, the entire backside of his light gray flight suit turned a much darker shade of gray which was now spreading down his legs. He waited a moment then shook, much like a dog does after a bath, and continued trotting towards his aircraft. Normally, such a sight would have brought gales of laughter from those observing it, but not today. We felt nothing but sympathy for him and knew that we could be in the same situation at any moment. We admired his dedication.

Some of the guys grew so weak that they were now bedridden except for the occasional trip to the outhouse. The word spread up the chain of command and soon a medical team arrived in the unit area to "help us."

The word spread that the team was setting up to give everyone a shot that would speed our recovery. Great! Where do I go?

It had been decided that the shots would be given to each platoon in sequence, so, we, in second platoon, would follow the guys in first platoon. The plan was that you would go in the front door of the tent, get your shot and exit the back door.

As we watched the guys from first platoon enter we noticed that not all of them were exiting the back door and those that were, had someone assisting them back to their tent. Hmmm! This was not looking good. What the hell was going on in there?

I found out as I entered the tent and saw the guy that was ahead of me draped over a chair with his buttocks exposed and a medic standing over him with one of those glass tubed horse needles with the three steel rings. The medic was straining to fill the needle with the contents of a bottle he was holding. As he pulled the bottle off of the needle and righted it, I couldn't help but notice that the contents of the bottle looked like and flowed like Karo syrup. No wonder that the medic had been straining as he pulled back on the plunger. I quickly looked around for a way out but was trapped like a rat. Another medic told me to drop my pants and prepare to assume the position. I don't know why, but I watched as the first medic plunged the needle into the right cheek of the guy ahead of me. The victim let out a whimper that gradually escalated to a loud moan as the medic squeezed the three rings together injecting the Karo like substance into his prey. The victim actually passed out and had to be picked up by two other medics and placed on a cot in the back of the tent to recover. That explained why not everyone who went into the tent was coming out.

As I reluctantly assumed the position, I asked the medic," Hey! What is that stuff?" He replied that it was Gamma Globulin and that it would help our systems fight the infection. He then apologized saying it was hard to inject since it was required to be kept cold and this made it very thick. While I did not pass out, it certainly was a pain in the ass.

It took about two weeks before we started to feel better but soon everyone was getting back to normal. We all were steering clear of the Kool-Aid bowl even though "Cookie" was swearing that it was good ice. Thanks anyway Cookie!

Summer and the heat dragged on and must have been having an effect on the enemy as well. It was now August and we were not getting that many missions down and the ones that we did get were usually those involving snipers or small skirmishes.

I was glad that things were quiet since I had requested an R&R to Hawaii to meet my wife who was now 7 months pregnant with our first child. The Commander was somewhat reluctant to approve it because most guys didn't go on R&R until the second half of their tour. However, since things were quiet and since I wouldn't be able to meet Nancy after the baby came, the Commander approved my R&R and I was off to Hawaii.

Nancy met me at the airport when I arrived and we had a great time for the next five days. We took in all the sights on Oahu and lounged on the beach as much as possible. We checked out the night life and even got to Don Ho's show which we enjoyed very much. Tiny bubbles and all of that. Those five days were over in no time and I was on my way back to Vietnam.

When I arrived back at Camp Evans, little had changed. The weather was hot and the NVA were not. We had gotten an interim Commander that no one seemed very thrilled about. While our previous Commanders would often go on missions with us, this guy seemed very uninterested in what we did. In fact, some of the pilots likened him to a pelican. I asked, "A pelican? What do you mean?" They said, "You know, you can't hardly get a pelican to fly unless you throw rocks at him." Oh! A pelican.

Anyway, what really made most of us pilots really dislike him was one day we started taking incoming mortar fire and, as usual, the crews on the "Hot" section started running for their aircraft to launch and go shoot at the bad guys. I was one of those crew members on this occasion and we all had to take a dive in the dirt as the rounds landed around us on our way to the helicopters. This was not unusual and quite often we would come back from the mission and have to tend to skinned knees, hands and elbows. We were just thankful that we didn't get hit by any shrapnel from the incoming rounds.

Well, our not so fearless leader was running to take cover in his bunker when the incoming started and banged his head on the beam over the doorway. We learned afterward that he went to our medic and insisted that he be put in for a Purple Heart Medal because of his "Combat Injury." The medic tried to talk him out of it but he insisted. I don't know if it was ever approved but it didn't matter. What pissed us off was that we regularly ran to our aircraft while under fire so that we could go attack the enemy and we never even thought about asking for or getting a medal for our actions. It was our job!! What a jerk!!

CHAPTER 14

Tiger! Tiger! Tiger!

We did get one mission down that turned out to be very interesting. We were told that the Division was going to conduct a search and clear operation in the mountains to our west and several companies of infantry would be airlifted in on a combat assault in the morning. This was going into an area we called the "Rocket Belt" because the NVA launched most of their 122mm rockets at Camp Evans from there. Apparently, intelligence reports said the NVA was building up troops in the area and had even set up a 37mm antiaircraft flak gun out there for protection. I was scheduled to fly mortar patrol that night and was off the next day to catch up on my crew rest. I was a bit disappointed since that meant I wouldn't be going out on the initial assault but maybe it would stir up some action in our area of operations over the next few days since things had been pretty dull lately.

That night, we dutifully conducted our mortar patrol in our Cobra and decided to cruise by the area to look for any enemy activity or lights on the ground in the target area. We had been told to stay clear of the area because of the antiaircraft gun but that was like telling a kid that the paint on the wall was still wet, don't touch it!

We were a bit on edge as we cruised over the area and this turned to stark terror as huge flashes started exploding all around us. OH! Crap!! The 37mm gun must have detected us and was trying to blow us out of the sky. I dumped the collective pitch, rolled the aircraft into about a 120 degree bank and pointed the nose straight down into a dive to get away. As we screamed toward the ground at over 6000 feet a minute, the flashes faded away behind us then stopped. I pulled out of the dive and, as our heart rate dropped below 200 beats per minute we headed back toward Camp Evans, having learned our lesson. The funny thing was that neither of us ever saw a muzzle flash from the gun even though we were both looking down at the suspected location when all the flashes started.

The next morning I was up early as everyone was getting ready to launch on the combat assault. I wanted to tell them to be careful of the 37mm gun out there. As I walked toward operations, the new CO, Major Kleese, stepped out of the tent. When he saw me, he started walking towards me with a wry smile on his face and a piece of paper in his hand. He said, "Bob, could I talk to you for a minute?"

"Yes, Sir!" I replied.

He said, "You guys didn't go out near the rocket belt last night, did you?" I began stammering and saying,"Well, ah … Well, ah..." He then broke out laughing as he handed me the paper.

It wasn't just a piece of paper but a photograph. The photo was of a Cobra helicopter, rolled on its side with two very frightened looking pilots looking directly at the camera. It was us from the night before. I was dumbfounded. The CO took pity on me and explained that a photo recon aircraft had flown over the rocket belt last night to take pictures of the area in preparation for today's combat assault. The flashes we had seen were his flash bulbs of sorts. These were small grenade like objects that he dropped and they produced a very intense white light when they detonated but were otherwise harmless. The resulting pictures his camera took, looked like they had been taken in broad daylight. Harmless maybe, but they sure scared the hell out of us. The CO took the photo back and said with a smile, "Next time we tell you to stay out of an area,...Stay out of the area!"

"Yes, Sir!" I replied.

The combat assault went off without a hitch and all the troops were on the ground and gradually working their way up the hillside. The good news was that none of the aircraft had been shot at by the 37mm gun or any other gun for that matter. The first day had gone well.

The next day I was on "Hot Status" and was ready to go if the troops on the search and clear operation ran into any trouble. It didn't take long. Around 9 AM the fire mission horn went off and we scrambled to our aircraft. We launched in under two minutes, as usual, and were told to head to the rocket belt area, "troops in contact."

Since it was a quick trip to the area, I immediately contacted the ground commander to find out his situation. He said that they had run into a company of NVA and there was a pitched battle going on and he needed our help. As we arrived overhead, I went through our normal protocol and had all his troops mark their locations. They had made it about one third of the way up the hill on one side but it was difficult to get an exact fix on them because of the trees in the area. Most of the trees were between 75 and 100 feet tall and were dispersing the smoke before it cleared the treetops. We finally got a good fix on their location and I rolled in with a marking pair. The ground commander said we were right on target and to keep firing into that area. We complied but the enemy wasn't giving up easily. Since we were down to about a half a load of rockets left, I called ops and told them to launch another section to help out.

The other section arrived in just a couple of minutes and I began briefing them on what was going on. I was getting ready to roll in and shoot at the enemy location to mark it when I noticed movement in a clearing further up on the mountainside. The clearing was about 75 meters across and was covered with scrub brush. It had a dirt trail running from upper right to lower left and was about 200 meters behind the NVA company's position. As I watched I saw an NVA soldier with an AK-47 rifle in his hands, come running out of the upper right treeline as fast as he could go. He was beating feet along the dirt trail towards where the NVA company was battling our troops. I thought, no way is this guy getting down there to shoot at our guys. I started to roll in to shoot him when I saw a tiger emerge from the same spot this guy had come from, and it was closing the distance between them very rapidly. I pulled out of my dive and watched as the guy glanced back at the tiger several times while running at full speed. The tiger was only one lunge away from the guy as they disappeared from sight into the treeline. The other section leader asked me, "Why didn't you shoot the asshole?" I told him I was afraid I would scare the tiger.

We couldn't figure out why the NVA guy didn't just turn around and shoot the tiger with his rifle. It was possible that he was out of ammo or it could have been primal fear took over and he wasn't thinking straight. Either way, we were pretty sure that the tiger won.

I completed the hand off of the mission after we fired the rest of our rockets and returned to Evans. The operation was a success because our troops beat the enemy into a full fledged retreat and found a bunch of 122mm rockets that were destroyed on the spot. OH! Yeah! They also found an abandoned 37mm antiaircraft gun. I still wonder if TIGER GUY was one of its crew.

Other than the Tiger Operation, September was very much like August and it slowly faded into October. It wasn't like you could tell. There were no leaves turning colors or a nip in the air or anything like that. It was still very hot every day and we didn't even get any apple cider in the mess tent. I was sitting out in my lawn chair on top of our bunker, reading a book when my attention was drawn by the loud noise of an airplane taking off to the north on the main runway. I looked up and noticed it was a twin engine C-7A Caribou operated by the Air Force and it was used to carry troops and cargo. I watched him rotate and climb into the sky. I had just flown out of here a few weeks ago on just such an airplane on my way to Hawaii for R&R. I couldn't help but feel a little envious of the guys on board heading for their R&R.

As I watched, the Caribou started a right hand turn while climbing very steeply. It was then that I noticed a CH-47 Chinook in the same area and I was horrified to realize that they were about to have a mid-air collision at about 1000 feet above the ground.

The two aircraft merged into one object and parts went flying in all directions. The Chinook stopped flying immediately and fell from the sky like a railroad boxcar. It twisted and turned on its way down and I saw at least two passengers thrown out during the fall. It burst into flames when it hit the ground. When I looked back at the Caribou it was also tumbling toward the ground. I noticed that the cockpit area had been nearly sliced off by the helicopters rotor blades. It sort of pinwheeled into the ground and landed with a very audible THUD! There was no post-crash fire from the Caribou.

Immediately, Hueys operating in the area began to land at the crash site to render assistance but it was too late. All 24 personnel aboard the aircraft were dead. It was October 3rd, just 3 days prior to my 22nd birthday. I was beginning to feel very old.

CHAPTER 15

The Move

The rest of October seemed to just slide by. The missions we had were nothing out of the ordinary. I flew about 40 hours that month which was about half what a normal month would have been. I was flying mortar patrol on the the 28th of the month and was due to land at midnight after my replacement got airborne. As I was watching my replacement crank up on the flight line, the artillery controller called me and said very cryptically, "Have you heard what's happening tomorrow?"

I said, "No, I haven't heard anything. What's up?"

He replied, "I can't tell you over the radio, but you'll find out when you get back on the ground."

He had piqued my interest, so, I called my replacement aircraft on the VHF radio to see if he knew anything. He replied that he was just taking off and that we could go ahead and land and get briefed on what tomorrow would bring. When I pressed him for some clue, he also said he couldn't talk about it on the radio but that we should go to Operations for a briefing when we got down.

As we landed we noticed a great amount of activity going on in our company area. Normally, everyone would be asleep at this hour. When we walked into the Operations tent, it was packed with people and they were very animated in their discussions. Okay, something very big WAS going on. The CO, XO and operations officer were huddled together looking over a map when I walked up. I asked, "What's going on?" The CO turned to me and said, "We are moving the whole damn Division to III Corps tomorrow!"

"What! Are you kidding, sir?" I asked.

"No, I'm not. I just got briefed by the Division Commanding General and they want us down there and operational by November 1st. The code name for this is 'Operation Liberty-Canyon.' and it is our only priority."

I thought, holy cow, they wanted to move 18,000 men and almost 450 helicopters over 500 miles, get set up and be fighting again in three days. I knew that the First Cavalry Division was "Airmobile" but this was a pretty ambitious plan. It was then that the CO gave me the bad news. He said, "Bob, I want you to stay here and wait for that Cobra that is in 15th TC maintenance to get fixed, then fly it down and meet us at our new home at Quan Loi. I've checked with them and they say it should be ready to go by the first." What could I say but, "Yes, Sir!"

The packing up continued all night long and by morning, all the aircraft were fueled up and loaded with as much essential equipment as they could carry. The rest of the day we continued to pack the CONEX containers with the less essential items that could be hauled overland by trucks.

On the morning of the 30th, my copilot and I watched as the entire Battery took off and headed south towards Quan Loi. We continued to watch as all the other helicopters in the division took to the skies throughout the day and by evening Camp Evans was a ghost town.

It was a pretty eerie feeling as the sun set since we no longer had U.S. Forces on the perimeter. It was now manned, very sparsely, by ARVN soldiers. I couldn't help but think about how they had thrown down their weapons and run away on so many previous occasions. We didn't have a nice warm fuzzy feeling about this. Since our tents were all gone, we took to sleeping in the bunker and praying that 15th TC would get that Cobra flyable very quickly.

The next morning, spooky Halloween, we wandered over to 15th TC to check on our aircraft and found out that it wouldn't be ready until the evening of the 1st of November. We complained but were told, "Hey, buddy, we want to get the F**K out of here too, ya know?!!"

There was another aircrew from 1st of the 9th Cav there waiting on one of their helicopters, as well, and we took to hanging out with them. When we bitched to them that our unit had only left us with 2 cases of C rations to eat and no heat tabs to warm them up with, they said they'd show us a trick that some LRRPs had showed them. One of the pilots told us to follow him and we walked to the perimeter and out to the wire. He bent down and pulled a claymore mine from its position in front of a sandbag. He then popped it open and removed the block of C-4 plastic explosive from inside. He ripped off a corner of the clay like material and put the block back into the claymore and repositioned it in front of the sandbag. We all walked back over to 15th TC area and on the way he was rolling the ripped off piece of C-4 into a tube like a cigarette. He told us to get our cans of C rations open and ready to be heated. As we did, he pulled out his lighter and lit one end of the C-4 "Cigarette" and placed it on the ground. I was shocked and amazed that it didn't explode. It burned with a blue flame and lasted quite a long time. As we heated our C rations the other pilot said, "Oh! By the way, don't stomp on it to put it out. You'll loose your foot." Good advice! It's amazing the things you can learn in a foreign country.

Throughout the day of Halloween, the ARVN troops continued to move into Camp Evans and as they did, we would hear explosions from wherever they were. One of the pilots from 1st of the 9th noticed my puzzled look as another of these explosions went off and said, "Don't worry, that's just the ARVN clearing all the booby traps that the 1st Cav troopers set before they left."

Don't worry? Really! I was worried. The pilot said that some of the infantry guys would take a hand grenade, unscrew the time delay fuse that it came with and replace it with an instantaneous fuse. They would then pull the pin while holding the spoon down and place the grenade under something that might be moved by the enemy when they arrived at Camp Evans. Only problem was that it was the ARVN that was moving in and not the enemy. The next day we watched as an ARVN armored personnel carrier (APC) arrived in our Battery area and began to flatten our revetments out on the flight line. The revetments were two walls made out of sandbags that protected the aircraft from shrapnel damage during incoming artillery. I watched as the APC nudged one of the revetment walls until it fell over. As it fell, there were two explosions on either end of the wall. Oh! Crap!! I was going to have to be very careful where I walked and with whatever I might touch for the next couple of days. This certainly would be the spookiest Halloween ever.

Late the next day, as promised, the 15th TC maintenance officer came to us and said that our aircraft was ready and we could pick it up anytime. It was already getting dark, and as much as we wanted to get the hell out of there, we decided the wise thing to do was to spend one more night before leaving on our 550 mile trip. Once again, we slept on the floor of our old bunker but didn't really get much sleep. Needless to say, both of us kept hearing things that go bump in the night and I was sure there were still a few rats around that wanted to take a bite out of me. We both slept with our pistols which was probably more dangerous than the enemy forces around us.

At first light the next morning, we loaded all of our gear into the empty ammo bay, topped off the fuel tanks and took off for Quan Loi. I was very happy to see Camp Evans in the rear view mirror as we headed south.

It took us six and a half hours of flight time and several refueling and pit stops but we pulled into Phouc Vinh (Our new Battalion HQ) about 4:30 in the afternoon. Initially the navigation was easy as we headed down the coast. After all, I had done that several times (in reverse) when I was picking up Cobras and ferrying them up north.

The navigation turned a little more dicey when we headed inland after refueling at Phan Thiet. The only navigational equipment that the

Cobra had was an ADF radio that would point you at a commercial broadcast station and since they were speaking Vietnamese on those stations, it was impossible to know what city or town they were in. We did have one other piece of equipment that came in handy on a few occasions. It was the FM homing function of our FM radio. It had a needle that would deflect left or right indicating the direction to turn in to head to the station that was broadcasting. When the needle centered up you were flying directly toward....or away from the station. The only way to know which it was, was to listen to the broadcast. If it was getting stronger, you were going towards the station, but if it got weaker or stopped you were going the wrong way. Really sophisticated, Huh? Anyway, the most reliable way was by map and time, distance and heading. We didn't need no stinking GPS. We were real aviators. (Even if we were real scared of going the wrong way, crossing a border and running out of gas.)

As we headed west from Phan Thiet, both of us were studying the map, trying to pick out landmarks or towns or anything that might confirm we were headed in the right direction. There were no water towers with the towns name painted on the side. In fact, there were no towns, just jungle. By using superior skill, cunning and a lot of luck (and most of our fuel) we finally saw Phouc Vinh up ahead and both of us breathed a huge sigh of relief.

After refueling and parking the aircraft we asked where operations was and were pointed in the right direction.

As we checked in with operations, the Battalion Commander saw us and walked over and welcomed us to Phouc Vinh. He asked how our flight down was and what kind of shape our aircraft was in. We told him the flight was fine and the aircraft was in great shape.

The Colonel said, "Very good! I need for you two to take that aircraft up to Quan Loi tonight because your buddies in Charlie Battery have been flying their tails off on fire missions since they arrived and could use you guys and that aircraft. But first, my operations officer will brief you on our current situation, then I want you to get something to eat before you head north. Okay?"

We replied, "Yes, sir!"

The Operations Officer took over as the Colonel walked away and took us up to the map on the wall. He showed us our new area of operations. The 3rd brigade of the division was based at Quan Loi, the 2nd brigade at Tay Ninh and the 1st brigade was arrayed between them and slightly to the south. Division headquarters was located at Phouc Vinh. This produced a kind of arc of protection for Saigon running from just west of the city, along the Cambodian border to about 100 miles northeast of the capital. We were a blocking force that would stop or blunt any invasion by the NVA across the Cambodian border aimed at Saigon. He then told us we were confronting 2 NVA divisions, the 1st and 7th and 2 Viet Cong divisions, the 5th and the 9th. Oh! Great!! I thought, 4 to 1 odds. Sounded like an even fight to me.

We copied down the new Charlie Battery frequency and call sign and got some other info we would need for locating Quan Loi then headed to the mess hall to get something to eat. By the time we finished, it was starting to get dark and we needed to get going since it had already been a long day. We took off heading north and were trying to follow Highway 13 which leads to An Loc, a moderate size town that lays 5 kilometers west of the Quan Loi airstrip. Our briefing by the operations officer indicated that once we got to An Loc we just needed to turn east and we'd see the runway at Quan Loi. That sounded simple enough.

The problems started when it became totally dark and we lost sight of Hwy 13. Apparently, they forgot to tell us that there is little or no traffic on the road at night and for good reason. It seems that the bad guys conducted numerous attacks and ambushes along the road both day and night so, anybody foolish enough to travel it at night was considered to have a death wish. This road was nothing like an interstate highway since it had no lights whatsoever.

Okay! Back to basics. Fly north for 30 minutes and look around. This was kind of dicey since Quan Loi was near the Cambodian border and we might inadvertently cross the border without knowing it. We tried calling our operations to see if we could FM home to them, but we were still out of range. The lights of An Loc were blocked by trees from our distance and our maps were completely useless since it was so damn dark.

We pressed on and as we were nearing the 25 minute point in our flight north, the UHF radio came to life. We had pre-tuned Quan Loi towers frequency into it once we took off from Phouc Vinh. Now we heard, "Quan Loi tower, this is Blue Max 69 Romeo One for takeoff. Fire mission." Followed by, "Roger, Romeo One, you're cleared for takeoff."

Oh! Great! That was Bill McCaslin taking off from Quan Loi on a fire mission, so, all we had to do now was scan the horizon and look for two helicopters climbing out of the trees and we'd know the airfield's location. In a few seconds, we saw them emerge from the darkness and we headed for that spot. I called Bill on the tower frequency and told him we were about 5 minutes to the south and asked him to flash his landing light to confirm that we were, in fact, looking at him. He flicked it on and off several times and I did the same. Bill called back and said, "Good to see you guys, it's been kind of busy around here since we arrived, we could use some help. Well, gotta go. I've got to contact the ground commander for this mission."

"Roger that, I'll see you at the house," I answered.

At that point the tower controller chimed in and said, "Blue Max 68 Oscar 1, Quan Loi tower, we have you in sight, no other reported traffic, you are cleared to land. Welcome to your new home."

I replied, "Thanks, tower. We'll need you to give us some idea on where we park when we get down. Okay?"

"Roger that, Oscar 1. It'll be on the north side, mid field," he said.

I tried operations again and they replied. They said that someone would be out there to guide me in when I landed. As I've said previously, I love it when a plan comes together.

As we were shutting down, a group of about 5 armorers and crew chiefs descended on our aircraft and began loading rockets and checking oil levels and other things. My crew chief, Russ Warriner, jumped up on the step as I was filling out the logbook and explained that they needed the aircraft right away since all the other aircraft had been flying missions since they arrived. He told me the CO wanted to see me in operations when I got done. As if to punctuate this whole conversation, the fire mission horn went off and two crews came running out to the flight line and clamored into their helicopters. Wow! Things sure did seem to be pretty busy around here.

Russ showed me where the operations bunker was and I went down the four steps into a beehive of activity. Some operations personnel were talking on radios and telephones, while others were posting things on the big map and still others were updating mission boards. It was quite a hectic scene. The Battery Commander saw me and, grabbing me by the arm, steered me back out of the bunker. Major Kleese said, "Come on Bob, let me buy you a beer and update you on what's going on."

We walked over to a tent that had its sides rolled up and several tables and chairs inside. The CO explained, "This is the all ranks club, but we'll probably be the only ones here tonight. It's been a busy day and the troops that aren't working are probably in bed."

Major Kleese walked over to a refrigerator, put some money in the jar on top then grabbed two beers out of it and handed me one. As we sat down at one of the tables, we paused our conversation since it was being drown out by a section of Cobras returning from a mission. After the Cobras shutdown, the Major continued to fill me in on all the missions the unit had been flying since arriving. It seems that the NVA was very unhappy about the 1st Cavalry Division moving into the area and were determined to kick us back out. Major Kleese went back to the refrigerator and got us two more beers and said as he handed me one, "Don't worry, you're done for the night but you will be flying tomorrow."

I thanked him for the beer and we resumed our talk. As I was about half done with the second beer, in walked Karl Schneider. He said, "Hey! Bob. Glad to see you. Do you think you could sit in for me for about 5 minutes while I get a shower? Everybody else is flying or something, I'm on Hot Status and I've been going all day long." (As if I hadn't)

I explained that I had just landed after flying all day too and was on my second beer and didn't think it was appropriate. Karl said, "Don't worry, I'll only be 5 minutes. If the horn goes off, just go get my aircraft cranked up and I'll be right there to take over. Okay?"

I looked at Major Kleese and he just shrugged his shoulders. I said, "Okay. But hurry up." He thanked me and trotted off. With a bit of disappointment, I pushed the remainder of my beer away while Major Kleese continued to talk about our new area.

A couple of minutes went by and suddenly, the fire mission horn went off. I looked at Major Kleese and said, "Well, I guess that's me."

I jumped up and ran to the flight line and began looking for Karl's aircraft. I grabbed one of the crew chiefs and asked, "Where is Mr. Schneider's aircraft?" He pointed me toward a Cobra just 2 revetments away and I ran to it. It was very dark on the flight line but I could see that the rotor blades had been untied and someone was climbing into the front seat. Instead of grabbing the "Chicken Plate" hanging on the step and putting it on, I left it where it was since I was sure Karl would show up at any second. I flicked the battery switch on and hit the starter trigger and the lights dimmed as the turbine engine began to whine and the rotor blades began to turn. It takes about 40 seconds for the start sequence and throughout it I kept looking for Karl to come running up. No such luck!

The crew chief arrived and looked at me strangely. He saw that the "Chicken Plate" was still hanging on the step and I had not put on my helmet yet. He grabbed the "Chicken Plate" and jumped up on the step handing it to me. At this point he was close enough to tell I wasn't Karl and said, "Mr. Hartley, what are you doing here?"

As I began to explain, a voice from the front seat shouted, "What the hell is going on back there?"

We were rapidly approaching the 2 minutes scramble time limitation and Karl was nowhere in site. I thought, "Well, I guess I have to do this."

I grabbed the body armor from the crew chief and slipped it over my head. Then he helped me with the shoulder harness as I pulled on Karl's helmet. Damn!! It was about 2 sizes too small and was crushing my head. Oh! Well, still no Karl and it was time to go. The crew chief closed up my canopy door and ran out front to guide us out of the revetment. I quickly called Quan Loi tower for takeoff clearance and they answered with, "Roger, Oscar 1, you're clear for take off, what took so long?" I answered, "I'll have to tell you later."

I then said into the microphone, "Who's that in my front seat?"

"It's me Gary, Who the hell is that?"

"It's me, Bob Hartley, Karl asked me to sit in for him while he took a shower. I guess he's still wet." So far, this mission was off to a very shaky start.

Gary called operations for the specifics on the mission. Ops said, "Roger, Oscar 1??? Head East for 2 kilometers, contact Iron Fist 19 on 33.5, troops in contact."

I rogered Ops and briefly explained what happened. Then I called my wing man and brought him up to date with what was going on. I said we'd be using my call sign for the mission and I told them that I had just landed at Quan Loi for the first time 45 minutes ago, so, I might need some help. It was just pure luck that the mission was only 2 kilometers east of the airfield and there was no real night time navigation required. We had taken off to the southwest and as we turned left to fly eastbound, we could easily see where the battle was since tracer rounds from both sides were flying everywhere. I armed the weapons system and was greeted by a bunch of unfamiliar lights on the panel. What the hell was this? I asked Gary and he said, "Oh! You don't know, but we have gotten almost all Cobras now and the new ones they just delivered have come with dual weapons in the turret. One minigun and one 40 mm grenade launcher. That's what the different lights back there mean."

I said, "Oh! Great, anymore surprises in store for me?"

Gary said, "No, that's about it."

Newer model AH-1G with Minigun on left <u>and</u>
40mm Grenade Launcher on right in turret.
Photo courtesy of Paula Huckleberry

So, let's sum up. I was in a new model Cobra, at night, in an area I was totally unfamiliar with, flying with a crew I usually never flew with, and I had a couple of beers under my belt, and we were on our way to administer deadly force in close proximity to friendly forces. That's about right. Oh! Wait, I forgot about the teeny tiny helmet I had on my head that was crushing the snot out of it. Yeah! That about sums it up!

I switched frequencies and called "Iron Fist 19" to tell him we were on station and ask him what his situation was. He explained that they were on patrol around the airfield and had run into a company size NVA unit that was preparing to attack the airfield.

I had him mark his unit's positions with star clusters just as a formality since I could easily distinguish the difference in the tracers from the enemy AK-47s and the U.S. M-16s. I told him I was coming in with a marking pair and to adjust my wingman. I selected a spot where 3 AK-47s were close together and firing at the U.S. positions and fired one pair of rockets.

As I pulled out of the dive, I saw a flash and wondered if I had gotten a secondary explosion. Iron Fist 19 called and said, "That's perfect, shoot up that whole area."

My wingman was already in his dive and firing as I climbed back to altitude. We normally start our rocket runs from 3000 feet above the ground per unit SOP but tonight, since we didn't have enough time to climb that high before we arrived on station, we were rolling in from 2500 feet. I checked with Iron Fist 19 again and he said, "Yeah! Keep doing it. We can hear them yelling every time you shoot."

I rolled in again and fired 6 more pairs of rockets into the area and noticed the same flash again as I pulled out of the dive. What the heck was that? Probably something else they forgot to tell me about.

On my third rocket run, I hit the button 3 times and no rockets fired. I quickly switched from outboard pods to inboard since there was obviously a problem with the outboards and punched the button again to launch rockets from the inboards but was greeted, instead, by a blast of tracers emitting from under my wings and converging on the target area. WHAT THE HELL!!

I released the firing button and pulled out of the dive totally confused. Again, the flash.

I said to Gary, "What the hell was that?"

He replied, "Oh! Didn't you know? We have XM-18 minigun pods on the inboards and 7 shot rocket pods outboard."

"WHAT???" I said incredulously, since our standard configuration was 4, nineteen shot rocket pods.

"That's the way they came. I thought you knew." said Gary.

Things were going so "smoothly" that I was sure something else was about to go haywire. Just then, Quan Loi tower called.

I answered saying, "Yes Tower, what's up. I'm kind of busy here."

Tower said, "Yes, Sir. But we've been watching you from here and thought you ought to know that every time you pull out of one of your rocket runs, there is a big explosion just under your aircraft and we were kind of worried about you." I thanked Tower profusely and said we'd be careful.

Apparently, the enemy was shooting an RPG at us armed with a B-40 warhead. The B-40 was designed to exploded after it had traveled a certain distance where the normal RPG round would explode on contact. Since we were pulling out of our dives just above his range, we could see the flash but not hear the booms, Thank God!

I told my wingman to hang back when I rolled in again and to watch for the muzzle flash of the RPG as it was launched, "... then, take him out!!" I said.

I rolled in again and fired a long burst from the wing mounted miniguns, then pulled up a few hundred feet early just to be on the safe side. As we were transitioning into a climb, we saw the flash again. My wingman radioed, "We've got him!" and began firing a bunch of rockets at the RPG site.

We made a few more runs on the target and got no more flashes as we pulled out of our dive. We were just about out of ammo so I called Iron Fist 19 and asked if he wanted another section of Cobras to finish up the bad guys.

He replied that the enemy had turned tail and was running away and his unit was now in hot pursuit. I told him "Good Luck! Give us a call if we can help."

He thanked us extensively and I couldn't help but think, "If you only knew how screwy this whole thing had been, you might not be so generous with your praise." I really needed that beer now!!

I called Tower again and said we were ready to land and he cleared us to do so. I told him that his call really helped save our ass and that we wound up shooting the guy that was doing it. There was a long pause then Tower called back and said, "Thanks for the info, there are a bunch of guys up here doing a jig in celebration right now. After all, we only get to clear aircraft for take offs and landings all day long. It feels good to help out."

I replied, "Thanks for having my back."

"Anytime, Oscar 1, anytime."

After we landed and I was trying to find where I would be sleeping that night, I saw Karl and said, "Where the heck were you when the horn sounded, I thought you'd come running after I got your aircraft cranked up."

He said, "I never heard the horn go off. I guess I had water in my ears or something."

"You had something in your ears all right, but I don't think it was water, you owe me big time Karl." I replied.

"Okay! Okay! I'm sorry. I owe you," Karl said.

I managed to find second platoons tent and the guys had set up a cot for me, so, I dumped my gear next to it and collapsed in a heap on top even though there was no air mattress or sleeping bag. When I woke up the next morning I was still in the clothes I had worn the day before. I guess I was pretty tired.

I took a cold shower and got some clean jungle fatigues on then wandered over to the mess tent for some coffee. Now that I was starting to feel human again, I walked into operations to see what was going on and Major Kleese spotted me. He said that they would get one of the other section leaders to take me up later that morning for a local area checkout since I'd never seen this place in daylight.

I have to apologize to whomever it was that conducted my local area orientation flight because I do not remember who did it. This was, unfortunately, a common event in flying the Cobra, since the seating was tandem and you could not see the other pilot's face. Quite often, you would not be able to recall who you were with on a particular mission. Anyway, it was a clear day and visibility was very good. We headed west after takeoff and I saw that the town of An Loc was only about 5 kilometers west of the airfield at Quan Loi. There was an ARVN compound on the south side of town that I should be aware of since they had some artillery guns there. Then we flew south along Highway 13 and I was shown where "Thunder 13" was located. This was another artillery fire base about 10 kilometers south of Quan Loi. It was important to know where these fire bases were so that you could avoid flying through the "Gun-Target line" to prevent being shot down by your own artillery. We then turned westbound and my copilot showed me some more fire bases. As I was annotating them on my map, I noticed on the horizon, a large, black mountain that looked very much like a volcano. I asked my fellow pilot about this and he said it was Nui Ba Den or "The Black Virgin." It was, indeed, an extinct volcano which had a commanding view of the countryside since its top was at about 3,200 feet above sea level. He told me that the U.S. Forces owned the top and bottom of the mountain but the bad guys owned the middle and had many caves and tunnels throughout it. He then said that this mountain had a "Twin Sister" about 30 kilometers northeast of Quan Loi that was called Nui Ba Ra near the town of Song Be (pronounced Song Bay). He said that it too was an extinct volcano, had a similar height of about 3,000 feet and had the same "ownership" arrangement. Both were very prominent landmarks and were good for keeping a pilot oriented during the day. He did tell me that I needed to be careful around them at night since neither of them had lights on top for security purposes. "Yes," I said, "I could see how an invisible 3,000 foot rock might be a problem for a pilot at night."

We landed at our sister battery's location at Tay Ninh in the shadows of Nui Ba Den, got some gas and took a tour of their battery area. Since Tay Ninh was the western most edge of our area of operations, we took off and headed back east. We were flying just south of the Cambodian border and my copilot was showing me that there was no clear delineation between the two countries on the ground as there had been up north in the A Shau valley. Other than the two mountains, there were not many landmarks to keep you from inadvertently flying across the border into Cambodia, so, you had to be careful he said.

As we flew eastbound, I noticed that the jungle gave way to what looked like an orchard of sorts. These were very uniformly shaped trees that seemed to be planted in rows. When I asked about this, my fellow pilot explained that this was the largest rubber tree plantation in Vietnam and I needed to know some things about it. He said that a large French tire company owned this and many other rubber tree plantations throughout this area of Vietnam but this one was the largest at over 31,000 acres and we were suppose to avoid shooting any bad guys in the plantation since the U.S. Government had to pay "War

Reparations" to the French, and the tire company, of up to $600 per tree for any damage we caused.

"WHAT!?" I said. "Are you kidding me?" I was incredulous. How could we, the American people, be paying the French for something that they screwed up to begin with? If I remember my grade school geography correctly, all of Southeast Asia used to be called "French Indochina" when the French colonized it and capitalized on the natural resources they found there, particularly rubber. The Vietnamese people were sick and tired of being conquered and abused by foreign troops including the Chinese, the Japanese, the French and now, the U.S. They finally defeated their last occupier, the French, at Dien Bien Phu and evicted them from control. But the U.S., under Eisenhower and Kennedy, decided to help the French save face by stepping in to "Stop the advance of Communism." So, as a way of saying thanks, the French decided to charge us for any damage to the natural resources that they were pilfering from the Vietnamese. As if this were not unbelievably convoluted to begin with, there was also a rumor that the South Vietnamese government was paying a bribe to the NVA and VC to stay clear of the Plantation because the French (or the French tire company) were paying the South Vietnamese Honchos under the table to make such an arrangement happen. Let me make it clear that I had no way of verifying this info but it was generally accepted as true. It was the U.S. Government and the American people that were ultimately left holding that bag of crap! I'm sure that some of the Head Honchos in the U.S. Government got a little taste of the action just because of the amount of money flowing around. As the saying goes, "It wasn't much of a war, but it was the only war we had!" and they had to make the most of it.

Sorry about the tirade, but I just had to get that off my chest. Back to my local area orientation. After we passed the Plantation, my copilot showed me the area called "The Fish Hook". It was a part of the border just northwest of An Loc that formed an image on the map that looked somewhat like a fish hook. This area was of particular concern since we knew that the enemy had large troop concentrations on the other side of the border there and speculation was that the NVA could punch through the defenses there and head down Highway 13 and straight into Saigon, so, it was sort of like a dagger poised over the heart of South Vietnam. This was the area where our guys had been conducting so many fire missions since we moved down here.

We passed just north of Quan Loi as we headed east. About 30 kilometers northeast of our airfield was the town of Song Be and the "Twin Sister," Nui Ba Ra mountain. It truly was a twin because it looked exactly like the mountain we had seen earlier near Tay Ninh. We flew around it and he pointed out the compound on top of the mountain that was occupied by U.S. Army Signal Corps folks who used the mountains height as a radio relay facility to enhance communications throughout the area. He also showed me the U.S. Army fire base called LZ Buttons. It sat near the base of the mountain on the northwest side near the town of Song Be. It had a battery of 105mm howitzers and just outside of the perimeter there was a refueling point and helicopter revetments along side a 3000 foot runway.

My tour of this portion of South Vietnam was over and we headed home to Quan Loi. Now that I was checked out, I would start being scheduled for missions the next day. When we landed back at Quan Loi, I had a chance to check out our new home. The runway was about 5,000 feet long and ran southwest to northeast. The whole base was a former rubber tree plantation, so, our tents were nestled in among the trees on the north side of the runway. We were about midfield and located right next to the ammo dump, a fact that I was not really pleased with. About 30 to 40 meters to our west was the control tower for the airfield and just past it was an artillery section consisting of an 8 inch howitzer and a 175mm Self propelled gun which were very large weapons. They would fire at irregular intervals both day and night and would scare the hell out of you whenever they did. We became somewhat used to them but when one of them fired at 3 AM while you were sound asleep, it took a while to get your heart rhythm back to normal. Overall, our area was pretty nice but I really didn't like our bunkers worth a damn. They were simple slit trenches about 5 feet wide and 8 feet deep dug by a back hoe. For overhead cover they had a half of a metal culvert pipe that was then covered with sand bags. Not very comforting at all. Four foot thick concrete would have been more to my liking. But this is what we had and we would make the best of it.

The unit now had all Cobras but the powers that be allowed us to keep 2 Hueys for backup since they were just going to be shipped back to the States anyway. All of our Cobras were now the latest version with the two weapons in the turret and very few hours on their airframes. Our armorers were rapidly changing the odd ball configurations to our standard 4 rocket pods of 19 rounds each.

The next day, as predicted, I was on Hot Status with Jerry Moses (Moe) as my wingman. The fire mission horn went off early in the afternoon, we scrambled as usual and got airborne in the allotted two minutes. Our mission was to head east for 4 kilometers and contact the ground commander because his troops were in a fire fight with a larger enemy force. Oh! Great! Here we are again with a large group of the enemy only a few thousand meters from where I sleep. Not Good!!

We contacted the ground commander and had him mark all of his positions, then I rolled into my dive to shoot a marking pair into the enemy's position. As I climbed back to altitude, the ground commander said my rounds were right on target and to let 'em have it.

Moe was already into his dive and proceeded to dump about 8 pair of rockets on the location. He began to pull out of his dive at what would be perceived as a normal recovery altitude but as as he changed the aircraft's attitude to a climb mode, the aircraft continued to descend on the same angle he had been diving on. He was experiencing a loss of power and I was wondering if he had been hit by ground fire. I called to him but he did not answer. Ever so slowly, his angle of descent began to flatten out but I wasn't sure he could regain control before hitting the trees. I was right! He hit the trees just over where his rockets had impacted a few seconds earlier and the only thing I could see of his aircraft was the rotor blades skimming through the treetops much like a weed whacker trims the grass in your front yard. There were leaves and branches flying off in every direction. Very gradually, his aircraft began to emerge from it's run through the jungle and looked like a submarine slowly surfacing in the ocean. As he broke free of the grip of the jungle, he called me and said he had some sort of power failure and needed to head back to Quan Loi. He said he didn't have any indication of his airspeed so he would just be using normal power settings and asked me to monitor his speed. I rogered him and said I'd follow him back to cover him if he had to put it down. I then called operations to give them a heads up and to have them launch another section to replace us.

We were on final approach as the replacement section of Cobras passed us on their way to help out the troops still in contact with the enemy. After we shut down, I walked over to Moe's aircraft to survey the damage. The first thing I noticed was that the rocket pods were totally jammed packed full of vegetative matter to the point that I couldn't see any of the rockets that remained unfired. I then walked around the front of his aircraft and saw why he was having airspeed problems. His pitot tube (the little probe sticking out of the nose of the aircraft that measures airspeed) was also packed full of tree parts and, thereby, totally eliminating any indication of speed. I glanced down to see the minigun and 40mm grenade launcher were also totally obstructed with green and brown stuff. However, considering that the aircraft hit the jungle going about 160 knots, it was in relatively good shape. The only other damage I could see was a few scratches and dents to the fuselage and the leading edges of the wings and a bright new green color to the frontal areas of the machine.

I asked Moe and his copilot how they were doing and, though a little shaken up, they said they were fine. The maintenance folks were able to replace the pitot tube very quickly and the turret weapons were able to be cleaned out but the real problem was the rocket pods. The armorers and the crew chiefs worked very hard at trying to clean out the tubes and pull the rockets that were jammed in place, but to no avail. It was finally decided to drop the pods and replace them with new pods. The old pods were turned over to the EOD (Explosive ordnance Disposal) folks to be blown up. The maintenance guys also found out that the original "Power Problem" that Moe experienced was due to an improperly set fuel control unit which they promptly fixed. The aircraft was back up and flying the next day but would retain its very distinctive bright green hue for the next several weeks.

The beginning of November not only brought us an new home and new aircraft but it also brought us some new faces. We, in second platoon, were getting a new platoon leader in Cory Couch. He was a lieutenant, soon to be captain, and would replaced Captain Frank Thornhill who was moving up to battalion HQ to take over as operations officer at the end of the month. It was a good career move for Frank and Lt. Couch proved to be a very worthy and capable replacement for him.

CHAPTER 16

Mac

We also had a new warrant officer who introduced himself to me as, "Francis X. McDowall but you can call me Mac." And we did.

Mac was a very energetic and enthusiastic about learning all he could about our mission, our tactics and the Cobra helicopter. While most new pilots kept a pretty low profile and tried to blend in, Mac was very inquisitive and always larger than life. He was very gregarious and had a great sense of humor, which was something we all needed just to get by.

We all liked him from the start and since I was a section leader, I was tasked with flying with him to teach him how things worked on our missions. Mac was a very quick study and was always asking questions about why I had done something one way instead of another. I could see early on that he was definitely section leader material and I decided to become his mentor and train him toward that goal. I was sure that he would learn very quickly and be able to be my replacement when I went home at the end of March. Because of this situation, Mac and I flew many missions together and some of them are very memorable.

Russ Juleen, Mac, Jerry Moses with Lt. Couch in background

One night, shortly after we met, I took Mac up on mortar patrol with me to show him how that mission worked. We were flying around Quan Loi and I was able to show him what out going artillery looked like so he wouldn't confuse the large muzzle blasts of our artillery pieces with the smaller flashes from an enemy mortar. As we were headed westbound around the LZ, I saw a flash from behind us and knew instantly what it was. I rolled the aircraft into a 90 degree bank and pulled the nose around very quickly so we were now facing the opposite direction and I was scanning the ground for signs of the enemy position because I knew that flash was from enemy fire directed at the LZ. As if to confirm my hunch, a large explosion erupted on the southwest area of the runway, right in the aircraft refueling point. The incoming round ignited one of the blivets used to store jet fuel and the resulting fire was now turning night into day in that area. Almost simultaneously, our artillery controller was on the radio screaming, "WE'RE TAKING INCOMING!!" to me.

I rogered his call and was preparing to fire into the general area where the flash came from but was purposely holding off in hopes that the enemy would fire again and I would be able to pinpoint his position. He didn't fire again, so, I was obliged to fire a few random rockets in his general direction to discourage him from trying an encore.

As I pulled out of my rocket run I noticed that the Hot Section was just taking off to come assist me and defend the LZ. Together, we made a few more rocket runs on the general area but the bad guys did not fire again. We saw that the fire department guys had knocked down the fire in the fuel point fairly quickly and heard the good news that no one was injured and we only lost one blivet and several hundred gallons of fuel.

After about 15 minutes, the Hot Section guys that had joined us were now heading back in and we resumed our patrol duties. As we were flying southwest bound and paralleling the two Hot Section Cobras as they were landing to the southwest on the runway, I caught a flash again from behind us and, this time, watched as a 57 mm recoil-less rifle round streaked down the runway, passing just below the two Hot Section Cobras on final approach, prior to exploding in the refueling point once more.

I did another quick turn and began firing into the general area once again to suppress the enemy fire. The Hot Section aborted their landing and climbed back out to rejoin me. This time, Mac and I saved our ammo and let the Hot Section shoot up the area. I wanted to have some ammo left if this scenario repeated itself. This time, as the Hot Section began its approach to the southwest again, I positioned myself so that we were headed TOWARD the enemy's position and kept my airspeed down to about 40 knots while "S" turning to stay oriented toward the northeast as long as possible. This would allow me to pin point the enemy's location if they fired again. They did not. We continued to circle the area but the enemy did not fire anymore that night.

As we circled and discussed what had just happened, Mac said he thought that the bad guys were watching us as we flew overhead and would only fire when they knew we were facing the other way. This seemed to be a fair assessment to me and I was surprised that neither I, nor any of the others pilots had ever made that observation before. It was true that as we circled the LZ, at some point we would have to be facing away from the enemy's out lying position and that time would be the safest time for the enemy to fire. Since I was now in agreement with Mac's conclusion, he said he had also thought of a possible solution to the problem. I said, "Okay, let's hear it."

Mac replied, "Well, since they are watching us and can tell which way we are heading by looking at our navigation lights (the red and green lights on the wing tips), I suggest that we swap the lenses so that it looks like we are going away, when, in fact,we are actually going towards them."

I was dumbfounded over the simplicity, and yet, the sheer brilliance of this idea. We talked about it some more and I was convinced that this was something we should pursue. The rest of that night was quiet and we had no more incoming.

The next morning, I grabbed Mac and we went over to see Major Kleese with Mac's idea. The CO listened carefully and after we cleared up a few sticking points, he approved Mac's plan.

One of the sticking points had been that the standard lighting configuration rule accepted worldwide was a red light was to be displayed on the left side of an aircraft or boat and a green one on the right. These rules were to aid in navigation and to help prevent accidents by eliminating confusion over which direction an aircraft or boat was headed in. The CO made us promise that we would only change the lights for mortar patrol and required us to brief all of our other pilots in our unit about the change. Since we would be in the Tower controlled airspace above Quan Loi, we were required to notify Tower that we were flying an aircraft with a "Non-Standard" lighting configuration. When we walked over and briefed the Tower controllers, they were fine with the plan and said they would notify any other aircraft operating at the airfield of the situation.

A couple of days later, when Mac and I had mortar patrol again, we put the plan into effect. It was about 11:30 at night and we were heading northeast on the south side of the LZ when the bad guys fired their 57 mm recoil-less rifle again, except this time we were heading directly at them. I pin pointed their launcher position, flicked the

Master Arm switch to "ARMED" and fired about 8 pair of rockets into their position. We then circled the area since there were several small fires burning where my rockets had landed and waited for the Hot Section to join us. We all circled the area for about 15 minutes and saw no further activity so the Hot Section went back in to land. Mac and I continued and completed our tour on mortar patrol without any further enemy action that night.

The next morning, the CO came to our tent to tell us that he had just heard from the commander of the 1st of the 9th Cav squadron that they had found a blown up 57 mm recoil-less rifle and 5 dead NVA during their "First Light" recon that morning. He added that they were recovering the weapon for us and that it would be put on display in front of our unit headquarters. I could tell that Mac was pleased with the way his idea worked out but he didn't gloat or boast about it at all. The mark of a true professional.

The author with 57mm recoil-less rifle and
12.7mm (.51 cal) antiaircraft gun

Mac was in my front seat on a mission near the "Fishhook" section of the border and we were shooting for an infantry company that had run into a complex of bunkers and dug in NVA. We had completely expended all of our rockets but were continuing to provide cover for our wingman since he still had a few rockets left. I had already called operations for another section to be launched since this operation was still on going. Mac was operating the turret weapons from his front seat gunners station and had run out of the 7.62 mm ammo for the minigun. He had switched over to 40mm grenades and was firing them under our wingman as he was pulling out of his last rocket run. The 40mm grenade launcher makes a very distinct "Bump, Bump, Bump..." sound as it fires. Suddenly, there was a very loud explosion that shook the entire aircraft. I was sure we had just been hit by some kind of enemy ground fire. I scanned the instrument panel to see what damage had been done. The "Master Caution" light was illuminated and the caution panel had a corresponding "#2 HYD SYS" light illuminated also. This indicated that one of our 2 hydraulic systems had failed and we were in an emergency situation. I then heard the hydraulic pump for the # 2 system start to whine and that meant the system was out of fluid due to some sort of leak. The good news was that the aircraft was still controllable but the bad news was that it would only be controllable for about 7 minutes since the good system was now bleeding its fluid over into the bad system and once it was depleted we were in big trouble.

All of that had taken about 3 seconds to determine and now I was concerned about Mac. I asked him on the intercom, "Are you okay?"

He replied, "Yeah, but my feet hurt!"

"What!! Are you hit?" I asked.

"I don't think so, but the explosion was right under my feet." he replied.

I had already turned around and was heading for Quan Loi which was about 5 minutes away. I called our wingman and told him what had happened and that we were heading home. He caught up with us pretty quickly and as he pulled alongside, he called to say, "Your turret is gone! There is just a bunch of junk hanging from where it used to be."

I can't say I was surprised by this revelation but I was too busy to worry about it right now. I called Quan Loi Tower to declare an emergency and asked them to have the Crash Crew standing by. They rogered my call and cleared me to land in any direction I wished. I told them we would be doing a running landing to the northeast so the Crash Crew could position themselves accordingly. I then called our operations and told them of my situation. The radio operator said he'd alert maintenance and the Commanding Officer and then he wished us good luck.

The runway finally came into view and we lined up for our running landing. This type of landing was preferable because it required less power changes than bringing the aircraft to a hover. We didn't want to hover just in case the other hydraulic system failed and the controls seized up since that would be catastrophic.

The running landing was perfect and we slid to a halt on the middle of the runway and adjacent to our flight line. The Crash Crew rolled up next to us and trained their hoses on us just in case. Our maintenance personnel were there in a flash and had the aircraft hooked up and ready to be towed almost before we could climb out of it. As I've said before, I love it when a plan comes together.

Mac and I surveyed the damage once the aircraft was safely parked in the maintenance area. All of the fairings for the turret were, indeed, gone, along with most of the minigun. But the majority of the grenade launcher was still there though pretty well mangled. Hydraulic hoses and electrical cables were ripped out and hanging down and the whole thing looked like it would take a considerable amount of time to fix. But the big question was...WHAT HAPPENED?

After some investigative work by our armorers and maintenance folks, it was determined that the 40mm grenade launcher had malfunctioned and a grenade had detonated in the turret. The explosion was totally contained within the turret except for the shock wave that stung Mac's feet. Mac's inquisitive nature got the better of him and he began to dissect the remnants of the 40mm grenade launcher. After delving into the maintenance manuals and studying the hunk of junk that once was the launcher, Mac solved the puzzle of what had actually gone wrong. With great satisfaction he showed us all that the feed paw that drags the next round to be fired into position, had broken while the round was only half way into the breech and the barrel of the gun had moved backward, as it was suppose to, and crushed the warhead until it detonated. Mac then conducted a briefing for all the other pilot on how to check the feed paw on their preflight inspections to preclude such an incident from happening again.

As a result of his self taught expertise and his enthusiasm in studying the weapons systems, Mac was appointed as the unit's Aircraft Armament Maintenance Officer. He worked tirelessly tinkering with the weapons systems in the hot sun out on the flightline and studying the manuals at night while the rest of us were just goofing off. Soon, all of our armament systems were in top notch condition and we were having very few jams or malfunctions, thanks to Mac. I was convinced, more than ever, that I had chosen wisely in selecting my replacement and was sure Mac would continue to excel.

I am fairly certain that Mac was with me on a mission one night to help out some LRRPs that had gotten themselves into quite a predicament. We were assigned as the Hot Section that night and the fire mission horn went off around 9 PM. We scrambled and got airborne very quickly and operations sent us the mission details. They said, "Head northeast for sixty kilometers and contact 'Sneaky Pete 15' on frequency 33.5, LRRP team surrounded."

"Oh! Crap!!" I thought. First of all, sixty kilometers was just about out of our area of operations and it was going to take at least 15 to 20 minutes to get there and secondly, by the time we did get there it was highly unlikely that they would still be alive since they were currently surrounded. I had Mac verify the mission info just in case they had made a mistake but operations said it was correct then added, "Good luck." to the end of their transmission as if to say, "Yeah, we know it's a long shot but we have to try to help them out."

I pulled the power up to the redline and had us going as fast as possible but the flight just seemed incredibly long. When we got into radio range, I called "Sneaky Pete 15" several times but got no response. My worse fears seemed to have come true. I tried several more times and finally, I heard the radio break squelch. This sound is when the normal static on the radio goes silent and you would expect to start to hear the voice of the person transmitting, but now I was just listening to an "open line." After about 15 seconds, I heard what sounded like someone whispering very softly. It was, in fact, Sneaky Pete 15 who was saying that he had to whisper because they had an NVA soldier, acting as a sentry, standing about 10 feet away from them. I found myself whispering each time I answered one of his transmissions, even though I was at 3000 feet above the ground in a helicopter with thundering rotor blades and a whining turbine engine making enough noise to wake the dead. The LRRP explained, in his whisper, that they had been following a battalion sized NVA unit for most of the day and had watched them make camp for the night just before sunset. At that point the LRRPs decided to back off several hundred meters and find a place to settle in for the night themselves. They had found a trench that all 5 of them could get into and had just settled in when, unfortunately, the NVA came walking back into their location and began to set up camp around them. Apparently, the first location for the NVA proved unsuitable and they decided to backtrack to this spot. The LRRPs had gone undetected so far but knew that with morning light, they would be dead men. What they wanted us to do was to shoot into the camp and during the ensuing confusion and melee, they would be able to get away. That sounded like a good plan but how, in hell, were they ever going to mark their location without giving away their position?

We had flown approximately 60 kilometers and were in the vicinity of the grid coordinates provided but it was a very dark night since there was a high overcast and no moon or starlight. We couldn't make out any geographical features like rivers or towns to orient us as to our location, so, we were unable to get a good fix on the LRRPs location as well.

I explained our dilemma to the LRRP and he said that he thought he could hear helicopters down to his south, so, I should fly north for a while. I did so and shortly he said he could see helicopters to his east and

I should turn west now. As I did so, he called back and said, "Yup! That's you. Keep flying west." I explained to him that even if he did vector me to a position directly over his location, he still had to have some way to mark his position so I could positively identify it to prevent shooting him. It was then that he explained he would mark by having a "Heat Tab" burning in the bottom of two "C Ration cans" which would be in the bottom of their trench. A "Heat Tab" was an Alka-Seltzer size tablet that comes with the C Rations and could be lit with a match to provide enough heat to warm the contents of the C Ration can. It burned with a very dim blue flame much like a can of Sterno. I thought, "You have got to be kidding me." The chances of me being able to spot that from 3000 feet would be slim and none. And besides, if I did see it, it would only be for the blink of an eye since it was in the bottom of the two cans and a trench. I was beginning to loose hope that we could ever pull this off when Sneaky Pete 15 called and said, "You're directly north of me, fly south." I did and a few seconds later he said, "Look Down!!"

I quickly rolled the aircraft into a 90 degree left bank, looked down and saw the momentary flash of what appeared to be a Heat Tab in the bottom of some cans. Unbelievable!! But it was gone as quickly as we'd seen it.

I told the LRRP that we had seen him. I said that he would have to vector us again but this time I would fire a marking pair of rockets when I rolled in and to be prepared to adjust my wingman. He told me the largest group of bad guys were to the north of his position and that they had all stopped moving around and were now watching the helicopters overhead. I told him I wanted to come in from the west and turn 90 degree to the left over his position so I'd be aimed at the largest group of bad guys. He agreed and said one of his men would shoot the sentry when our rockets hit the ground and they would be up and running to the south. We had a plan!

He vectored us back around and, once again, said, "Look Down!" I did and immediately saw his Heat Tab. I continued the left hand roll past the 90 degree mark and simultaneously entered a very steep dive. I imagined a spot about 30 meters north of where I'd seen the Heat Tab, lined up on it and fired a single pair of rockets. It was like shooting into an inkwell. As I was pulling out of my dive, I heard the LRRP on the radio, in a very loud and booming voice say, "That's it!! You got 'em. Shoot! Shoot!"

My wingman could see several small grass fires burning from my rounds and used them as an aiming point to fired about 8 pair of rockets into the area. We must have hit them pretty good because they were now shooting wildly into the sky in an attempt at self defense. As my wing man climbed back to altitude, I decided to hold off on shooting anymore until I could be sure the LRRPs were clear of the area. I called Sneaky Pete 15. No answer. I called again, still no answer. I was worried that maybe one of our rounds had hit them or perhaps the enemy had discovered them while they were running away and eliminated them. I called again in desperation. Finally, they called back and said, while panting very heavily, that they were now about 2 kilometers south of there and continuing to run and that we had done a great job and should finish shooting up that whole area.

We were very relieved to hear from them and didn't need to be told twice to finish shooting up the area. Once we expended all of our ammo on the target, we turned toward home feeling very satisfied that we were able to bail the LRRPs out of a very bad situation once again.

Over the next few months, we had an unusual number of missions to help out the LRRPs. Either they were conducting higher number of dangerous missions than usual or they were just having a string of bad luck. Anyway, one day in February of 1969, most of us in the second platoon were sitting around out in the "backyard" of our tent, just shooting the breeze and waiting for a mission, when a group of 5 infantrymen walked up. The obvious leader of the group said, "Who's Blue Max 68 Oscar 1 and Papa 1?" His demeanor seemed to indicate that the owners of those call signs might be in a heap of trouble and that he and his team were here to exact some sort of retribution. Steve Woods and I gingerly raised our hands to indicate that we were the guilty parties.

It was then that they broke into wide grins and said, "We're the LRRPs from Company E of the 52nd Infantry Battalion." And after saluting us he said, "Let me shake your hand, Sir. I can't believe how many times you guys have saved our asses. We'd have been dead several times over if it weren't for your help."

They then gave us two cases of beer as a way to say, Thanks! We sat around talking about several of the missions we'd been on with them and they told us that they were the team we'd fired for back in November when the NVA battalion had made camp around them. We all had a good laugh as we thought of the NVA soldiers wondering, "How in the hell did those helicopters find us out in the middle of the jungle on such a pitch black night?"

As they were preparing to leave that afternoon, the leader of the group stood up and issued the command, "Attention to Orders." This military command means that all personnel within earshot of the speaker must stand at attention and listen to the reading of an official order. They were presenting us with another token of their appreciation. It was the award of the "Blue Max." The citation in part reads, "the officers and men of Company E, Long Range Patrol (LRP) Air Mobile (AM), 52nd Infantry Battalion, 1st Cavalry Division to Battery C, 2nd Battalion, 20th Artillery, 1st Cavalry Division for Conspicuous Gallantry in support of long range patrol ground operations against hostile forces in the Republic of Vietnam during the period 1 November 1968 to 31 January 1969."

They had painstakingly hand drawn the award on parchment paper, duplicating as much as possible, the look of an actual certificate that would accompany the presentation of a medal like the Bronze Star or the Air Medal or Distinguished Flying Cross. We solemnly accepted this award on behalf of all of the officers and men of the unit. We all considered it the most meaningful award we had ever received.

The "Blue Max" award certificate

Mac and I continued to fly together on a regular basis and he was certainly with me on many of the missions I will write about from here on but I just can't be certain which ones they were. I think it was in February that he got checked out as an aircraft commander and began flying as a wingman for me and the other section leaders. After I went home at the end of my tour in March, I heard that he was appointed as a section leader and was doing well. I was very proud of my protege. I was assigned to Hunter Army Airfield in Savannah, Georgia as an instructor pilot in the AH-1G Cobra. It was there, toward the end of August, that I learned that Mac had been killed in combat at Quan Loi. I was very saddened at the news and was determined to find out exactly what had happened.

I finally learned that Mac had been asked by the unit commander to take his section up to Song Be and stand-by there as a ready reaction force since there was intell that the NVA was going to attack Quan Loi that night with a large ground force and attempt to overrun the LZ. Mac and his wing man flew to Song Be, as directed, and settled in for the night. About 4 AM they got the call that Quan Loi was, indeed, under heavy ground attack and his section was needed to help repel the enemy forces. Mac launched immediately and flew back to Quan Loi where he and his wingman engaged the enemy and help to break the attack while dodging heavy antiaircraft fire. When they had expended all of their ammo, Mac elected to remain overhead to direct artillery fires on the remaining enemy forces. This choice meant that he and his wingman would not have enough fuel to return to Song Be to rearm and refuel. Initially, the enemy assault had broken through the perimeter and there were bad guys inside the LZ but with Mac's assistance, the assault was crushed and most of the NVA were withdrawing. Since they were nearly out of fuel, Mac and his wingman landed at Quan Loi and parked in their normal revetments. As their rotor blades were coasting to a stop and Mac was still sitting in the aircraft filling out the logbook, one of the remaining NVA soldiers ran up and either fired an RPG, or threw a hand grenade or satchel charge (it remains unclear which) into the cockpit with Mac. He died instantly.

I am still very proud of my protege. I will always miss my friend.

Mac was awarded the Distinguished Flying Cross and The Purple Heart posthumously and a memorial to him can be viewed in the main atrium at the Atlanta Hartsfield-Jackson International Airport in Georgia. While those honors are very nice and fitting, Mac's true legacy is that today, across this land, an untold number of Vietnam veterans were greeted with a "Good morning, Dad!" or "Good morning, Grandpa!" by at least two generations of children who would never have been born had it not been for Mac's skill and courage in intervening in battle on their behalf so many years ago.

CHAPTER 17

The Last of the Hueys

After the move to Quan Loi, our unit had gotten its full compliment of Cobras but we still had a couple of Hueys that they allowed us to keep to augment the Cobras in case, say, a turret blew up or something. It was a nice convenience that we could use to move our personnel around and make required soda and beer runs among other things. I distinctly remember three missions I flew in our last Hueys.

On the first one, I was on a day off since I had flown mortar patrol the night before. It was afternoon and I had already caught up on my sleep when the CO came to me and asked if I would take one of the Hueys and fly down to battalion HQ at Phouc Vinh to pick up some new enlisted men that had been assigned to our battery. I said, "Sure."

I grabbed my crew chief, Russ Warriner, and told him to get the aircraft ready for the flight while I went and rounded up one of the new pilots to be my copilot for the trip. This would be a relaxing cruise at altitude with the doors open and the wind blowing through our hair and no worries over combat. Russ would get a little flight time which would help him get his flight pay for the month and we could just enjoy the scenery during the flight. I let the new pilot do the flying while I just kicked back and relaxed.

The new troops were standing out on the flightline when we arrived at Phouc Vinh and Russ helped them load their duffel bags onto the floor of the cargo area. There were more men than seats, so, some of the newbies had to sit on their bags in the middle of the floor. Soon, we were off the ground and headed back to Quan Loi following Highway 13 northward. It was a beautiful sunny day and we were cruising at 3000 feet where the air was a bit cooler. Quan Loi was just coming into view when we heard what sounded like a sledgehammer being dropped on the floor in the cargo area. I turned around quickly to look at Russ and find out what the noise was, though I had my suspicions. All the new guys were looking at me with big wide bug eyes indicating that they had heard it too and weren't real pleased with it. I locked eyes with Russ and he gave me the universal shoulder shrug that meant he didn't have a clue either. About that time, my copilot told me we had a "Master Caution" light illuminated. I checked the caution panel and saw that one of our fuel boost pumps had failed. This was normally not a big problem and could be remedied by descending to a lower altitude, however, I was beginning to suspect the real cause was that we had just been SHOT!

I told Russ my suspicions and asked him to check with each of the new guys to make sure they were okay. After he had checked them all out and given me a thumbs up, I turned back and looked at the fuel gauge. YUP!! We had lost 200 pounds of fuel in a very short time and I was now convinced it was due to a bullet hole in our underside. CRAP! I took control of the aircraft and headed us directly at the airfield. By estimating the rate of fuel loss I was pretty sure we would have enough to make it home but if the engine did flame out I could still land it on the highway beneath us. I couldn't help but think, "Some freaking day off!" We did manage to land at Quan Loi with about 200 pounds of fuel left in the tanks but it didn't stay there very long. As it poured out onto the ground beneath the aircraft, we were all rapidly climbing out of the aircraft just in case there was a fire. As one of the new guys grabbed his duffel bag and tried to pull it out after him, we heard a loud "RIP". He tugged on it again and it came free, revealing a bullet hole in the floor that had jagged metal edges that had snagged his bag. It turned out that the bullet had not only punched a hole in the fuel tank and taken out the boost pump but had pierced the floor of the cargo compartment and lodged in this guys duffel bag ... that he had been SITTING ON!!

He unpacked his bag out on the flightline, a few meters away from the still dripping Huey, and pulled out a totally spent 12.7mm bullet from an enemy antiaircraft machine gun. We told him to hang onto that bullet since it surely was the one with his name on it. The 12.7's maximum effective range is about 3000 feet above the ground so the gunner was just very lucky to have hit us and we were certainly very lucky that it didn't do more damage. I was going to need another day off.

The next adventure in one of our last Hueys was on an admin type flight up to Song Be. We had a couple of crews temporarily based there to support a large ground operation in the area and I was asked to fly a relief crew and some hot chow up to those guys. It was late afternoon and after we had dropped off the crew members and chow, we repositioned to the "Hot" refueling pad to take on some gas while we waited for the returning crew members to show up. The crew chief that day was someone I was not familiar with but he was doing a very good job. As we landed on the pad, I rolled the throttle down to flight idle, the crew chief jumped out and closed the cargo door over so he could access the fuel port. As he pumped the fuel, I watched the gauge and waved at him once we had the desired amount of fuel loaded.

I was rolling the throttle back up as he climbed back on board and was waiting for him to plug back into the intercom system when, BANG! A shot rang out. I quickly turned around to see what had happened and my eyes met with the crew chief's. He was looking at me with a puzzled look on his face and his eyes were wide with surprise. He was holding his helmet jack in one hand and the intercom cord in the other but the connection had not been made yet and his hands appeared to be frozen in time. He looked from me, slowly down at his right leg and my eyes followed his. That is when I noticed the pool of blood that was slowly growing around his foot. WHAT THE HELL!!

He finally plugged his intercom in and said in a somewhat monotone voice,"I think I've shot myself."

I quickly rolled the throttle all the way off and was scrambling to get out of my seat. My copilot was already out of his and grabbed the first aid kit from the bulkhead. The bullet had gone through the crew chief's calf, without hitting a bone, and buried itself in the floor of the cargo compartment. We managed to get the bleeding stopped, even if we did use most of the bandages in the kit. After all, nobody ever accused us of being medical personnel... other things maybe, but not medical personnel. I got on the radio and called operations and told them what had happened. They said there was a Medevac Huey stationed at Song Be and they would get them to pick up our crew chief and take him to the hospital at Quan Loi. Okay! Now that that problem was taken care of, I had to find out how, exactly, he managed to shoot himself.

He was wearing an army issued .45 caliber pistol in a holster on his right leg and when he climbed back into the aircraft, the handle of the pistol got caught on the metal tube that makes up the front edge of the nylon bench seat. This action must have cocked the hammer all the way back and also depressed the safety that runs along the back of the pistol grip. At this point the weapon was fully cocked and the safety had inadvertently been eliminated. Only a touch of the trigger was necessary now and it was provided by the victim himself. As he reached down to get his intercom cord to plug in, he, somehow, managed to touch the trigger and BANG. The Model 1911 .45 Caliber pistol is considered a very safe weapon because it has several safing mechanisms incorporated into its design but this incident just goes to show that no weapon is totally foolproof.

My final Huey story also has to do with weapons systems that are not foolproof, in a way. We had a crew chief that seemed to have a black cloud over his head at all times. Don't get me wrong, the guy was very conscientious in his duties, kept a well maintained ship and was an all around good trooper but things just sort of happened to him on a regular basis. Sergeant Olney was crewing for me on my last Huey mission. All of the Cobras were already paired up for the day's missions and we had a lone Cobra left and Sergeant Olney's Huey, so, it was decided to make a fire team out of this odd couple. My platoon leader, Frank Thornhill, would be the section leader in the Cobra and I would fly the Huey as his wingman. Lt. Jackson was my copilot and he was in his final stages of training to become an aircraft commander, so, he would be flying in the left seat and doing all the shooting while I monitored his performance.

As it turned out, it was a very busy day and our "Odd Couple" section was launched on a fire mission early in the afternoon. The mission was to head southwest about 20 kilometers to help out some Armored Cav guys in APCs (Armored Personnel Carriers) that had been ambushed by the NVA as they tried to cross a river. When we arrived, there was one APC, on fire, sitting in the middle of the shallow river. The other APCs we arrayed on the western bank of the river, firing their .50 cal machine guns at the enemy positions on the eastern bank. Frank checked in with the ground commander and determined that all the friendly forces were on the west side of the river and we were cleared to fire on any position on the east side.

Frank had elected to attack from the north and break to the right, over the friendly troops. Lt. Jackson positioned us to cover Frank and to be prepared to continue the attack once the ground commander gave us the corrections to Frank's marking pair of rockets. The ground commander called as Frank was pulling out of his dive and said his rounds were right on target and to continue to shoot that area up. I moved the Master Arm switch to "Armed" as Lt. Jackson rolled into his dive and began punching the fire button to launch our rockets. The airspeed increased as did the wind noises outside as we bore in on the enemy's position but NO rockets!! I glanced over and saw Lt. Jackson furiously punching the fire button but to no avail. With the airspeed approaching the redline, Lt. Jackson pulled out of the dive without firing a single rocket. As I looked down and moved the Master Arm switch to the "Safe" position, I expected to hear Sgt Olney's M-60 machine gun firing to cover us during this highly vulnerable phase of flight but heard only one "POP." The enemy decided to take advantage of this apparently "Toothless Tiger" and unloaded on us. After the bullets stopped flying and we had gained some altitude back, I asked, "What the Hell just happened?" Lt. Jackson said that the rockets just wouldn't fire and Sgt Olney said his M-60 malfunctioned. I called Frank and told him of our problems and that it would take a few minutes for us to reset everything. He rogered my call and said to let him know when we were ready.

I turned to Sgt Olney and said, "Check to make sure all the contact arms are in place."

He replied, "Yes, sir!" and promptly climbed out onto the skid and peered over the back of the rocket launcher. The contact arms were electrical contacts that were mounted on metal spring-loaded arms on the rear of each rocket tube. These arms could be pulled back slightly, then rotated 90 degrees out of the way to facilitate the loading of the rockets. As you might imagine, it is critically important that the arms be rotated back into position once the rockets are loaded so that the electrical firing circuit will be completed. Both Lt. Jackson and I had checked these contacts during our preflight inspection earlier that day but it was one of only a few possibilities that could explain our inability to fire the rockets. Sgt Olney climbed back in and said all the contact arms were in place and, so, I mentally eliminated that as a cause. I then pulled the "Rockets" circuit breaker to reset the system and hoped we were back in business.

I then turned my attention to the M-60 malfunction and asked Sgt Olney what he was doing to fix that problem. He replied that he had switched guns and was now ready to go with his other M-60. I told Frank that we had reset everything and were ready to try it again. He replied, "Okay, I'm rolling in again, cover me."

Frank fired about 6 pair of rockets into the enemy position and was pulling out of his dive as Lt. Jackson rolled in and began pushing the fire button again. And again...NOTHING!! As we pulled out of the dive, I heard a single "POP" from Sgt Olney's "other" M-60. The sense of deja vu was overpowering. Again, we took heavy enemy fire during our pull out but were lucky and weren't hit. I figured that the enemy was laughing so hard, that they couldn't shoot straight with all those tears in their eyes.

I gave up on the rocket system but was determined that we would provide some sort of covering fire for our section leader. As I turned to confront Sgt Olney, I remembered that his nickname among the other pilots was "Single Shot ONLY" and now I knew why. Usually, the M-60 machine gun was a very reliable weapon, so, I knew that with both of them having this kind of malfunction, that the common denominator had to be the operator. Without becoming too irate, I asked him what the problem was and if he could come up with something to provide some covering fire. He said that he had an extra barrel for the M-60 and thought that he could get one working by swapping out the barrel. I said, "Okay, get going, he's about to roll in again and I want you to be shooting when he pulls out of his dive."

I called Frank and told him our rocket system was totally inop but that we would try to provide some covering fire when he pulled out of his dive. As he prepared to roll in again, I turned to see how Single Shot was doing. I watched him flick down the lever that would allow the bad barrel to be removed on the M-60. He had the new barrel in his lap as he pulled off the old one and turned to lay it down on the seat behind him. I was astounded as I watched the new barrel slide off his lap, hit the floor with a "Klang" and then bounce out the door. HOLY CRAP!! You have got to be kidding me!! We were now, officially out of operable M-60 machine guns AND spare parts not to mention, rocket systems. We had fired a grand total of TWO bullets at the enemy and I was about to go nuts. I asked Single Shot if he had an M-16 as his personal weapon since all enlisted men were issued one of these rifles. He said, "No but I have a 12 gauge shotgun." While disappointed, I said, "Okay, fine. Get it and shoot towards the enemy location when Captain Thornhill pulls out of his dive. Oh! And try not to hit him."

"Yes, Sir!" He replied.

After informing him of our current situation, Frank said he'd finish firing the last of his rockets in about two more runs and we could head home. He had already called operations and told them they would need to send out another section to "Finish the Job"

As Frank rolled in, we flew above and parallel to him so that Sgt Olney could fire his shotgun to cover him. As Frank began his pull out of the dive, I heard the reassuring "Boom, Boom, Boom" of Sgt Olney's shotgun. But...Wait. Only three shots?? Frank was only half way through his break. I turned to see what was wrong and was greeted with the self congratulatory smiling face of Sgt Olney. I asked him what was wrong and the smile suddenly turned to a frown as he explained, "I only had 3 rounds."

It is a very good thing that I had my seat belt and shoulder harness on because I do believe that if I did not, I would have gone back there and thrown him out. Once I recovered my composure, I pulled out my own .38 cal Smith & Wesson pistol from my survival vest to give to Single Shot as one last ditch form of firepower to try to cover Frank on his last run. As I was struggling to get it free of the holster I saw Lt. Jackson looking at me with wide eyes and a terrified look on his face. Apparently, he thought that I had lost it and was going to shoot Single Shot. I said, "It's not what you think." And he relaxed a little, but not much. I then told Sgt Olney to come get my pistol and fire the six shots in it as Frank pulled out of his next dive. He did as he was told and Frank finished firing his rockets at the same time, and with that, we were heading home. All told, when Single Shot finished firing the six bullets in my .38 pistol, our aircraft had expended a grand total of 12 pieces of ordnance on the bad guys, that is, if you count the M-60 barrel that fell overboard. I'm sure we really impressed them with our overwhelming and deadly firepower. I could just picture them rolling on the ground, holding their sides while laughing hysterically. Oh! Well.

As we flew home, we passed the section of Cobras that had been sent to replace us and Frank briefed them on the radio as they flew by. It was then that Lt. Jackson asked if I would fly for a while so he could have a cigarette "because he really needed one." I said, "Sure," and took the controls.

As he fished out his cigarette pack and lighter, he fumbled the lighter and it fell down into the chin bubble where it would remain until we got on the ground. He just stared at it for a moment and then said, "What else can go wrong today?" He knew that I didn't smoke so he asked Sgt Olney if he had a lighter. Single Shot said, "Yes, Sir, here you go." and handed Lt Jackson his Zippo. I could see the relief spread over the Lieutenant's face as he put a cigarette in his mouth and flicked open the lighter. He spun the wheel once, then again and yet again but no flame was forth coming. He closed the lid, turned the lighter over and pounded it into the palm of his other hand. Once again, he flicked it open and tried to light it again and again. No flame. He just stopped, his head slowly sank forward until his chin was on his chest and I saw his shoulders twitch up and down several times. I think he was crying.

We landed a few minutes later, Lt Jackson retrieved his lighter and lit up, with great relief, as I filled out the log book on my LAST Huey mission.

CHAPTER 18

Settling In

By mid November we were getting used to all the new things in our current situation. The last of the Hueys had been turned in and replaced with new Cobras, the new personnel were quickly learning the ropes and helping out immensely and we were getting used to our new home at Quan Loi. And speaking of new things, I got a message that I was to report to the Commanding Officers tent immediately for a briefing. "A briefing at the CO's tent? What the hell was this about? Did I do something wrong? Was I about to get chewed out for something?"

These and other questions continued to pop into my head as I walked toward his tent. This was definitely out of the ordinary since all our briefings took place in the operations bunker. I was feeling a bit of dread as I knocked on the small wooden square hung just outside the door of his tent, just for that purpose. Major Kleese said, "Come in," but I couldn't discern his mood by the way he said it. As I pulled back the flap of canvas to enter, I noticed several other people were inside. Besides the CO, the executive officer and Ops officer were there and had very serious looks on their faces. Since this seemed to be a somewhat formal occasion, I came to attention and saluted Major Kleese and said, "You wanted to see me, Sir!"

He replied, "Yes Mr. Hartley, perhaps you can explain this to us," while handing me a piece of paper. I thought, "I really am in trouble but I have no clue as to what this is about."

I took the paper from him and began to read. It was a telegram forwarded through the Red Cross saying, "Congratulations on the birth of your son STOP Mother and child doing fine STOP" and was signed by my father-in-law. Stunned, I looked up to see all three faces now had broad grins on them and their hands were outstretched, wanting to shake mine. After a round of congratulations, Major Kleese pointed out that the telegram said the birth was on the 10th of November and it was already the 13th. There's nothing quite like a super fast telegram to announce important news.

The CO said I should get over to the MARS station across the runway to book a call back to the States so I could talk to my wife and get all the details. MARS stands for Military Affiliated Radio Stations and is a network of military and civilian HAM radio operators, operating high frequency radios, allowing military personnel stationed overseas to talk to loved ones back in the States. In order to use the service you had to "Book" the call since there were a lot of troops trying to call home. MARS gave you an appointed time to be back at their station and then they would "try" to place your call.

My call was scheduled at 9 AM on the 14th, so, I was sitting in the radio station at 8:30, just to be sure. The military personnel there briefed me that I should talk for at least 30 seconds and when I was done, I had to say "OVER" very loudly so that all the radio station operators that were listening in, while rebroadcasting our transmission, would then know to flip their switch from "Transmit" to "Receive" so I could hear my wife's reply. They said my wife had also been briefed on this procedure and to remember that there may be as many as 6 operators listening in, so, be careful what you say. Great! Nothing like an intimate call with your wife to start off your day.

Atmospheric conditions were good that day and my call went through on the first try. I asked my wife how she felt, how the baby was doing, if she was still in the hospital or if she'd been released yet and finished with "OVER."

All the appropriate switches were thrown and I could hear her answering my questions and asking some of her own. While I had no problem recognizing her voice, it sounded somewhat strange in that the pitch of it wobbled up and down throughout the call and I assumed mine was doing the same on her side. Anyway, we were on for, perhaps, 5 minutes and it was time to say goodbye. It felt very strange saying, "Goodbye, I love you dear...OVER." And listening to her say the same. While it was very nice to talk to her, it was also a very bizarre experience.

Our new area and living conditions were definitely better than those we left behind at Camp Evans. We now had a mini Post Exchange that had been set up adjacent to our area and we could buy things like books and magazines as well as snacks and even liquor and beer. There were a couple of concessions co-located with it as well. One was a laundry and alteration service, one was a barber shop, and finally, one was a knick-knack shop selling plaques, local collectible items and things like Zippo lighters with your unit crest on it. These shops were all run and staffed by local Vietnamese workers and we were not used to having such close contact with so many locals. At Camp Evans, we only had a few, older local workers inside our perimeter and they were only there to burn the deposits we made in the latrines. They were driven around and supervised while inside the perimeter by U.S. Military personnel. While it was very convenient having these shops nearby, many of us felt somewhat uneasy about having so many of the locals in our area and near our equipment all day long.

Of particular concern was the barber shop. Prior to having this convenience, we had all cut each others hair with a set of clippers while sitting outside our tents. Some of the haircuts didn't come out looking very professional but it wasn't like we were trying to pick up "chicks" or anything.

The disturbing thing about the Vietnamese barbers was that they were all "military aged males," a term used to indicate possible Viet

Cong soldiers. After all, most military aged males were in the South Vietnamese Army or the Viet Cong. Additionally, they all had straight edged razors as part of the tools of their trade. I, and several of the other pilots, refused to get our hair cut at this shop for several months and when we finally did, we told the barbers, "No razors out," and sat in their chairs with our pistols in our hands. I know that most of you are probably thinking that we were very paranoid but let me tell you a story.

Shortly after my son, Rob, had been born and I had made my MARS call, I was sitting out by the flight line with several other pilots one afternoon, waiting for the mission horn to go off. We were just getting some rays and bullshitting about nothing in particular. I turned my head to the right to look at the latest speaker and noticed something quite unusual going on behind him. I saw one of the "barbers" out near the runway strolling around near the control tower. He was about 40 meters away, smoking a cigarette and looking around. I stopped the speaker by putting up my hand and saying, "Look at this." Motioning with my head toward our "barber." We all continued to watch him as he walked up to the base of a radio tower that was next to the control tower and put his back up against one of the legs of the tower. He then started to walk towards our flight line and seemed to be taking very deliberate steps. We all pretended not to notice him as he passed by us. He stopped about halfway up our flight line, adjacent to our operations bunker, pulled out a piece of paper and wrote something down. He then walked toward the barber shop location in a rambling manner. As he passed out of sight, we all looked at each other with our mouths agape.

As if on cue, we all said simultaneously, "Are you shitting me? That son of a bitch just plotted the coordinates of our flight line and ops bunker." We were amazed. The key to our analysis was that while the control tower did not have a light on it at night, the radio tower stood about 50 feet higher than the control tower AND had a very bright red light on top to warn aircraft at the airfield of the obstruction. This made it a very convenient "aiming point" for the enemy to use to fire mortars or rockets at us at night and would help them make adjustments to their shooting so they could hit our aircraft and ops bunker.

We all decided we needed to go tell the ops officer about our observation and get the MPs (Military Police) to come arrest the asshole. After we had detailed our observations, the ops officer told us that we were making mountains out of molehills, not to worry about it and summarily dismissed us. We tried to re-emphasize our point but he would have none of it. As we left operations, we continued to grumble about the ops officer's decision and some, including me, decided to spend the night in the bunker.

I really hate to say, "I TOLD YOU SO!!" but, I told them so. That night, we got hit by, not one, but three mortars from different directions. While we were very lucky that no one was killed and none of our aircraft were seriously damaged, the operations bunker took a direct hit and our fearless ops officer had the CRAP scared out of him. And guess what? The "barber" didn't come to work the next day. Imagine that!

Shortly after that incident, we were informed that the military intelligence folks had gotten word that the NVA was offering a bounty of $10,000 to anyone who killed a Cobra pilot. Makes you all warm and fuzzy inside, doesn't it? Paranoid, Indeed!!

Several weeks after, when all the hub bub had died down, we had another situation that helped to reinforce those good ole paranoid feelings, again.

It started late one afternoon. I was scheduled to fly the first period of mortar patrol that night and because of that, the crew members involved were allowed into the mess tent early to eat dinner before their scheduled takeoff. My copilot and I were nearly done eating when they opened the doors for everybody else in the unit. As the tent began to fill up, I told him to take his time but I was going to go get my gear and I would meet him at the aircraft. I worked my way through the crowded tent and once outside I noticed that the rest of the personnel in the unit were in line waiting to get inside. It wasn't like our mess sergeant had made anything special, just that everyone must have been hungry.

I felt all alone as I made my way across the company area towards our tent, it seemed everyone was at the mess tent and the rest of our area was deserted or at least, I thought so.

As I turned the corner around the operation bunker, I saw a "military age male" Vietnamese, in civilian clothing, standing at the entrance of our bunker. Initially, I thought little of it but then it hit me. Hey! Wait a minute, it's after 6 pm and all civilian contractors were suppose to be off base by 5 pm. At about the same instant that I realized that this wasn't right, the guy standing by the bunker said something to an unseen person inside the bunker. A second "military age male" Vietnamese stuck his head out of the bunker and the two of them looked at me momentarily before they took off running toward the wire and the jungle beyond. I started to run after them but only got a few steps before I realized that I didn't have my pistol with me. It was hanging with the rest of my flight gear by my bunk and I had no idea if the men I was chasing were armed. I decided to go back to the bunker and see what they had been up to.

As I had mentioned, these bunkers were just a long trench about 5 feet wide and covered with half of a culvert pipe with sand bags on top. There was an opening on either end with a set of 5 or 6 steps leading down. As I looked into the entrance where these guys had been, I didn't initially see anything out of the ordinary. I decided to go down the steps to look around inside but I didn't have a flashlight with me so, I waited a moment for my eyes to adapt to the darkness inside. As they did, I noticed a wire running across the second step down. Without entering, I bent down to take a closer look and saw it was a trip wire that ran up either side of the inside face of the beams making up the doorway. As my eyes followed the wire up the beams, they came upon two hand grenades that had been mounted on the inside of the beams. Had I entered and stepped on that step, the grenades would have gone off and I would have had a very bad day. I quickly ran back to the mess tent and told everyone, "Don't go in the bunkers right now, they are all booby trapped."

I quickly explained to Major Kleese and our operations officer. Major Kleese wanted me to show him and our operations officer went to call the Military Police and E.O.D.

I got a flashlight and showed Major Kleese the booby trap I had found. We then went around looking at the entrances to the other bunkers and found they had all been booby trapped! I then explained to the CO that I was due to takeoff on mortar patrol and that I should get going since I was pretty sure we were going to be hit that night. He agreed and said they'd handle it now.

We took off and flew the first 2 hour segment of mortar patrol without incident. But about 9:30, as we rested in our tent between segments, I heard the mortars start their "thump, thump" sounds as rounds were being launched in our direction. We ran to the bunkers to take cover, and I momentarily paused at the entrance thinking about the booby traps. I had been assured by several of the other pilots, that E.O.D. had been through all the bunkers on Quan Loi, while I was flying, and given them the all clear after removing the explosives. Even so, I was a bit reluctant to enter until the mortar rounds started to explode in our area. Talk about motivation!

As we stood around inside the bunker we could hear the other mortar patrol aircraft firing rockets at the mortar position. There must have been more than one mortar because the rounds kept coming in and exploding in our area despite the attack by our Cobra. The mortar patrol ship was now in his second firing run and we could hear his rounds impacting south of the runway. We also heard the "Hot Section" aircraft cranking up to go reinforce him. Once they had taken off, the volume of incoming rounds dropped significantly and soon stopped altogether.

We found that while our aircraft sustained only minor shrapnel damage and no one was injured or killed in the attack, several of the mortar rounds had detonated in the tops of the rubber trees and rained down shrapnel on our tents. They now looked like Swiss cheese and would have to be repaired or replaced before the next rain. Of more concern was that the shrapnel had also torn through our cots and air mattresses making them less than serviceable. We were just happy that we weren't sleeping in them at the time.

CHAPTER 19

The Missions Continue

L ate in November there was a large operation planned for an area about half way between Quan Loi and Song Be that would have several battalions of infantry sweeping through the jungle and small villages to clear out enemy troops that had been operating in the area. The intell guys had been getting a lot of reports from local villagers about NVA soldiers terrorizing them and stealing their rice and livestock.

We would be supporting the troops by escorting the lift ships during the initial insertions and throughout their sweep if they ran into any tough resistance from the NVA. The combat assaults into the various landing zones that morning met no resistance at all from the enemy and we were all glad about that. Once our troops were on the ground and maneuvering through the area, they encountered only light resistance from small groups of NVA soldiers. In fact, the resistance was so light that none of our crews were launched on a fire mission because the infantry was having no problems dealing with the bad guys they came across.

Early that afternoon, my section was tasked to provide cover for a combat assault of a company of ARVN troops that were taking up a position to act as a blocking force while US troops swept another area and funneled any escaping NVA toward the ARVN position and into a "Kill Zone" between the two forces. The ARVN did have their own helicopters and conducted their own combat assaults but today, due to the joint operation between the U.S. and South Vietnamese, the lift ships would be from the First Cavalry and be flown by our crews during the assault.

The landing zone was expected to be "cold" like the others had been throughout the day and the artillery prep was only to be 5 minutes long also indicating that little resistance was expected. My wingman and I located and joined up on the lift ships and escorted them to the LZ. There were ten helicopters assigned to this lift but the size of the landing zone would only accommodate 5 at a time. The flight leader told the other 5 lift ships to hold off to the west and once his group had dropped off their passengers and taken off, the other Hueys could land with their group of ARVN soldiers.

All went according to plan. As the first 5 Hueys landed in the LZ, my wingman and I were about 1000 meters behind them keeping them covered. As we got closer to the LZ, I could see that the landing aircraft had blown down the elephant grass and directly behind the tail rotor of the last aircraft was a stick about 8 feet tall and about 5 inches around that had been hidden by the grass. The stick was black and looked like it could seriously damage the tail rotor, so, I radioed all the lift ships to warn them of its location. The Huey flight leader reiterated my warning and the location of the stick to the other 5 helicopters waiting to land.

By this time, the first group of Hueys had discharged their passengers and taken off allowing the elephant grass to stand back up, obscuring the black stick again. The next flight of 5 were on final approach and we had positioned ourselves behind them to provide cover once again. As the first 4 aircraft passed over the spot of the stick, they blew the elephant grass flat again and it was easy to see it. I could tell that the last of the Hueys was purposely hanging back so that he could see the stick prior to landing. I also noticed that most of the ARVN soldiers already on the ground had positioned themselves near the tree line around the edges of the LZ and were now looking back towards the center of the LZ to watch the landing aircraft. As the last Huey slowly began settling towards the ground while steering clear of the stick, all hell broke loose. Suddenly, there were tracers flying in all directions and people running all over the place. The ARVN soldiers on one side of the LZ seemed to be shooting at their counterparts on the other side and vice versa. All of the Hueys aborted their landings and immediately started climbing out of the area. I could not identify what had caused this sudden fire fight so I held off shooting until I could talk to a commander on the ground to find out where the bad guys were.

The Huey flight leader called the ground commander and asked him what all the shooting was about. The commander replied that the "Stick" was actually a King Cobra snake that was standing up to see what was going on and his troops, who were obviously deathly afraid of snakes, had all tried to shoot it. "Oh! Yeah, by the way, we have some wounded troops down here that need medical evacuation," he said.

I couldn't help but think, "You have got to be shitting me! How could a commander take a total lack of discipline by his troops so lightly?" With allies like this, who needs any enemies? We were lucky none of the aircraft were hit during the melee.

A few days later I was on "Hot" status and we got scrambled for some troops in contact. I pulled in maximum power once we were off the ground so that we could get to the battle site as quickly as possible. After about a 10 minute flight we arrived over the unit that was having the fire fight with the bad guys. As I reduced power to loiter in the area while I figured out who was where and how I was going to set up our attack, something strange happened. As I lowered the collective pitch to reduce power, the nose of the aircraft started an uncommanded turn to the left. This would be a normal reaction to a reduction in power that the pilot would compensate for by adding right pedal to reduce the pitch in the tail rotor. However, I had added right pedal but with no effect. Something was seriously wrong with my flying machine! I pushed the right pedal as far forward as it would go but nothing happened. I then tried moving the pedals back and forth but they were having no effect one way or the other. I found that by pulling power back in, the nose would move to the right and almost resume a normal attitude. All of this took less than a minute to analyze but I now knew that I had a tail rotor failure in a fixed pitch setting and it was not a good thing.

I called my wingman and told him of my predicament and asked him to call operations to launch another section to come help out the troops below us since I was going to have to head back to Quan Loi immediately to deal with this emergency. I then called the ground commander to tell him that we had a malfunction and had to return to base but that another section of Cobras were on the way.

With that out of the way, I pulled in enough power to straighten out the nose and turned toward Quan Loi. The amount of power required to keep the nose straight was producing an airspeed of 150 knots. This was not exactly a normal landing speed for a helicopter, jumbo jet yes, helicopter NO!

I called Quan Loi tower and declared an emergency. They responded that I was cleared to land and that they were rolling the Crash Crew out to standby for us. I could see the runway coming into view up ahead and knew that I had to start slowing down to land. The longer we flew, the more gas we used and that was, thereby, reducing our weight. This was a problem because we wanted the aircraft to weigh as much as possible so that it would require more power to stay in the air and hence, keep our nose straight. The other problem was that as we slowed down and the nose swung left, then the fuselage would roll to the right because of the impact of the airstream on our right side. This was a danger because if we rolled more than 15 degrees, the mast would be bumped by the rotor hub causing the rotor to separate from the aircraft which would then plummet to the ground causing our ultimate demise. That was something I wanted to avoid.

Even if I did manage to get the aircraft slow enough to do a running landing, there was the distinct possibility that when we touched down and I reduced pitch (and power) to put the weight on the skids, the nose would turn left causing us to roll over to the right while going 60 to 70 knots. Once again, something I wanted to avoid.

The U.S. Army flight school at Ft. Rucker Alabama does an excellent job of preparing it's students and graduates to handle emergency situations. They teach students how to safely land a helicopter that has experience a total engine failure by letting them actually DO it. They teach students how to do a running landing in case of a hydraulics failure by letting them actually DO it. But when it comes to tail rotor failures, they tell you how to handle it since it is too dangerous to DO it.

I quickly reviewed in my mind what they TOLD me to do. I lowered the pitch (and hence the power) until the nose had swung left a very uncomfortable amount. I was watching the attitude indicator and stopped my power reduction once my angle of bank got to around 12 to 13 degrees. I was hoping that this power reduction would be enough to get us down to the runway and slowed enough to do the running landing. We were about 3 miles out on final approach and the airspeed was still around 120 knots and we were only descending at 200 to to 300 feet per minute. I was worried that we may not get low or slow enough to accomplish this landing.

Ever so slowly, the airspeed was starting to bleed off. At about 1 mile out, we were now down to about 90 knots but as we slowed, the nose swung further to the left. I continued to watch my roll angle very carefully and kept it between 12 and 13 degrees. We were nearly touching them as we passed over the last of the trees on our approach. I purposely tried to get that low so I would have only about 50 to 60 feet to lose to get to the runway and it might take half or more of the runway to accomplish that.

It was now time to start doing what Ft. Rucker had published in its training manual to resolve this situation. The manual said to slowly start rolling off the throttle and pull up on the collective pitch to replace the lost lift. This seemed counter intuitive but the theory seemed to make sense. The theory said that by rolling off the throttle slowly, you reduced the rpm on both the main rotor AND the tail rotor simultaneously. This reduction in rpm caused the main rotor to loose lift and the tail rotor to loose thrust. The good news was that the loss of lift could be replaced by pulling up on the collective pitch. Okay! It was time to put the theory to the test. We were now at about 3 feet over the runway. As I slowly started to roll the throttle off, the nose swung even further left and I was sure that we would start to go round and round to the left at any second but as I pulled up on the collective pitch to replace the lost lift, the nose slowly came back to the right. I liked that a lot so I tried it again. Once again, this maneuver caused the nose to move even further to the right. As I continued to very delicately manipulate the controls in this manner, I was suddenly distracted by flashing red lights off my left side. I was so busy that I could barely spare the time to glance left to see what this was but I did so anyway. It was the crash crew in their fire truck racing alongside of us so they could be the first ones at the scene of the accident, well, actually the second ones. I and my copilot would be the first ones. While I really appreciated their zeal and enthusiasm, I really didn't need the distraction right now.

We touched down on the heel of our right skid, at about 65 knots, just passed midfield. I was able to keep the aircraft headed straight down the runway by rolling the throttle on or off slightly. I was beginning to wonder if we would stop before running out of runway since we were still sliding along at 50 knots. I slowly lowered the collective pitch to the bottom and we finally began to shudder to a stop amid a huge cloud of dust and smoke. Before I could regain my composure and shut down the engine, both of our canopy doors were yanked open and the firefighters were there ready to cut our seat belts off and drag us from the aircraft. I yelled at them, "Whoa! Whoa! Whoa! Hold everything! We're okay." Another fireman now jumped up on the skid and shoved a fire hose into the cockpit. Thank goodness he didn't start spraying the place down.

Our maintenance folks showed up in a few minutes and were ready to tow the aircraft back to our area just after we climbed out of it on wobbly legs.

The maintenance officer and a technical inspector came to us the next day and apologized to us for getting us into our predicament the day before. Apparently, the aircraft had just gone through some maintenance on the tail rotor and they had missed installing several bolts that resulted in the pitch change mechanism for the tail rotor becoming disconnected. Of course, it didn't happen until I picked the aircraft up to a hover during our scramble on the fire mission. No wonder I have so many gray hairs now.

November 1968 was a very busy month. The enemy had been very active in the III Corps area around Saigon. This was partly the reason our division was moved from up north, near the DMZ, where things were quiet, to its current locations at Quan Loi, Tay Ninh and Phouc Vinh. Intelligence and surveillance showed a very large build up of enemy troops and equipment on the other side of the border in Cambodia. General Westmoreland and the other top brass were concerned that the NVA was gearing up for a major assault on Saigon and feared it would be as devastating as the Tet Offensive was earlier that year. It was thought that, in our area, the enemy would attack around Loc Ninh and plunge southward through the An Loc, Quan Loi area continuing along Highway 13, straight into the heart of the capital only 76 miles away.

During the Tet Offensive in February, the NVA was so sure of their superiority that entire companies of troops were seen marching, IN FORMATION, down Highway 1 on their way to attack the Imperial City of Hue. It was thought that this type of activity may recur if such an attack was attempted on Saigon. It was known that a very effective weapon against troops in the open was the Flechette rocket, more commonly called "Nails" by the aircrews. As a result, our unit was directed to have one Cobra, with a full load of 76 of Nails, on standby, 24 hours a day to respond to such an attack.

One day in late November, my copilot and I were assigned as the crew for the day on the Nail Bird. The problem with being the Nail Bird crew was that you probably weren't going to fly that day unless the "Invasion" happened. Another reason we probably wouldn't fly was that most of our fire missions were close air support where our troops were in close range of the enemy. That proximity precluded the use of Nails since shooting them was like shooting a shotgun and our troops would likely be within the spray pattern on most missions. In fact, we were not permitted to shoot Nails within 1000 meters of friendly forces for safety's sake. So, in effect, being the Nail Bird crew was akin to having the day off.

Anyway, that afternoon, I heard the fire mission horn go off and watched as the hot section crews ran to their aircraft and launched toward the west. As I was settling back into reading my book, the field phone in our tent rang. The field phone was a directly wired link between operations and each of the flight platoons, the CO's tent and maintenance. It was kind of an upgraded version of the cans and a string type phone. I answered it and was told by the operations officer that the Nail Bird was needed and to take off immediately, a general's aircraft had been shot down just north of An Loc.

Oh! Crap! This really was something big. I grabbed my copilot and we scrambled to get off the ground. As we were climbing out of Quan Loi, operations sent us our mission information over the radio. They said, "Head northwest for seven kilometers and contact Saber Six on frequency 34.5, an aircraft has been shot down by heavy weapons."

Saber Six was the commander of the First of the Ninth Cavalry and was in charge of the rescue-recovery mission. As we were coming up on An Loc, I could see a lot of aircraft flying over an area just north of the city along Highway 13. I noticed that two of our Cobras were following a Huey around at about 3000 feet above the ground, so, I called them on our internal frequency to find out what was going on. It was the section that had just taken off a few minutes before me and they said that the Huey they were following was Saber Six and that the bad guys had three .51 cal antiaircraft machine guns triangulated around this section of the highway.

Apparently, the general's aircraft had been flying along the highway below 3000 feet and was shot down as it flew into the trap. They pointed out where the general's aircraft had crashed and that any aircraft going in to assist would come under intense fire by the .51s. The First of the Ninth had several other Hueys in the area that were carrying their "Blues" (infantry guys) whose job it would be to secure the crash site once they were on the ground. Saber Six had several of his Cobras and OH-6 scout aircraft in the area as well. These scout teams were probing around the edges of the conflict area trying to locate the exact positions of .51s without becoming a casualty themselves. The OH-6 "Loaches" were flying at treetop level and very fast in hopes of seeing the gun emplacements and then being out of sight before the enemy gunners could react. If they saw a gun, they would throw out a smoke grenade as they passed and then all the Cobras present could stand off, out of range, and pummel the area until the gun was neutralized.

Another facet of the operation was, of course, the urgency of getting to the downed aircraft as quickly as possible to provide medical assistance to any survivors before they succumbed to their wounds. I'm sure the thinking was to use my Nail Bird to blanket suspected gun areas with the Flechettes in hopes of getting lucky in hitting some of the enemy gunners. The gunners on those weapons had to be exposed to the sky so that they could swivel their guns around as they shot at the aircraft. Even though the Flechette rounds most effective range was 1500 meters, we knew they would still wound and possibly kill at greater ranges but that the density of the coverage would be much less. To make up for the lost density, we would simply fire more rounds at a given target. After all, death by a thousand paper cuts was death, nonetheless.

I positioned my aircraft about 100 meters behind Saber Six so I could better see the areas he was likely to point out as he briefed me on where he wanted me to shoot. I called him on his frequency and told him I was the Nail Bird he had requested and that I was directly behind him. He said,"Glad to have you here. We've got some .51s around the downed aircraft and can't get in to help them, so, I want you to..." Suddenly, his voice was interrupted by the sound heavy weapons fire as bullets flew very close to his aircraft. He continued his transmission but now he was screaming, "we're taking fire! We're taking fire!" His aircraft made a very steep turn to the left and I could now see the stream of tracers passing off his right side. I immediately pointed the nose of my aircraft almost straight down and saw the spot in the trees where they were coming from. I flicked the Master Arm switch from SAFE to ARMED and began firing my Nails at the .51 caliber gun position. I had only fired two pair when the enemy gunner switched to firing at me. Now that I was below 3000 feet and getting lower all the time, I was well within the effective range of the enemy gun. If I pulled out of my dive too early, I would present the enemy gunner with a relatively easy shot at me, so, my plan was to drive right in on him, shooting the whole time and pulling out only at the last possible second so I could scoot away at treetop level until I was clear of the area.

The Flechette rockets we had now had been improved because a florescent red dye powder had been added to the warhead so that when the nails were fired out of the rocket, the pilot would know that the warhead had functioned properly and ejected the 2200 hundred nails contained in it. From the pilot's point of view, this appeared as a puff of red smoke as each rocket reached rocket motor burnout range and the warhead fired, ejecting the nails and powder.

As I now was closing the distance between myself and the gun, I was furiously firing rocket after rocket and the red cloud between me and my target was growing to the point that I could no longer see the trees but only the tracers emerging from the red cloud and zooming past me. I took some comfort in thinking that if I couldn't see the guns location anymore due to the red cloud, then the gunner couldn't see me either. It was now time to stop shooting and pull out of the dive since we were getting pretty close to the ground and the airspeed was pushing past the redline. It worked exactly as I had planned and we continued to fly outbound at treetop level for a couple of miles before climbing back to 3000 feet. We had not been hit but both of us were pretty nervous after the close call.

As we rejoined the group of aircraft over the area, I looked down at the spot that the gun had shot at us from. There was now a red circle surrounding the spot in the trees where the gun was located. Saber Six called me and said, "Nice shooting! I'm going to have one of my little birds (OH-6) go check it out."

He vectored the OH-6 toward the red spot in the jungle. The little bird said he could see the red spot and headed toward it at max speed and treetop level. As he crossed over the spot, we all heard him say, "Whoa! Oh! Man, that's amazing." He pulled the aircraft into a nose high attitude, climbed slightly then spun around to go back the way he had come. As he approached the red spot, he slowed to almost a hover until he was directly over it. He then said, "Well, you eliminated these guys. There are only three bloody blobs down here stuck to that gun. Nice job!"

With one of the legs of the triangle eliminated, it would be possible to approach over this area toward the downed aircraft to complete the rescue and extraction. Even so, Saber Six had me fire the rest of my Nails into the areas suspected of having the other two .51s just to be on the safe side. Since I was now out of ammo, I was released to return to Quan Loi to rearm and refuel.

We learned that they were able to rescue the general and most of the crew of the downed Huey but one crewmember had been killed.

The next day, Saber Six had some of his men deliver the gun that we had shot up and our CO had it put on display outside of our orderly room. The gun actually had some nails imbedded in the barrel, the receiver and the metal legs. The guys who delivered it said they had to pry the bodies off of it because they were, literally, nailed to the gun. Quite gruesome!

The author with the captured .51 cal. Antiaircraft
gun and holding an AK-47

It was now December and the missions continued to come down. The NVA was continuing to press the offensive in our area of operations. Russ Juleen was my wingman and we were launched on a fire mission for a Special Forces camp northeast of Song Be. When we arrived over the camp, we called them to find out their situation and were told that they were getting sporadic mortar fire from a group of trees about 2 kilometers north of their camp. They said that over the last few days the enemy would fire a few rounds into their compound at different intervals during the day and they were tired of it. The Green Beret on the radio said that because of a slight valley between them and the trees, they actually saw the bad guys set up the mortar on the south side of the trees that morning, fire several rounds and then disassemble the weapon and disappear back into the trees. Their camp was just outside the range of the normal "Tube" artillery, so, they had called for support from us.

The treeline in question was a very thick grove of trees about 50 meters long on each side and square in form. This grove was surrounded on all sides by wide open fields of low grass that would allow us to see anyone or anything leaving or entering the trees. In essence, whoever was currently in those trees was now trapped there with no avenue of escape.

Russ and I decided to attack the treeline from the east so that the sun would be behind us allowing better visibility into the trees. Between us, we had 152 rockets with a mix of 10 pound and 17 pound warheads, 3000 rounds of 7.62mm minigun ammunition and 300 rounds of 40mm grenades. Each of the rockets had a bursting radius of between 10 and 15 meters, so, the ordnance we would expend on this grove of trees would be sufficient to kill anything or anyone in there many times over.

We set to our task. We made rocket run after rocket run. With each pass, the trees were showing the damage. Many of them had been blown down while others were stripped of their bark and treetops. Just for good measure, we reset our ROCKETS circuit breakers and made one last run on SALVO and 19 pair. Using this procedure, we were able to fire the last few rockets that had hung up on our first runs. We then proceeded to fire all of our 40mm grenades into the area and half of our minigun ammo as well. We'd save the other half for self protection on our trip home.

We were quite pleased with the devastation we had wreaked on this small grove of trees and we made one last, low pass over it to survey our handiwork. I passed over the western edge of trees and looked down as I started a slight climb. It was then that I saw something absolutely amazing and pretty disheartening at the same time. Two water buffalo were walking very slowly, one could almost say sauntering, out of the treeline and into the open field. The disturbing part was that they were not staggering or all bloody or even distressed in any way. They walked side by side for a few meters, paused and ate some of the grass, then proceeded on their way. When Russ saw them, he began laughing on the radio. He couldn't believe that those animals were not only alive but, apparently unscathed by our "devastating" attack.

The author and a crew chief reloading the
minigun after "devastating" attack

We told the Green Beret that we had shot up the area pretty good but were now out of ammo. He thanked us for our help and released us to go home. I couldn't help but think that they may be taking more mortar fire later that afternoon since we may not have done much except kill trees.

When we got back to Quan Loi, Russ was having a great time telling everyone about how "effective" our overwhelming firepower was against two water buffalo. He couldn't get through telling the story without breaking down into uncontrollable laughter each time he got to the point where the water buffalo walked out of the trees. It was Russ' idea to alter my call sign slightly from Blue Max 68 Oscar 1 to Blue Max 68 OX CART 1!! Whenever he said it, he would burst out into gales of laughter and holding his sides while tears streamed down his cheeks. Very funny. Eventually, the new call sign was shortened to just OX and it became my nickname for around camp as well. What really bothered me about that mission was that while it appeared we had very little effect on our target that day, the converse was always something that we dreaded because we all knew of situations where a single rocket went astray while being fired in close support of our troops and one or more of them was wounded or killed by it. As a result, it was very dangerous to underestimate the lethality of our weapon systems.

I mentioned earlier that we had an officer's club in our area. When we first arrived in Quan Loi, we were told there was an officer's club on the other side of the runway near the east end of the LZ. They said it had been established in the deserted mansion of the Frenchman who owned the local rubber tree plantation. I never got the story as to why he abandoned the building. Perhaps because of the threat from the communists, who weren't too happy with his kind or maybe he just decided he'd made enough money to retire to the French Riviera or some such place. It really didn't matter. The army took it over and turned it into a club.

One night, a bunch of us that weren't flying mortar patrol or on "Hot" status, decided to go over and check out the club. The first problem was getting a vehicle that could get us there. We talked to the

CO and asked to take his Jeep but he said "NO" quite emphatically. We finally talked the supply sergeant into lending us his ¾ ton truck after swearing to him that we were only going to get something to eat.

When we pulled up in front, we were all very impressed with the structure. It was 2 stories, made out of concrete, had very large windows and doors and at least 8 bedrooms upstairs. The dining room was spacious as was the bar area. All together, I would estimate, the place was about 10,000 square feet in total area. While I'm sure it was very spectacular in it's heyday, it was now in desperate need of some basic maintenance.

The meal we had was very uninspiring and we all thought that our mess sergeant did a much better job than this cook. The bar was also a let down since the drinks were expensive and seemed to be watered down. Several of us decided to call it an early night and wound up walking back across the runway to our area. It was during that walk, while we vented over how unhappy we'd been with the club, that we decided we could do a better job.

Site planning and construction began almost immediately. After getting the CO's permission to do it, we selected a spot just across from the operations bunker where it would be centrally located for easy access from each of the flight platoon tents. Since the enlisted men would not be using the "Officers" club, they did not assist us with the construction. So, we had about 30 officers, all pilots, as a work force. Some of them had previous experience in construction and kept the rest of us in line. We begged borrowed and stole some of the major pieces of lumber necessary for the frame but the greatest portion of the wood came from empty rocket boxes (we shot a lot of rockets). When you weren't busy flying a mission you were expected to be helping with construction. Most of us unskilled laborers would just sit around with a hammer pulling apart rocket boxes, salvaging not just the wood but the nails too.

In just a couple of weeks, we were almost done with our project. We had a bar long enough that about ten to twelve people could belly up to it at once. There was a separate room that had several tables in it.

These tables were large enough that 6 to 8 guys could sit around them while playing poker or other card games. The interior walls were covered with plywood that was then scorched with a blow torch to bring out the grain in the wood. The same technique was used on the surface of the bar and then sealed with varnish to produce a very impressive finish.

We supplied the bar by taking up a collection of a few dollars from each guy then going to the Post Exchange Annex, that had just opened on our side of the runway, and buying a bottle of each of the most popular types of booze and several cases of beer. We had calculated that if we charged a mere 25 cents a drink, we would clear a profit of 10 cents per drink. Once we paid all the initial investors back, we could use the profits to get a wider variety of booze and beer and possibly even add some snack food. It was all working very well up to the point that the supply boat didn't make port. It was either blown off course, torpedoed or hijacked. It didn't matter which, all we knew was that we were running out of supplies. At one point, the only booze we could get was some rot gut vodka and they were totally out of mixers. We resorted to borrowing canned grapefruit juice from the mess hall and mixing it with the vodka to produce our version of a Salty Dog. The only problem with it was that the mess hall's grapefruit juice tasted more like battery acid than grapefruits, so, that drink wasn't such a great seller.

This sorry state of affairs lasted only a couple of weeks before our supply lines returned to normal. We were once again able to buy cases of Cokes and other soft drinks as well as a wide variety of booze and beer. The only fly in the ointment was that when you bought a case of soft drinks or beer, you HAD to take a free case of Carling Black Label beer because the ship bringing it over had sprung a leak and the Black Label beer cans were all rusted (the days before aluminum cans) and the beer tasted like crap. The Post Exchange system came up with this method of getting rid of the bad beer because the South Vietnamese government prohibited them from dumping it in the ocean or selling it to its citizens, even at a great savings. So, the answer was to force us to take it and dispose of it however we saw fit. Good Plan!!

Anyway, we were back in business and doing well. The word had spread around Quan Loi of our establishment and, as a result, officers from other units began showing up to patronize our little tavern. I remember one night in particular. When I walked into the club I noticed two new guys at the bar. One was an Army Ranger and the other was a Green Beret. Both were captains and they were having a polite disagreement over which group was the most fearsome fighters. The Ranger said his brethren were much tougher than the Special Forces soldiers and to prove it he told the Green Beret to, "Wait here, I'll be right back." He went outside and was gone for about 10 minutes. All of us were beginning to think he had passed out somewhere when the door opened and he walked back in carrying a snake that he was holding very tightly just behind the head. This disturbed most of the occupants of the club because you could hear chairs scooting back across the floor as the Ranger passed by with this unknown variety of serpent that was about four feet long.

He walked up to the Green Beret and said, "Watch this!" Whereupon he grabbed the body of the snake about 4 inches below his other hand and then proceeded to bite through the neck of the snake. Apparently, the snake did not like this very much and the rest of his body began to flip around like some kind of out of control bullwhip. This action continued for several minutes even after the head and body had been separated by the Ranger's teeth.

The Green Beret observed this demonstration without showing any emotion whatsoever. Once the Ranger had rinsed his mouth out with a beer, the Green Beret said, "Very interesting. But now it's my turn and we'll let these pilots here decide whose demo is more impressive. Okay?" The Ranger agreed to the terms and we agreed to be the judges of this little competition.

The Green Beret got up and went outside. He was gone for only a few minutes and returned with something cupped between his hands. He slowly put it down on the bar and removed one hand while pinning the critter to the bar with the other. We could now see that it was a tree frog. He then asked our bartender for a fresh beer and wanted to know what time it was. I'm sure we all had very quizzical expressions on our faces as the bartender delivered the beer and said, "It's 9:25"

The Green Beret turned to the Ranger and said quite emphatically, "Now YOU watch this!" He now picked up the live frog that was struggling to get away, and shoved the whole thing into his mouth. He kept his lips closed but his jaw in the open position and we could see the frog's legs pushing out his cheeks while attempting to escape. At one point, one of the frog's legs poked out of his mouth and the Green Beret used one finger to gently push it back in. He did not bite the frog but made two attempts at swallowing it before he succeeded. He then used his fresh beer to wash it down.

Whoa! Quite impressive but it was going to be hard to come up with a clear cut winner. We began our deliberations, the Green Beret interrupted us and said, "Not yet, I'm not done."

"Okay, what's next?" we said. We figured he go outside again and get another critter to add to his "Dinner" but he just sat at the bar and told story after story about his exploits.

He finally asked the bartender, "What time is it now?" to which our guy said, "It's 9:55, why?"

The Green Beret said, "That's long enough. Do you have a bucket or something?"

The bartender bent over behind the bar and retrieved a steel pot which he thumped down on the bar, rather unceremoniously. I'm not talking about some sort of cooking utensil, though it was used as that too, but the steel outside shell of an infantry helmet that was suppose to protect our brains from being penetrated by enemy bullets. The steel pot rolled around on its top a bit, then was seized by the Green Beret. He pulled it over in front of his face with one hand while he stuck the fingers of the other down his throat. He retched twice and up came the frog and some beer. The frog blinked a couple of times to clear his eyes then climbed up to the edge of the helmet and launched himself about 6 feet down the bar, paused momentarily then launched himself again, this time landing half way up the wall. From there, he climbed the rest of the way up and disappeared into some crevices that were the result of our fine carpentry. Most of us had our mouths hanging open in disbelief as we looked back at the Green Beret. He then said, "Okay! I'm done."

That remark reminded us that there was still a wager that needed to be resolved. One glance at the Ranger told us that he accepted his defeat. His chin was resting on his chest as his head slowly and almost imperceptibly swung from side to side in the "NO" movement. Who knew that a tree frog could hold his breath for 30 minutes while inside the human stomach? Apparently, the Green Beret knew but it was a moment of enlightenment for the rest of us. We all broke into simultaneous applause and started slapping the Green Beret on the back, while unanimously declaring him the winner. The loser had agreed to by a round of drinks for the bar which set him back about three dollars.

CHAPTER 20

LZ Dot

I was up for mortar patrol once again. I had already flown one segment and was preparing to take off at midnight to relieve the other mortar patrol bird that was currently circling Quan Loi. Since this wasn't a scramble type mission, we were taking our time during the start and run-up to do a complete systems check. As we sat running at flight idle, going through our checklists, I heard the fire mission horn go off.

We watched as the crews for the "Hot" section came running out of their tent. As they arrived at their aircraft, the front seat pilot unhooked the tied down rotor blades and quickly donned his "chicken plate" (armored vest). He then climbed in, put his helmet on and began belting in. The rear seat pilot put on his "chicken plate" and climbed in but didn't start strapping in right away. Instead, he immediately flicked the battery switch on and hit the START trigger, even before he was seated. The anti-collision light and navigation lights dimmed as the aircraft battery labored under the strain of starting the turbine engine. I could hear the low whine of the turbine as it began to accelerate. The lights were slowly returning to full brightness as the engine came to life.

I had decided to maintain my position in the revetment until they were airborne and on their way. I turned my attention to the wingman's aircraft to see how he was doing and noticed that his lights were still dim and seemed to be getting dimmer. I could hear the whine of his engine also, but it was not accelerating as it should. I called operations and told them that Romeo One's wingman was unable to start and they might want to consider launching another section. They replied, "Roger Oscar One, standby."

By this time, Romeo One (Bill McCaslin) had completed starting his aircraft, so, I called him to let him know that his wingman was having problems starting and I had already told operations. He rogered my transmission and called operations to find out what they wanted him to do.

Operations answered his question by calling me and saying, "Oscar One, you go on the fire mission with Romeo One and we will get someone to replace you on mortar patrol."

I rogered operations then called Bill and said, "I'm flying your wing tonight Romeo One, let's go!"

Bill rogered me then called tower for takeoff clearance. As we climbed out of Quan Loi, I assumed my wingman position, slightly behind and off to one side of Bill's aircraft.

Operations sent our mission. We were to fly west for 30 kilometers and contact the ARVN liaison officer, LZ Dot was under heavy ground attack and about to be overrun.

LZ Dot was an ARVN fire support base with 6, or so, howitzers and was base for the 36th ARVN Rangers. The base occupied the top of a knoll that gave a commanding view of the countryside around it. The barbed wire perimeter fence enclosed an area about 70 meters in diameter. The howitzer guns were arrayed around this circle like spokes of a wagon wheel with each pointing outward in defense of the LZ. Bulldozers had scraped away every bit of vegetation inside the barbed wire and an additional 50 meters outside the wire to produce a no mans land that would reveal anyone attempting an attack. In the center was a complex of subterranean bunkers that made up the Tactical Operations

Center (TOC), troop quarters and an ammunition storage facility. The liaison officer that we were to contact was a U.S. Army officer (usually a Major) that was to coordinate with and advise the ARVN on integrated operations with U.S. Forces. The total number of friendly forces located at LZ Dot would have been around 200 people.

As we cleared the trees on our climb out, we could immediately see LZ Dot. It, and the entire area around it, was illuminated by artillery flares. We had been told by ops that the supporting artillery was coming out of fire bases south of LZ Dot, so, Bill had elected to fly by Dot on the north side so we could look down on it to evaluate the situation while simultaneously staying clear of the inbound artillery rounds. The artillery flares were igniting at about 4000 feet above the ground while we were flying at about 3000 feet. The flares would slowly descend on their parachutes and eventually burn out at about 1000 feet over the LZ. At any given moment there would be between 10 and 15 flares illuminating the fire base and they allowed us to see all of what was going on as we flew past on the north side.

The entire LZ was swarming with people and looked like a fire ant nest that had just been stomped on. I was pretty sure they weren't friendly forces since they were shooting into the bunker complex and streams of tracers were coming out of the complex at them. I saw one person shoot an RPG into the bunker, so, I knew he was a bad guy.

I listened as Bill called our point of contact on the ground. When the liaison officer keyed his mike to respond to Bill, the radio came alive with the sound of the major screaming over the noise of very close machine gun fire and explosions going off in the background. He was saying, "We are being overrun. Everybody outside are bad guys and they are trying to get in here. All the friendlies are...LOOK OUT!, LOOK OUT!..POW!, POW!, POW!....BOOM!! Sorry, some asshole just tried to throw a satchel charge in here, I shot him. Please, Max, just shoot anybody outside, and HURRY!"

We had seen the explosion of the satchel charge next to the central bunker and knew that was where the major was located. We would later refer to him as John Wayne when retelling the story.

Even though we were all very hyped up now, Bill replied very calmly, saying, "I'm rolling in with a marking pair, adjust my wingman."

John Wayne replied, "Roger, HURRY!!" as the battle noise continued in the background.

Bill called me and said, "I'm rolling in from west to east with a left break to the north. Cover me."

I rogered him and watched as he made a left turn back towards the LZ and lowered his nose into a dive pointed at the open area just next to the bunkers. I had positioned myself to be able to roll into a dive as soon as Bill began to pull out of his dive so I could cover him and await John Wayne's adjustment. Bill fired a single pair of rockets, which landed exactly where I would have aimed, and began a gradual pull out of his dive.

Suddenly, from all around the LZ, streams of tracers from seven 12.7mm (.51 caliber) antiaircraft machine guns converged on Bill's aircraft. His aircraft lights went out immediately but I could still make out the shadow of his helicopter at the very focal point of the streams of tracers. I was sure he was being hit many times.

I quickly reached over and turned out all of my aircraft lights then picked out the closest .51 cal. Gun. The one I selected was on the north end of the LZ firing south at Bill. I rolled in on him and began shooting in an attempt to protect Romeo One. My rockets began to explode right where I saw his muzzle flashes but he continued to fire. As I was firing my third pair, I saw that his stream of tracers were starting to move. He never stopped shooting as he swung his gun around towards me. The arc of his tracers carved a curve in the sky as they swung around and then settled on me as their new target. Though I was concentrating on him, I could see out of the corner of my eye that the other 6 guns were now swinging the arc of their tracers around to engage me and soon I would be in the same predicament as Romeo One. Even though I had turned out my lights, they could still see my position by watching my rockets red glare as I fired. I was sure they would still be able to see me if I stopped firing because of all the light from the artillery flares. I decided that the best defense was a good offense, so, I continued my dive determined to eliminate the gun position in front of me. The best plan was to drive right in on him, shooting all the way, then break to the left at treetop level, heading north, away from the LZ and all the guns and light.

The tracers from the other 6 guns were distracting because they were coming from our right and crossing in front, above and below us. I tried to ignore them and concentrate on the gun directly in front of me. I found it interesting how the tracers from his gun seemed to initially "float" up at us but as they got about half way up they suddenly seemed to accelerate till they zoomed by our canopy. Each of the tracers from his gun initially looked like it was going to hit you right between the eyes but at the last moment it would veer away to the left or right. This concerned me because it meant he had us bracketed and there were four other regular bullets, that we couldn't see, between each tracer and that his cone of dispersion would get smaller as we got closer. I had no choice but to press the attack. If I pulled out now, I would present him with a broadside and a much larger target to hit. Quite simply, it came down to him or us.

I kept yelling at myself in my head, "Don't get target fixation!... Don't get target fixation!..." After all, I didn't want to take out this gun emplacement by driving a Cobra into it.

I had now fired about 14 or 15 pair of rockets at this guy and we were getting pretty low, so, I decided, "One more pair and we're out of here."

I fired the last pair of rockets, began a left hand bank and pulled the nose up out of the dive. I watched the rockets go directly into the spot where his muzzle flashes were coming from. We were only about 50 meters from him when the rockets went off and almost instantaneously there was a huge secondary explosion that momentarily blinded us. As the initial "Flash bulb" light faded, we saw a fireball where the gun had been and the sky around us was filled with tracers tumbling end over end like some sort of Fourth of July celebration. We got him!!

All we had to do now was stay over the trees as we headed north, away from the LZ, and into the darkness until we were far enough away to climb back to altitude.

Since I had banked about 90 degrees to the left, I looked out the left side of the canopy to see how high we were from the treetops. Here's where things get really screwy. As I am looking "down" out the left side of the canopy, I see spent parachute flares drifting "up" at me from where the jungle and trees should be. I quickly looked out the right side of my canopy and saw treetops racing by.

WHAT?!?! That makes NO sense!! I know I must roll the aircraft level before we run into the trees but the TREES aren't where they're suppose to be. We must have been tossed around by the secondary explosion. I know that I am experiencing a phenomena known as spatial disorientation and I have very little time to sort it out.

The logic of the visual presentation says I should roll the aircraft to the left another 90 degrees but my body is screaming at me not to do that because it "feels" like I'll be rolling the aircraft upside down and crash, inverted, into the trees. Unless you have been in a similar situation, I can not convey to you how powerful the feeling is, despite the visual cues and what logic is telling you.

I knew I was in trouble but I also knew there was a way out. I immediately looked at the instrument panel and found the attitude indicator. We had been trained in flight school to depend on our instruments, so, I concentrated on what it was telling me now. The instrument was telling me I was in a 90 degree RIGHT bank even though I "KNOW" I banked LEFT when I pulled out of the dive. The instrument was calmly telling me to roll the aircraft to the left to fly straight and level and RIGHTSIDE UP!

I did as I was told and started rolling the aircraft to the left. I was sure we would impact the ground any second but suddenly, as the indicator approached the 45 degree mark, my internal gyros all reset themselves, the world resumed its normal position in the universe and we were again flying right side up. HALLELUIAH!!

It was now time to figure out where we were and where we were going. We were only about 30 feet over the ground, going full speed at 190 knots, and flying directly into the MIDDLE of the LZ. I guess you could say we got turned around.

My primary concern at this point, though certainly not my only one, was the spent parachute flares that were drifting down all over the place. The canopy of each of these parachutes was at least 10 feet in diameter and if I hit one, it would get wrapped up in the main rotor or tail rotor and we would certainly crash right in the middle of this hostile territory. Even if either or both of us survived the crash, I was pretty sure our welcoming committee would dispatch us in short order. As I bobbed and weaved, banked left and right to get around the suspended parachute hazards, I couldn't help but think that it looked like I was trying to swim through a sea of suspended jellyfish, while trying to avoid being "stung".

While I was going through my radical maneuvers, I heard a noise that was vaguely familiar but it seemed far away. A momentary respite in dodging the flares allowed me a split second to realize that the noise was coming from our minigun, which was blazing away at 4000 rounds a minute. My copilot was using the minigun like some people use their garden hose to water flowers. He was walking the steady stream of tracers from left to right, and back again, in front of the aircraft like someone sweeping a sidewalk with a broom as they walked along. I took a momentary glance out in front of the aircraft and that picture remains burned into my memory. I saw a lot of bad guys, all firing their AK-47s at us while the minigun tracers swept them away like the aforementioned broom. They were falling like pins in a bowling alley.

Also included in my picture was a huge amount of 12.7mm tracer rounds crisscrossing right in front of us as we passed the bunkers in the middle of the LZ. Apparently, the operators of the other 6 antiaircraft guns were pretty pissed off at what we had done to their buddies and since they could easily see us, now that we were illuminated by the flares, they wanted to exact retribution.

It took what seemed to be an eternity to cross the rest of the LZ. I was concentrating on getting to the darkness that I could see on the south side. I continued to dodge the parachutes while keeping my speed as high as possible since I knew I would need it when, and if, we cleared the LZ.

Finally, the barbed wire perimeter fence flashed by under us, another 50 meters and we were over the trees and disappearing into the darkness. The tracer fire that had been following us was quickly dissipating, so, I pulled in maximum power and did a cyclic climb, which entails pulling back on the stick to trade airspeed for altitude thereby "zooming" upward to get back to safety. The climb to 3000 feet took about 20 seconds and brought our airspeed back to about 60 knots.

Later, as I objectively looked back on the entire attack sequence, I'm sure the whole thing, from when I rolled into my dive until I was back at 3000 feet on the south side of the LZ, was not more than 90 seconds in total duration, if that long.

As we leveled off, I immediately started looking for Romeo One. I was actually looking for the flaming wreckage of Romeo One's aircraft since I was sure he had been shot down. I asked my copilot if he saw anything that might be Romeo One and he replied in a rather grim tone, "I don't think he made it."

I decided to call him on the radio to see if there was any response. "Romeo One, this is Oscar One, what's your position?" No response. "Romeo One, this is Oscar One, what's your position?"

"Well, hello there Oscar One! Glad to hear from you, we didn't think you'd make it through all those bullets down there," Bill said.

"Well, we thought the same thing about you! Where are you?" I asked.

"We're on the south side of the LZ at 3000 feet. Where are you?" He asked.

CRAP!! That's where we were. "QUICK, TURN ON YOUR LIGHTS!!" I demanded.

As I flipped on my lights, Bill did the same and I saw his aircraft fill my windshield as he streaked by from left to right only about 30 feet in front of us. We were so close that neither of us had time to react and I wound up flying through his rotor wash which felt like hitting a huge pothole.

"HOLY CRAP!! That was close!!" I transmitted.

"Let's not do that again!!" Bill answered.

As my heart rate slowly dropped back down below 200 beats per minute, I joined back up on Bill's wing and said, "Where do you want to shoot next?"

He said, " Let's put some around the TOC to help those guys out then we'll fire up those holes in the wire. I guess I'd better call ops for another section, we'll be expended soon and this looks like it might take awhile. Oh! And let's climb up to 4000 feet to stay away from those twelve point sevens."

"Good idea!!" I confirmed.

We rolled in from 4000 feet and pulled out of our dives by 3000 feet to stay out of the 12.7mm guns effective range while firing a bunch of rockets all around the TOC. The place was still swarming with bad guys but after a few runs, there weren't as many that were moving. The 12.7mm guns were still firing at us on each pass but they weren't nearly as close as they had been previously.

Bill decided that we would use the rest of our rockets on a breach in the wire on the east side of the LZ. The bad guys had blown or torn a hole in the wire there and were streaming into the LZ at that point. The hole formed a bottleneck that forced them together as they ran through it. We were in the process of firing the last of our rockets into that hole to stem the flow of bad guys when we heard a strange voice on the radio that took both of us by surprise. It was kind of like when you're all alone, working intently on a project, then someone, you didn't know was there, leans over your shoulder and says, "What cha doing?" And scares the crap out of you!

The voice simply said, "Can we play, too?"

Bill called the disembodied voice back and said, "This is Blue Max 69 Romeo One...who's that??"

The voice replied, "This is Spooky 15, we saw you guys shooting up the place and wondered if we could help you out?"

"Spooky" was the call sign for a rather elite U.S. Air Force unit. The unit flew old WWII, C-47 cargo planes. These were similar to the old DC-3, two engine, tail dragging passenger airplanes from the 1930s. They had been significantly modified and now had three 7.62mm miniguns mounted on their left side. They would carry as much as 24,000 rounds of ammunition for these guns which were exactly like the one we had in our turret but had been modified to fire at 6,000 rounds per minute instead of our paltry 4,000 rounds per minute. The pilot could fire one gun at a time or all three simultaneously, thereby raining down 18,000 rounds per minute on the enemy. It was a very fearsome weapons system.

When the unit initially started operations, the enemy had thought it was some sort of dragon in the sky that was attacking them and this was seized upon by the U.S. Air Force, who then nicknamed the aircraft "Puff the Magic Dragon" from the then very popular song by Peter, Paul and Mary.

Bill called "Spooky" back and said it was okay with us but he needed to check with our contact on the ground. Bill then called "John Wayne" and told him that we were just about out of ammo but that "Spooky" was on station and another Blue Max section was on its way.

We were glad to know that "John Wayne" was still alive when he responded, "Yeah! Tell him to shoot up the whole damned place, all the friendlies are still in the bunkers."

Bill passed the info along and we watched as the AC-47 gunship rolled into a gentile 30 degree left bank, pointing his wingtip at the perimeter of the LZ. Three streams of tracers began spewing from the aircraft and were pouring into the area between the wire and the jungle, ricocheting in all directions. My copilot made the observation that, "It looks like a cow pissing on a flat rock." Which, indeed, it did!

As we were watching the show, the other Blue Max section arrived on station. Bill briefed the section leader on what was going on and warned him of all the 12.7mm guns surrounding the LZ. Once the new section leader checked in with "John Wayne" we were released to return to Quan Loi.

As we were on final approach, we saw another section taking off and listened in as their mission was issued by operations. They were told to head west to LZ Dot. This was turning out to be a major operation.

Once we had rearmed and refueled, I was told I would resume my rotation on mortar patrol as the rest of the unit was flying mission after mission out to LZ Dot. As I circled Quan Loi at 2 AM, I could see the parachute flares and an occasional explosion out at LZ Dot. I was somewhat jealous of the sections that were out there shooting up the enemy but the jealousy quickly faded as I thought about my duel with the antiaircraft gun a few hours earlier.

I was shaken awake at about 10 AM by the operations officer who wanted to know if I'd gotten enough rest because they needed another section out at LZ Dot and all the other pilots had been flying all night in support of Dot and had just gotten to bed a little while ago. I said, "Let me check on my other guys and I'll let you know."

I felt terrible waking up the others but they all elected to go on the mission. Apparently, the attack on Dot had been repelled, friendly troops had been inserted into the LZ that morning and were now tracking down the retreating elements of the attacking forces. The NVA would occasionally set up an ambush for our guys that were tracking them and the resulting fire fight was what we had been called in to assist on.

As we circled just to the northeast of the LZ trying to discern friendly from enemy troops, I kept glancing at the LZ where there was a lot of activity going on. The ground within the wire was littered with bodies, from the night before, that were now being picked up and stacked in one area. There were many more bodies still draped in the wire and a large pile of them clogged the area of the bottleneck where the perimeter was breached on the east side during the attack. While talking to the ground commander of the unit tracking down the fleeing NVA, he told us that, so far, the friendly forces had found nearly 300 dead NVA soldiers and there were numerous blood trails where the wounded and dying had been dragged away.

We fired for the ground commander, helping him break through the ambush, then his troops resumed chasing the enemy and we were released to go back to Quan Loi. On the flight back, I thought over the attack on LZ Dot and almost, I repeat, ALMOST, felt sorry for the NVA soldiers. I certainly wouldn't have wanted to be in their shoes, er, Ho Chi Minh sandals.

I didn't know it but, evidently, Bill McCaslin thought I did an exceptional job at LZ Dot, because he recommended me for the Silver Star Medal for my actions that night. Division headquarters liked to reserve the Silver Star Medal for ground actions, so, they awarded me the Distinguished Flying Cross instead. I was perfectly fine with the change because it honored my flying skills and of course was created by Congress to honor Charles Lindbergh's transatlantic flight in 1927. Other recipients include Chuck Yeager, Curtis LeMay, Francis Gary Powers, Jimmie Doolittle as well as most of the astronauts who walked on the moon. I was very honored to be included in that select club.

The author with his newly awarded Distinguished Flying Cross

CHAPTER 21

Mortar Patrol Dominates

I t seemed that during the last half of November and all of December and January, mortar patrol and night missions dominated most of the action we were involved in. That is not to say we didn't have many day missions. We certainly did, but they were mostly small skirmishes and sniper fire incidents. No big operations where hundreds of troops were involved. Maybe I just remember more of the night missions because so many of them were very intense and out of the ordinary. The first one started out like most mortar patrol missions. Boring! I had flown the first period from 6 pm to 8 pm and was on my second period from 10 pm to midnight.

As I watched my replacement crank up at about 11:50 pm, I saw the classic flash from a recoil-less rifle being fired from their favorite spot. The round went streaking down the runway and into the refueling point where it exploded and set the fuel bladders ablaze. I quickly rolled in on the recoil-less rifle site and fired about 6 pair of rockets into it. As I was pulling out of my dive I started seeing flashes from around the outskirts of the LZ. There were at least 3 mortars firing simultaneously and their rounds were now exploding all over the LZ. I picked out one of the mortars and began firing on him but the other ones continued to pump round after round into Quan Loi.

It was then, right about midnight, that the ground assault began. Tracers were now flying out from the defenders of the LZ but many more were flying into it from the attacking enemy forces. I continued to shoot at the mortar tube positions while ricocheting tracers from both sides tumbled through the air around me.

I was joined by the other mortar patrol aircraft that managed to get airborne despite all the incoming rounds and we continued to shoot at any mortars we saw as well as the attacking enemy infantry.

Once we had suppressed most of the mortar fire, the "Hot Section" got off the ground and joined us in the fight. I was just about out of ammo and was pretty low on fuel since I'd been airborne for over two hours and fifteen minutes. The ground assault was still raging and the fuel point was still on fire, so, I called operations to ask what they wanted me to do.

After a long pause, operations called back and said it was too dangerous to land, so, I should go to Song Be and refuel and rearm there and come back as soon as possible. I rogered their transmission and asked them to call Song Be and have them turn on some lights since Song Be was normally blacked out at night for security purposes. Ops assured me they would and I headed toward Song Be as I started getting an intermittent MASTER CAUTION light and 10% LOW FUEL warning light. This warning meant that I had only about 20 minutes of fuel left before the engine would flame out and it was at least a 10 to 15 minute flight to Song Be. The other thing that was a major concern was that there was a 3000 foot mountain at Song Be that I would have to avoid running into in the dark.

Another factor that I had to account for during the flight was that due to the design of the Cobra, I had to slow down every few minutes and point the nose of the aircraft up toward the sky to balance the remaining fuel load. Because of its narrow design, and since it normally flew nose down, the fuel in the aft tank would flow forward to the front tank and uncover the aft fuel boost pump. If I allowed that to happen, the aft boost pump would suck air and the engine would flame out even though I still had fuel indicated on the gauge. So, we flew along, porpoising through the sky while looking for any lights on the ground that might indicate we had arrived at Song Be. Nothing!

We called Song Be operations over and over but got no response. We were out of radio range of our operations at Quan Loi, so, there was no use in calling them to help. The fuel gauge was now indicating less than 100 pounds or about 8 minutes of fuel left and that was only IF the gauge was correct. We still couldn't see anything.

I decided we needed to take our chances with the enemy, so, I slowed down to about 40 knots, turned on our landing light and slowly started to descend, hoping that I would see the mountain before we ran into it. I dropped down low until we were just over the trees and began looking for any clear area we could land in. A field, a road, a river bed, anything. All we saw with our landing light was jungle and treetops. If we could find a place to land, I figured we could hide out in the jungle until morning when someone would certainly come looking for us. I was half expecting to start getting shot at by any bad guys in the area since we were such an easy target but, luckily, that didn't happen.

We were at 5 minutes remaining on fuel when we saw the road. We started following it to see if we could find a spot wide enough to land on without hitting the trees on either side. Surprisingly, the trees on both sides of the road were gone as the road now crossed a large open field. As I began to slow down and prepare to land, I recognized the "field". It was the cleared area around the airstrip at Song Be and I knew if we continued another 50 meters we would come across the aircraft revetments and the refueling point. Sure enough, there they were! I hovered into the refueling point and set down. I looked down at the fuel gauge and it was showing we had 20 pounds of fuel left. I told my copilot to go wake up the personnel that ran the pumps so we could get refueled and as he climbed out of the front seat, the engine quit. That was a little too close for comfort.

It took about a half an hour to get refueled and rearmed and we were on our way back to Quan Loi. I told the personnel at Song Be to turn on some lights and keep the pumps going because I was sure they were going to get additional business during the night.

As we were taking off, I saw the landing lights of three aircraft approaching from the southwest. I called on our VHF air to air frequency and it was, indeed, our other aircraft arriving to rearm and refuel. They informed me that the battle was still going on and that ops wanted me back ASAP. They said that the refueling point at Quan Loi had been hit very hard and it was estimated that it wouldn't be back in service for a few days at best. When I arrived back at Quan Loi, the battle had waned significantly and I was asked to fire on one group of bad guys that just wouldn't quit. They finally retreated after I dumped a half a load of rockets on their position. Operations told me to come in and land because they wanted me to save as much fuel as possible since our fuel point was out of action. It was kind of a pain for the next couple of days since we had to go to Song Be to refuel after every mission but they soon had our system up and pumping again.

It was around this same time that all of our pilots were called to a meeting at the mess tent for a very important briefing. It was being conducted by our operations officer and our maintenance officer and they seemed to be in a very serious mood as we filed in. The operations officer started by telling us of a situation that had happened to our sister battery at Phouc Vinh. He explained that a section of Cobras from that battery had been scrambled to shoot for an LZ that was under attack two nights ago. The attack was much like the one that had occurred at LZ Dot, in that the enemy had breached the perimeter and was running around inside the wire. The lead Cobra had told the ground commander that he was rolling in with a marking pair of rockets and to adjust his wingman.

What the lead Cobra pilot did not know was that the aft lug on the bomb rack that held one of the rocket pods had broken, allowing the rocket pod to pivot on the front lug to the point that it was now pointing up through the rotor blades. When the pilot fired his marking pair of rockets, the rocket from the broken pod went up through the rotor, hitting one blade and cutting about 3 feet off of the tip. This resulted in such a severe aircraft vibration that the crew nearly lost control. They reported that everything was just a blur. They couldn't make out the instrument panel and that the only thing that helped them stay oriented was the artillery parachute flares drifting down over the LZ. (Imagine that!!) The pilot somehow managed to land on the LZ that was in the process of being overrun and he and his copilot somehow evaded the enemy troops and got into one of the bunkers to take cover. The attack was repelled and the crew and aircraft were recovered the next day.

At this point the maintenance officer took over and explained that the failure occurred because the armorers were using the bomb shackle lugs to adjust the elevation on the pods and had unscrewed the aft lug until there was only one thread holding it in place. As the pilot maneuvered the aircraft on the way to the LZ, a simple turn could have produced enough "G" loading to rip the shackle from the pod causing the problem. Our maintenance officer explained that they were going through all of our aircraft, inspecting and making sure we didn't have any "unscrewed" lugs on our aircraft but that we should keep and eye out for this in the future. Future, my ass. When we left the meeting, every one of us headed straight to the flight line to check the aircraft we were currently assigned to fly. Through our own research we found that there were two different lugs that could be used. One had 15 threads and the other had 19 threads. We knew that at least 8 threads had to be engaged to adequately support the pod, so, we knew we didn't want to see more than 7 exposed threads on a shackle during our preflight inspections. After all, we had enough things to worry about on a mission without being concerned about dangling pods.

One night, I was section leader of the "Hot Section" and was just chilling out when the fire mission horn went off. We ran to the aircraft, got cranked and I started to back out of the revetment as operations was calling us with our mission. My copilot replied, "Send it."

Ops answered with, "Our mortar patrol bird is taking heavy antiaircraft fire over An Loc. Go help him."

As I was taking off, the mortar patrol bird was calling saying he was still under fire from a 12.7mm antiaircraft gun on the southeast side of the town. As I cleared the trees, I armed the weapons system and started searching the sky for the mortar patrol bird. I spotted him almost immediately. He was hard to miss as he pulled out of a dive and tracers from the antiaircraft gun streamed up at him. He was instantly on the radio yelling, "Taking Fire!! Taking Fire!!" Since mortar patrol was always flown as a single aircraft mission, he had no wingman to cover him during his pullout.

The location of the gun shooting at him was about 7 kilometers from me and I knew that the max range of the 2.75 inch folding fin aerial rocket was 9 kilometers under ideal conditions. Nevertheless, I decided to take a shot at the gun since they were currently firing at my compatriots and the sound of my exploding rounds might distract them enough to save my friends. I knew I had to be very careful since the guns location was only about two hundred meters outside of the civilian populated town of An Loc.

I was currently in the "Go Fast" mode with my nose down and maximum power pulled in and the rocket pods pointed at the ground a few meters in front of us. Now I transitioned to a max climb mode by pulling the nose up until it was pointed about 30 degrees above the horizon and I maintained max power. The 2.75 inch rockets flight is very dependent on the relative wind as it impacts the front of the rocket pod. Normally, we wanted the relative wind to be directly impacting the front of the pods since this would make the rockets fly straight. But now, since I wanted maximum range, I wanted the relative wind to be coming down in front of the pods so the rockets would turn upward when fired. As I climbed out with a nose high attitude and max power, it felt like we were in an elevator going straight up. This produced the perfect angle of attack for max range on the rockets and I fired 4 pair in rapid succession.

The rockets did exactly what I expected. As they cleared the end of the rotor blades, they immediately turned upward as if heading to the moon. I watched as they climbed very steeply until the rocket motors burned out at about 1000 meters after launch. The rockets then entered a parabolic ballistic arc that would, hopefully, bring them back to earth near the target some 7000 meters away. It seemed to take a very long time for them to get there but suddenly 8 rockets started to explode all over the spot that the gun had been firing from. As the fourth rocket detonated we saw a large secondary explosion where the gun had been. I'm not sure if we hit the gun or, perhaps, the mortar that the gun was protecting but we hit something that exploded in a large fireball. We joined up on the mortar patrol bird and surveyed the area where the gun had been. There were a few small fires burning, so, we decided to shoot up the area to make sure they weren't going to try anything else that night.

The mortar patrol crew said they saw me shooting at something as I took off but were totally surprised as my rounds started to impact at the gun site because I was such a long distance away. I have to say, I even impressed myself with that shot and still consider it one of my best, even if there was a significant amount of luck involved.

The next time I came up in the rotation for mortar patrol, I went out to the flight line to do a preflight inspection of my assigned aircraft at about 4:30 in the afternoon. I was due to take off on the first period at 6 pm and I needed to look the aircraft over and do a run up to test all the systems out. During the preflight inspection, I climbed around the aircraft, checking fluid levels, checking for leaks and any damage that may have happened on its last flight. After checking the engine and transmission compartments on the left side, I climbed up on the left wing to inspect the rotor. As I looked over the top of the rotor blades for any damage, my head was about 11 to 12 feet above ground level as I stood atop the wing. From this vantage point, I had a good view of our entire flightline and the runway. I had only begun to look over the rotor blades when, suddenly, WHAM! I heard an explosion behind me from the direction of the control tower. I turned quickly to see what it was and saw a second explosion, WHAM!, about the size of a hand grenade, go off between the runway and the first of our revetments. I also noticed that the smoke from the first explosion was on the opposite side of the first revetment. I knew immediately that we were under attack by a 60mm mortar. I was in the fifth revetment down the line and now saw a third round hit next to the third revetment.

The Blue Max flightline at Quan Loi
The author hovering out of revetment

Crap! They had our revetments bracketed and were walking the rounds down the line towards me! The rounds were landing every 2 to 3 seconds and would be impacting in my area very shortly. No time to climb down from the wing! I jumped toward the wall of the revetment, landed badly, wrenching my back, and rolled up against the wall. Here, at least, I was partly protected. If I tried to run, I might not make it very far and I wasn't too sure my back would cooperate. WHAM! The next round hit even closer. I was very concerned that one of these rounds would land in the little box at the end of every revetment wall that contained fifty to sixty of our rockets for rearming our aircraft. WHAM! That one sounded like it had hit the revetment next to mine. I was next. I could hear the fire mission horn blaring in the background but I knew no pilot in his right mind would be running out here right now. WHAM! This one hit just on the other side of the wall on the end near the runway. I felt its concussion and had dirt rain down on me. The next one would be IN my revetment! I tried to think small. I cuddled up to the wall as closely as I could and I waited. And waited. And waited.

Unbelievably, they had stopped firing. I lay there for several more minutes because I was sure they would resume where they left off but that didn't happen. Eventually, I heard voices of people coming my way and struggled to my feet, holding my back. It was the "Hot Section" crews scrambling to take off and go shoot at the mortar. When they saw me they became very concerned that I had been hit because I was shuffling along holding my back. I said, "No. I did this to myself jumping down off an aircraft, so, don't let me slow you down. Go shoot those assholes!" I told them that the first four aircraft down the line might have some damage from the rounds but the rest were okay since the rounds never got that far. They said that their aircraft were in the unscathed group and they quickly mounted them. Soon they were airborne and on their way to avenge my aching back.

I was out of action for a few days as I recuperated with the aid of a few muscle relaxant pills that our "Doc" (actually an E-5 medic) gave me. He wanted to know if he should put me in for the Purple Heart Medal since I was wounded in "combat." I said, "Not only NO! But HELL NO! This is my own stupid fault. There are people who deserve that medal for what they've done. I don't! Besides, I have a goal and that is to get through this year without 'Qualifying' for one of those and I wouldn't want to break my current streak."

A few days later, after my back had improved, I was again on HOT status and was scrambled to assist some infantry guys that were pinned down by a sniper. The location was only a few kilometers southeast of Quan Loi and we arrived on station very quickly. Once there, we slowed down to loiter speed while I called the ground commander and began to identify where all his troops were. As I circled the area, I suddenly felt a BANG in the controls like I had just flown through another aircraft's rotorwash. I knew that that was not the case since my wingman was behind me and there were no other aircraft in sight. I became dismayed when I noticed that to fly straight and level, I had to hold the cyclic stick nearly all the way to the left so that it was touching my left leg. Something was definitely wrong and I told my wingman and the ground commander that I had to return to Quan Loi immediately. I called operations and told them to launch another section to replace me and to have maintenance standing by when I got back.

I didn't want to try hovering the aircraft since there was some sort of flight control malfunction going on so, I did a short running landing and stopped the aircraft abeam of our maintenance tent. The maintenance guys were out by the time I shut down. They hooked up the ground handling wheels and towed the aircraft clear of the runway and right into the maintenance tent. Since this particular aircraft was only a few hours short of it's 100 hour inspection, the maintenance officer decided to go ahead and start the inspection early in hopes of finding the problem and getting the inspection complete at the same time. Since most of the inspection panels would be removed during the inspection, it would aid in finding whatever the problem was with the controls.

I briefly looked over the aircraft in hopes of finding something simple that could be corrected quickly but was unsuccessful. I was assigned a different aircraft and went back to flying missions, confident that the maintenance folks would find the problem and correct it.

Two days later, my crew chief, Russ Warriner, came to tell me that the inspection on the aircraft was nearly complete and they had not found any discrepancy in the flight controls. They were preparing to close up all the inspection panels and take the aircraft out for a test flight.

I decided to take another look at the aircraft to see if I could spot something before they flew it again. I took my flashlight and started looking in all the holes that were open. I wasn't sure what I was looking for but knew that my eye would catch anything that was out of the ordinary. I had gotten to the area under the transmission and had a feeling that something here was wrong. Everything I could see seemed normal. Nothing bent or broken caught my eye but I had a feeling that something was missing. I decided to do a mental inventory of the parts that I normally inspected in this area. I looked over the 5 transmission mounts and reached up and touched each of them. They seemed okay. Next I looked over the bottoms of the flight controls hydraulic servos. I grabbed each one and shook it. They were all secure and their hydraulic lines were routed correctly and tight. Next, I looked at the lift link...it was NOT THERE!! What the Hell!!

As you may recall from earlier in this book, the lift link is a 8" long steel bar that connects the transmission and rotor system to the fuselage of the helicopter. Without it, the rotor would go up and the fuselage AND crew would go down with disastrous results. Apparently, the only thing that kept me and my copilot from becoming a lawn dart that day was the 5 transmission mounts. These are solid rubber plugs the size of a beer can that are mounted on one side to the fuselage and on the other to the transmission. They are designed to dampen out vibrations from the rotor system to the airframe of the helicopter. They are held in place by a bonding material (read GLUE) and have no solid connection to support the weight of a 9000 pound machine. Had I tried to pull out of a dive that day, the rotor would have complied but the transmission mounts would have failed and we would have made a very large crater and fireball somewhere in the vicinity of the sniper.

On closer inspection of the attachment point on the transmission, I noticed that the flange had snapped off cleanly leaving no jagged, telltale fragments that might catch one's eye during an inspection. The lift link itself had fallen over sideways and was laying on top of the airframe beam that it's bottom end was still bolted to. The reason so many eyes had missed this potentially catastrophic fault was like looking at one of those picture puzzles of two nearly exact copies of the same picture. Often, in the second picture, they change the color or position of an item or REMOVE it entirely from the photo. That was the case here.

I called over Russ and our maintenance officer and asked them to show me the lift link. As they looked into the hole below the transmission, their eyes slowly got larger and their mouths began to gape. The maintenance officer said rather sheepishly, "I was just going to test fly this aircraft."

To which I replied, "Maybe you should postpone that for a little while."

The maintenance officer sent an emergency notification up the chain of command and the Army issued an immediate inspection order for all Cobras in the inventory. The inspection reveled several more aircraft that had cracked flanges that resulted in their immediate grounding until repairs could be completed. I like to believe that I helped prevent someone else from becoming a large lawn dart.

As I have mentioned previously, about 5 kilometers to the West of Quan Loi was the South Vietnamese town of An Loc. Located adjacent to the town was an ARVN (South Vietnamese Army) artillery fire base. Their weapons consisted of a battery of six 105mm howitzers which they would fire in support of their troops in the field. Generally speaking, their artillery supported their troops and ours fired for our guys. At Quan Loi, the U.S. Army had a battery of 105mm howitzers in addition to a battery of 155mm howitzers and a single 8 inch howitzer and one 175mm self propelled gun.

During takeoffs and landings, the control tower would advise us if any of these various artillery groups were currently firing and on what azimuth so that we could avoid being hit by their outgoing rounds. In the interest of safety, each of the U.S. Artillery groups had what they called a "Bird Spotter". This was a safety person that scanned the area in front of an artillery piece just before it was fired to make sure no aircraft were approaching the danger zone.

One night, while I was on mortar patrol, my artillery controller called me to say that the 175 mm gun and the 8 inch howitzer would be conducting sporadic H&I firings over the next couple of hours and they would be firing on an azimuth of 040 degrees, so, I should avoid flying in this area until advised. Additionally, they advised me that the ARVN artillery unit at An Loc would be firing in the same general direction and their gun-target line would go over Quan Loi.

H&I firings are Harassing and Interdicting shots designed to keep the enemy from using the same trails and assembly areas since they never knew when these rounds would start landing.

I rogered the controller's warning and moved my orbit to the South side of the LZ. From that position, we were able to see the huge flash of the large American artillery pieces as they fired and observe the impact of the rounds when they landed.

At one point we watched as the 175mm gun fired and saw its round explode about 25 kilometers to the northeast. The initial explosion was followed by a secondary blast, a fire and more explosions. They had obviously hit something but we had no idea what it could be. We reported this to the artillery controller who passed it along to the gun crew. They were all very excited to know they had actually HIT something besides trees and the ground. Division artillery made note of the coordinates where this round hit and would send out a scout team in the morning to check it out. To capitalize on this lucky "Shot in the Dark," the other artillery units began to shoot into the same coordinates in hopes of catching the bad guys with their pants down.

There were now many flashes of outgoing artillery rounds being fired from Quan Loi. We were concentrating our attention on the area of impact to see if there were any more secondary explosions. Suddenly, our artillery controller was screaming on the radio that Quan Loi was taking incoming. We quickly switched our attention back to the immediate area surrounding the LZ but saw none of the distinctive flashes from enemy mortar or rocket fire. As we scanned the area, another volley of rounds landed near the runway and once again, the controller was yelling that they were STILL taking incoming.

I had noticed one peculiar thing just before the last incoming rounds landed and that was that the ARVN artillery unit had fired its guns only seconds before the impacts. I thought, "Nooo! It couldn't be, could it?" I started toward the ARVN compound and kept staring at it as I closed the distance. Again, I saw their guns fire and watched as their rounds landed on Quan Loi. Holy Crap!! Those assholes were firing on our base camp. I immediately told the artillery controller what was going on and he said he would call them and order a ceasefire. He also said, "If they fire again, shoot back."

Apparently, either the ceasefire order was lost in translation or there was a communications failure because, they did fire again and the rounds landed on Quan Loi. I armed my rocket system, selected a spot about 50 meters outside their perimeter and fired 3 pair of rockets.

The explosions got their attention. They stopped firing and immediately called Quan Loi to complain about the wayward Cobra that was firing at them. Imagine that!!

The next day a joint investigation was launched and found that the ARVN artillery unit was not using the correct propellant powder charges in their guns causing their rounds to fall far short of their intended destination. While there was some equipment damaged at Quan Loi and some shattered nerves, no one was injured or killed but the ARVN didn't know how close they had come to being taken out by a "Friendly" Cobra.

CHAPTER 22

Figure the Odds

We were well into 1969 and the enemy activity around Quan Loi had died down significantly. Most of our fire missions were at a distance from our base camp and as a result we would have to fly for 15 or 20 minutes just to get to the grid coordinates of where the action was taking place. That's why we were surprised one day when my section was scrambled and told to head east for six kilometers to assist in the recovery of a downed helicopter crew. We had operations confirm that they said six and not sixty, just to be sure. As we turn east after takeoff, we could see another Cobra flying in circles over an area about six kilometers from us.

We called on the frequency we had been given and the Cobra responded. He said that he and his OH-6 Loach had been doing a recon in that area when the scout aircraft sighted what appeared to be some trucks parked in the jungle. As the scout flew over the area a second time to confirm his observation, he began taking intense automatic weapons fire. They were hit but managed to fly the aircraft clear of the jungled area and land it in a nearby rice paddy about 100 meters from the treeline. The pilot and crew chief had gotten out of the downed aircraft and were taking cover behind a rice paddy dike because the enemy was still shooting at them from the treeline. The Cobra had been shooting up the treeline to suppress the enemy fire and was now almost out of ammunition.

As we arrived overhead, we could see the downed Loach and the two crewmen laying behind the dike a short distance away. The Cobra marked the enemy's location in the treeline for us by firing the remainder of his ammo at them, whereupon, we took over and began to shoot up the area. Several more aircraft from their unit started arriving in the area and their commander decided they were going to try to extract the downed crew. He then asked me if I would provide some heavy suppressive fire to the treeline as he had one of his Hueys come in from the southwest, land next to the downed crew, pick them up and fly back out the way they had come in.

I assured him that we could do that and asked if he wanted me to scramble another section to help out. He replied, "The more firepower, the better! Do it!"

I called ops and told them we needed another section on station ASAP. They replied that the fire mission horn was going off and that we would be joined shortly by another of our sections.

As I saw our other section take off, I called them on our air to air frequency and explained what was going on. I told the section leader to just shoot at the treeline that I would be shooting at so we could provide intense suppressive fire while the crew was being extracted. He replied, "Roger that! We're ready to go."

The rescue Huey was inbound from the southwest, going as fast as he could, and we began to fire up the treeline again. We had formed a daisy chain so that as one of our aircraft was pulling out of his rocket run, the next one was already shooting and he would be followed by the third and fourth, then, the first would be attacking again. This worked well and provided a continuous stream of rockets impacting the treeline as the Huey touched down next to the downed crew. They were aboard in a flash and the Huey lifted off heading back the way he had come in with his nose down while he accelerated to maximum speed. It was my turn in the firing rotation and as I pulled out of my rocket run, I was watching the departing Huey when, suddenly, his nose went up and he began to loose speed. As I watched him settle towards the ground, I knew he had been shot down also. The pilot did a very nice job of landing the powerless aircraft and soon, all aboard were out and taking shelter behind the dike of the next rice paddy.

This development seemed to shake up the entire command structure. Soon, this operation was attracting a lot of attention from not just the First Cavalry Division Headquarters but from General Westmoreland's headquarters in Saigon.

A third attempt to rescue the downed crews was successful and they were taken back to Quan Loi. We wound up being involved in the operation for the rest of the day. Several more scout aircraft were shot down that day as they tried to develop targets for all the attack assets that were now on station. The artillery folks were firing a lot of rounds to the north side of the truck park to prevent the enemy from escaping through the jungle that way.

The Air Force had several Forward Air Controllers (FACs) in the area that were directing fighter-bombers in on targets in the enemy truck park area. F-4 Phantom jets were coming in dropping a lot of high drag bombs and I particularly liked watching the A1-E Skyraiders do their dive bombing. The Skyraider is a propeller driven, single seat fighter-bomber that can carry a huge amount of ordnance. The truly amazing aspect of this aircraft is its ability to dive straight down. They do this to be very precise in the delivery of their bombs. After all, it's hard to miss when you are directly over the target and headed straight down at it. You just have to let the bomb go. The interesting thing about their technique was that when they rolled into this vertical dive, the airplane did not appear to accelerate downwards but seemed to hang in the air like a balloon. Quite impressive and accurate.

Meanwhile, we were tasked with suppressing the treeline while maintenance recovery teams rigged the downed Huey so it could be picked up by a Chinook and taken back to Quan Loi for repairs. My unit eventually had three sections committed to the operation and I and my wingman wound up flying back and forth to Quan Loi to rearm and refuel at least six times that day.

On my last flight out to the battle area, I couldn't help but notice that there were at least 5 different "Command and Control" Hueys flying around in circles over the battle area. Generally, you could tell the level of command by how high a particular aircraft was flying in the stack. The company and battalion commander's aircraft would normally be flying at about 3,000 to 4,000 feet above the ground, followed by the full colonels and one star generals at 5,000 feet and two star generals and above at 6,000 feet. That day we had the full circus in attendance and it was a miracle that there wasn't a mid-air collision.

I reported back in and asked what target they wanted me to shoot now. This question was followed by several minutes of silence as the various levels of command consulted with each other. Finally, the unit commander called me and said they wanted me to destroy the OH-6 scout helicopter that had started this whole thing since it was still too close to the enemy to allow any attempt at recovering it before nightfall. They did not want the enemy to capture the radios during the night, so, I was elected to do the dirty work.

Since I would be destroying a valuable piece of government property, I requested the initials of the commander so I wouldn't wind up paying for an un-flyable helicopter for the rest of my life by monthly deductions from my pay. Once I had written his initials on my canopy in grease pencil, I told my wingman to hang back and keep me covered but to not shoot at the helicopter. I didn't want him to be involved if there was going to be any repercussions later.

I armed the weapons system, rolled into a dive and unleashed 5 pairs of rockets on the OH-6. Almost all of them were direct hits. The aircraft exploded into pieces and began to burn. I had accomplished what needed to be done but I didn't feel good about it. At least the bad guys weren't getting any radios tonight.

The commander thanked us for our support throughout the day and said we could dump the rest of our rockets into the truck park area and head for home. He also said that it had been decided to put in a B-52 strike on the area that night just to make sure the bad guys wouldn't be using any of those trucks ever again.

That evening we saw the night turn to day and the ground shake under our feet as the B-52 "Arc light" attack rained down on the truck park.

You may think that this story ends here but you would be wrong. Please bear with me while I explain.

Let's flash forward some 13 years, to 1982. I had just been promoted to CW4 (Chief Warrant Office grade 4) which, at the time, was the highest rank for a warrant officer in the U.S. Army and I was reassigned to Heidelberg, West Germany. My new unit was the 207th Aviation Company and our job was to provide aviation support to a four star general who was the Commander-in-Chief (CINC), United States Army, Europe. Our mission was to fly the CINC, his staff, visiting dignitaries and other VIPs wherever the needed to go, throughout Europe, North Africa and the Middle East. To accomplish this mission, we had 12 Beechcraft Super King Air executive airplanes, 10 UH-1H model Huey helicopters and 6 UH-60 Blackhawk helicopters.

When I received my orders assigning me to the unit, I also got a letter from a CW4 Fred Santoro explaining that he was currently a member of the unit and had been assigned as my sponsor to assist me with my family's move to Germany. He said his job as my sponsor was to help me and my family during the move so that we could get settled into our new quarters as quickly as possible, get my kids registered for school and iron out any bumps in the road we may encounter during the move. My wife, Nancy, and I thought that this was a very nice program and were very appreciative of the help Fred and his wife, Michelle, provided us.

Fred was also one of the unit's instructor pilots and helped me with my local training and check ride once I arrived in the unit and had gotten my family settled.

We became good friends very quickly and flew many missions together during my 3 years there. During one of those early missions, I believe it was to Athens, Greece, Fred and I had gone out to dinner and were relaxing over a couple of beers. We were comparing notes on where each of us had been assigned, checking to see if we had any common friends or acquaintances and generally telling "War Stories" about our adventures. It was during this exchange that Fred told me that he had been based at Quan Loi at the same time I was there. He mentioned that he had a been shot down just east of Quan Loi in his OH-6 Loach after discovering a truck park. Then he said that the Huey that had rescued them was shot down just after it picked them up.

Suddenly, things snapped into place and I said, "THAT WAS YOU?!?!"

Fred said, "What? Do you know something about that?"

"I should say so!" I answered, "I was the section leader of the first section of Blue Max Cobras that showed up after you got shot down. We were covering the Huey when they picked you up. I'm glad I have this opportunity to apologize for not doing a better job. It must have been very crappy to be shot down twice in one day."

At this point, Fred dissolved into near hysterical laughter. I began to think that I had pushed him over the edge by bringing up some very bad memories.

As he slowly regained his composure, he explained, "I was shot down a total of THREE times that day!" Once again, he lost control and began laughing uncontrollably. I'm sure that the expression on my face, and my jaw hanging open, had something to do with sending him back into hysterics since he was now pointing at my face with one hand while holding his side with the other.

As his mirth receded and he wiped the tears from his eyes, he told me "The Rest of the Story."

It seems that when the second rescue Huey actually managed to pick them all up and returned them to Quan Loi, Fred decided that he needed to get another Loach and go back out to the battle area to "teach" those NVA bastards a thing or two.

Apparently, it was the NVA that was doing the teaching that day. Fred managed to get shot down for the third time and was on his way back to Quan Loi for yet another aircraft when his commander told him to "STOP!" He was running out of aircraft and couldn't afford to have Fred "Teaching" anymore lessons.

As an officer in the U.S. Army, your promotions and selection for advanced training are controlled by how well you do on your Officer Efficiency Reports (OERs). These are a sort of "Report Card" written by the officers above you in the chain of command. Your immediate supervisor is your "Rater" and the next level of command is your "Endorser." These reports are kept in your file in Washington D.C. and are critical for anyone wanting to make a career out of the U.S. Army.

Because of his performance that day at Quan Loi, Fred's rater wrote, in his very official OER, that, "Fred is a Magnet Ass and managed to get shot down three times in one day!" While I'm sure that the writer thought that this statement would be viewed as derogatory, those in Washington reading it, must have thought that it indicated incredible bravery, tenacity and devotion to duty because Fred WAS promoted to CW4 and received advanced training in the form of the Fix Wing Qualification Course and the C-12 King Air Qualification Course. Figure the Odds!

CHAPTER 23

Flight Suit?

I t was my "Day Off" and I had caught up on my sleep from the previous night of mortar patrol. It must have been a Monday because I was experiencing some intestinal distress. You may be wondering why Mondays and cramps go hand in hand. It is quite simple. Monday was the day of the week that everyone was required to take a Chloroquine tablet to ward off malaria. This was a large orange tablet about the size of a quarter and was used to prevent a particular strain of malaria. We were also required to take a small white tablet every day to prevent a different strain of the disease. In true military fashion, these tablets were handed out by our medic as we entered the mess tent for our evening meal. The little white pill was never a problem and the guys took it every day without any complaints but the large orange tablet caused everyone to have cramps and need to use the latrine within an hour or two of taking it.

Some guys became very adept at palming their pill or hiding it in their mouth and we would see the orange pills in the trash cans or scattered on the ground outside the mess tent after dinner. Those that avoided taking the orange pill reasoned that the white pill was for the type of malaria that would kill you but the orange pill was for the strain that would only make you wish you were dead and since the orange pill made you feel that way every week anyway, they'd just take their chances. Anyway, I was a good soldier and took both types of pills and just dealt with the cramps.

So, I was just finishing my visit to the latrine about 9 PM and as I was leaving, another of our warrant officers was just entering the facility. Those pills really worked well. As I walked back towards my tent in my skivvies and flip flops, I heard the unmistakable sound of 107mm rockets being launched our way. I knew I didn't have enough time to get to a bunker, so, I yelled, "INCOMING" and hit the dirt. The first rocket hit the ground back in the vicinity of the latrine and several others impacted near my tent. As soon as it was quiet again, I was up and running as fast as my flip flops would carry me. The closest place of protection was the operations bunker, so, I ran in there just as I heard the next volley of rockets taking off. I heaved a sigh of relief as I entered but that was short lived. A very strange scene greeted me.

The Commanding Officer and the Operations Officer were standing on the far side of the bunker. They were staring, with mouths agape, down and to my right. They had simply glanced at me when I entered and returned their gaze to the couch to my right. I saw our Operations Sergeant seated at his radio console behind the CO and Ops Officer and he too was looking at the couch to my right while talking on the radio. I overheard him saying that it might be awhile until the "Hot Section" was airborne. Apparently, he was informing the mortar patrol aircraft that there was some sort of problem with launching the "Hot Section." All of this had transpired in less than 10 seconds and now I followed everyone's gaze back to the couch.

As I looked at the empty couch trying to determine what was so interesting, the next volley of rockets began impacting outside. It was only then that I saw something move UNDER the couch. Whatever it was, it recoiled with each impacting round. It was then that I heard the whimpering. I thought, "What the Hell?" and leaned over to look under the couch. I saw that it was a person curled up in the fetal position and shaking like a leaf. I thought it might be a new guy and this was his first encounter with incoming but I was totally amazed that he could fit under the couch.

I looked back at the others and said quietly, "Who the Hell is that?"

The CO looked back at me and mouthed the name of one of our section leaders. I was shocked, to say the least. At the same time the CO said out loud, "Bob, we are short a section leader (as he motioned toward the person under the couch) for the Hot Section and the others are waiting out on the flight line for him, would you mind taking his place?"

Hell yes, I minded!! But considering the other pilots were out there waiting on their "Fearless Leader" and were in danger, I said, "Yes, sir! Right away."

I turned and headed back out of the bunker and towards the flight line, again running as fast as my flip flops would carry me. I was about halfway there when I heard another volley of rockets taking off.

Crap!! I took another dive into the dirt just as the rounds started arriving. The first few hit at a distance but then one hit a treetop near me and I could feel the heat of the blast and heard the whizzing and WHACK of the shrapnel as it hit the ground around me. I took a very quick inventory and decided that I hadn't been hit, so, I was up and running again.

As I arrived at the section leader's aircraft, the other crew members gave me a strange look as they came out of hiding from behind the revetment wall. Their looks became even stranger when I said, "Come on, let's get airborne!!" Do you think that maybe the looks were because I was climbing into the back seat of the Cobra in my flip flops and underwear? I'd have to explain later that it was my new "Comfortable" flight suit authorized by the CO.

As we climbed out after takeoff, I noticed that the incoming rounds had again hit the refueling point and a small fire was burning there. I called operations and told them of this so they could get the fire crews out there before it got totally out of control and shut down the refuel point.

We then rendezvoused with the mortar patrol aircraft and he showed us where all the rockets were being launched from. He had fired almost all of his ammunition into the area but the enemy continued to launch more rockets. I decided that my section would fire about half of our rockets into the area in hopes of discouraging the enemy from continuing their assault. If nothing else, we might cut some of the remote launch wires or knock over some of the launchers. "Besides" I thought, "I was still pretty pissed off at having to dive into the dirt twice tonight. It was time for some NVA assholes to eat dirt."

We spread our 76 rockets over the suspected area and the mortar patrol bird finished up his remaining ammo and returned to Quan Loi. We continued to orbit the area for about 20 minutes but there were no further rocket launches. Operations called and said that they were sending up another mortar patrol bird and once he was on station, we could return. I rogered them and we continued to circle the area. As things calmed down, I noticed that my hands, elbows and knees were beginning to hurt and I was coming down with the "Shakes." The "Shakes" are what happens when you come down off an adrenaline high and, apparently, I was having significant withdrawal symptoms. I was shivering and cold and the pain that had been masked, was now making itself known. As we orbited, I turned up the cockpit lights and looked at my elbows and knees. They were bleeding pretty good and making a mess on the radios and the floor. I'd have to apologize to the crew chief when we landed.

Soon, the other mortar patrol bird was airborne and we were back on the ground. I walked over to the operations bunker to check in with the CO and partly to see what happened to the section leader under the couch. As I walked in, the CO said, "What the Hell happened to you?" My shakes were gone but I was still bleeding from my elbows and knees and I presumed that the blood was what he was talking about.

I said, "I took a dirt dive on the way to the aircraft. What happened to the couch section leader?"

He replied, "He had some sort of breakdown and is over at the medic's tent getting something for his nerves. You need to get over there and get those looked at." Indicating my bloody wounds. I thought, "There is no way I'm going to the medic's tent while that guy is there getting treatment for his 'Nerves'. I'll deal with this myself."

It was then that the CO turned to a private standing next to him and said, "Bob, I want you to know that because of your radio call about the refueling point being on fire, I sent Private Smith here, over there with the water truck he uses to fill up our shower tanks, so that he could help put out the fire. I'm putting him in for the Bronze Star Medal for Heroism. What do you say to that?"

I was incredulous! Are you kidding me? Besides everything else, I thought it was pretty well known that you DO NOT use WATER on a FUEL fire!! I did think it was brave of the young man to drive his truck to the refuel point during the attack even if it was not the brightest thing anyone has ever done. I did learn later that the firemen at the scene told him to, "Get the Hell out of here!"

I didn't answer the CO but turned to the private and said, "Congratulations," and walked out.

As I walked into my tent, the other guys in my platoon looked at me in my flip flops, underwear and coagulated blood and in unison said, "What the Hell happened to you?" It seemed to be the question of the day.

I gave them the short version, then got some water and began cleaning up my scrapes and scratches before going to bed.

CHAPTER 24

SHORT!!

Right around Christmas I officially became a "Short-timer". This term refers to someone that has less than 100 days left before they are due to return to the States. The Army was very specific when they sent us to Vietnam. They said our "Tour of Duty" would be exactly 365 days. Not 364 or 366 but exactly 365 days. They used the date we first entered the "Combat Zone", added 365 days to it and that was your DEROS date. DEROS was an official acronym that stood for Date Expected Return from Over Seas. By this method of calculating, no one would have to worry about leap year or any other situations that might expose them to more than 365 days of danger in a combat zone. I never really figured out why the Marines did a 13 month tour of duty. Was it just to prove they were better than the Army or Air Force? Who knows?

Anyway, now that I was "Short," I could refer to myself as a "Double Digit Midget" and tell the other guys that, "I'm so short that they no longer have to open doors for me, I'll just walk under them." There were a million such jokes about being "Short" and new ones being created every day but, in truth, I was starting to get a little nervous that the odds were starting to pile up against me making it out of here in one

219

piece. The good news was that there wasn't much enemy activity going on around Quan Loi. This made me feel a little more hopeful of making it to my DEROS date without becoming a casualty of war.

Just as I was starting to think, "I might just make it out of here," we were all called into the mess hall for a briefing by our CO. The CO said that since we had done such a great job of discouraging the NVA from attacking Saigon through our sector, north of the city, the enemy had moved its forces to the west and was now threatening an attack on Saigon from the infamous area called "The Iron Triangle" near Cu Chi. This area had a labyrinth of underground tunnels replete with barracks for troops, hospitals, ammo dumps, storage facilities, etc, etc. Earlier, the Air Force had tried to collapse the tunnels by bombing the area repeatedly with B-52 "Arc-Light" strikes but the complex went too deep to be seriously damaged.

Another tactic that was tried was putting "Tunnel Rats" into the complex to root out the enemy. A Tunnel Rat was an infantryman, usually of somewhat smaller stature, that would climb down into the tunnel entrances when they were discovered. Because of the darkness and small spaces, he would only carry a .45 caliber pistol and a flashlight while exploring the tunnels. He had to be careful of the numerous booby traps and ambushes the enemy would set for those foolish enough to venture into their lair. While these brave men did have some notable success in finding and destroying enemy weapons caches, strategically, their efforts were not great enough to rid the area of these subterranean fortifications.

As I sat in the briefing, I couldn't help but wonder, "What good was a bunch of helicopters going to do in solving the problem of the tunnels in the Iron Triangle?"

As if he were reading my thoughts, the CO said, "As a result, General Westmoreland has tasked the First Cavalry Division to send a task force to Cu Chi to supplement U.S. troops currently in the area and to conduct intensive operations in the Iron Triangle area to choke off any enemy resupply efforts from across the Cambodian border. In short, the plan is to starve them out. Our unit has been selected as part of the task force. We fly out to Cu Chi in the morning."

Somehow, I sensed, that this would not be a short term operation since it usually took longer than a few days to "starve" a well stocked enemy into submission. But I had nothing else to do till my DEROS date arrived, so, what the hell, let's go.

The next morning we launched six of our Cobras (3 sections) and one Huey that the commander had borrowed from battalion headquarters. We had left behind the other 6 Cobras, several of which were in maintenance and the others were to continue the mission of mortar patrol around Quan Loi.

When we arrived in Cu Chi, we were told that we would be staying with the guys from the local CH-47 unit whose call sign was the "Muleskinners." This was the 242nd Assault Support Helicopter Company assigned to the 25th Infantry Division. They were very good hosts and helped us in many ways. The accommodations were better than what we had back at Quan Loi and the chow was superior. I might actually begin to like this place.

Another added luxury that the Muleskinners had in their area was a swimming pool. They had taken a damaged and unserviceable 5000 gallon fuel bladder, cut it open, steam cleaned it and mounted it in a wooden frame. While it wasn't your classic concrete and plaster pool, it certainly served our purposes and was quite refreshing at the end of a long day.

We learned from our hosts that just before our arrival, their unit had lost several aircraft when a group of enemy sappers had broken through the perimeter at Cu Chi and set demolition charges in some of their Chinooks.

This development concerned me. While I really liked our new accommodations, I was not too keen on the uninvited guests that showed up in the middle of the night and tried to spoil the party. I think that some of the enthusiasm that the Muleskinners showed at the arrival of six Cobra attack helicopters in their area was more out a sense of protection and survival than out of just the camaraderie of fellow aviators. I might be wrong.

Soon, the sweep and clear operations in the Iron Triangle began. As the U.S. and South Vietnamese forces swept through the area, they would uncover and destroy every tunnel entrance they found, burn and blow up any food and weapons caches discovered and defeat any enemy troops encountered. Occasionally, when the enemy resistance was unusually strong, they would call for us to launch a section to assist them in defeating the pocket of resistance so they could move on.

I remember one particular instance when my wingman and I arrived overhead of an Armored Cavalry unit that was locked in an intense firefight with a large enemy force. There were 8 armored personnel carriers (APCs) arrayed in a semicircle around a thicket of bamboo. The APCs were all firing their .50 caliber heavy machine guns into the thicket and the enemy was returning a huge volume of small arms fire at the APCs. The return fire was so intense that I could see enemy tracers ricocheting in every direction off each of the APCs. The ground commander was having a difficult time hearing me when I checked in with him on the radio, just because of the din of the ricocheting rounds.

He explained that he wanted us to shoot the bamboo thicket because that was where all the bad guys were. I told him we could flatten the bamboo thicket but he had to guarantee me that all his personnel were inside their APCs with the hatches closed because I would be firing Nails (Flechettes) and anyone outside would be subject to being hit. He said, "Okay, let me tell them to close their hatches. I'll get right back to you."

"Okay," I said, then added, "In the meantime I'm going to mark the target with a pair of 10 pound H E (High Explosive) rockets to confirm that I am looking at the same bamboo thicket that you are looking at."

He rogered my transmission and I rolled into my dive and fired one pair into the bamboo. As I pulled out of the dive, I started taking intense enemy small arms fire. It sounds like your standing next to a popcorn machine when all the rounds are flying around you but the sound changes when you are actually hit. Today, I was lucky and took no hits.

We had started carrying Flechettes on our inboard rocket pods just in case we came up against a large group of enemy soldiers out in the open during this operation. They would also serve us well in case the enemy tried another ground attack on Cu Chi while we were in residence there.

The ground commander called me back and assured me that all his people were closed up and in their APCs. He said that my marking rounds had hit the correct bamboo thicket and I was cleared to fire my "Nails."

I called him back and said, "Roger that. I must say again that this will be 'Danger!! Close!!' and all personnel must be under cover."

He reassured me once again and I told him we would now be rolling in on the bamboo thicket with Nails.

I rearmed the weapons system and selected the inboard pods. I told my wingman to fire about half of his Nails into the same spot when I pulled out of my dive. He rogered me and I prepared to enter a very steep dive. I chose a steep dive because it would help limit how far an errant rocket could travel, just to be on the safe side. The bamboo thicket was about 30 meters in diameter and very distinguishable from the rest of the jungle since the bamboo was a much lighter, almost florescent, shade of green. This thicket was about 30 to 40 feet tall and very dense, thereby providing good cover for the enemy.

I rolled into my dive and fired 10 pair of rockets in rapid succession. The red marker dye from my rockets was now staining the grove of bamboo, providing an unmistakable target for my wingman. As I pulled out of my dive, I watched him roll in and dump about 10 pair of his Nails onto the target. Neither of us had taken any enemy fire during our pullouts.

Perfect! I could even see that there was now a divot in the jungle where the bamboo had been.

I called the ground commander and told him that his folks could open up their hatches and get some fresh air because we were done for

ROBERT F. HARTLEY

now. I said he could recon the thicket to check for any resistance, we'd be standing by.

He rogered me and soon, I saw the hatches on the APCs open up and several of them were now moving towards the red spot that used to be the thicket. The commander called me as his lead APC drove into the red area of the bamboo and said his men were getting absolutely no resistance and that there was nothing there but a bunch of red chop sticks. There wasn't a piece of bamboo taller than 6 feet left in the entire area.

Excellent! Now that's the way to cut grass.

The ground commander released us to return to Cu Chi and said he'd let us know what the body count was once they searched the area. We found out later that there was only 15 bodies found but there were many blood trails that lead to well camouflaged tunnel entrances in the area. These were all explored by the Tunnel Rats and then destroyed.

That evening our CO came up to me and said, "Bob, you've done an excellent job out here but you are only a couple of weeks away from your DEROS, so, I want you to go back to Quan Loi, take a break and just help out with the mortar patrol duties until it's time for you to leave. I have an aircraft that needs to go back for maintenance, so, I'd like you to fly it up to Quan Loi tomorrow. Okay?"

"Yes, Sir!" was my reply but I had mixed emotions. While I was very happy that I was getting close to going home, I was somewhat reluctant to release the reins and let others take over before the job was done. While it made sense logically, it was very difficult to accept emotionally. I had great confidence in my protege Francis "Mac" McDowall and the other new pilots but, somehow, I felt I was deserting them. I would just have to wrangle with this while I cooled my heels back at Quan Loi.

I checked in with the Executive Officer (XO) when I got back to Quan Loi and he said that he and the CO had talked and I would only be responsible for flying mortar patrol every few days. He did tell me that they had been getting mortared and rocketed almost every night since we had left for Cu Chi, so, he said, "Don't think you're getting off easy being here. In fact, there has been a report that the psychic, Jeane

224

Dixon, renown for predicting the assassination of JFK, just reported a vision she had of An Loc and Quan Loi being the center of a big battle and that it concluded with both places being overrun by the NVA with heavy losses for U.S. Forces."

Great! Just what I wanted to hear. As if to confirm the prediction, we got mortared that night. The next day I decided that I was moving into the bunker for the rest of my time at Quan Loi. I chose to stay in the bunker closest to the flight line reasoning that if there was a ground attack, I could get out to one of the remaining Cobras and get airborne rather than being stuck on the ground. Besides, I'd be able to inflict more damage on the enemy from the air than I would being on the ground fending them off with my pistol. By the way, Jeane Dixon's prediction did prove true! However, the battle for An Loc was not to take place for several more years.

After I cleaned out some of the spiderwebs and sprayed the bunker down with insecticide, I took my bunk apart and reassembled it down in my new home. While I felt a little safer sleeping there, the accommodations were not exactly 5 star quality. There was no electricity so, no fan to move the hot air around and the only light I would have to read by was a flashlight. I decided I could tough it out for the ten nights I had left until I caught a flight out of there.

The time passed slowly and the handful of mortar patrol missions I flew were uneventful. Two days before I was to fly out, I was told that the mission in Cu Chi was over and all the aircraft and crews would be returning to Quan Loi tomorrow. This news cheered me up a bit since I would be able to see all the other guys and say goodbye properly. I was looking forward to it.

My last full day at Quan Loi dawned bright and beautiful. I was in a very good mood. I had some chores to take care of that included turning in things like my pistol, flight gear, etc, etc. I wanted to get these mundane tasks accomplished early so I could spend some time with the guys when they returned from Cu Chi. I was sure they would have some very interesting stories to tell about their adventures. I finished with my "out-processing" by noon and had a leisurely lunch while waiting for the inbound task force to land. I stopped by operations and asked if they had heard from the flight of Cobras from Cu Chi and the operations sergeant said they were just getting ready to take off, so, they were about an hour out. I thanked him and decided to go lay in my bunk and read until they arrived.

About an hour later, as I lay reading, I could hear the growing thunder of six Cobras flying in close formation and at high speed as they approached Quan Loi. I delayed getting up because I knew that when they landed, there would be a lot of red dust blowing around as they jockeyed for position to enter the revetments and shut down. I figured I'd just lay there until I heard the last of the engines winding down, then I would walk out to the flight line to greet the returning winged warriors.

It was a good plan but doomed to failure. As I lay there, the noise of the hovering aircraft built to a crescendo that suddenly was punctuated by a very loud BANG and the sound of something whirring off into the distance. This was followed very quickly by the sound of a Cobra's throttle being chopped to idle and the whop, whop... whop.....whop........ whop of the main rotor slowing down as the pilot performed a hovering autorotation.

WHAT THE HELL? I quickly ran up the four steps of the bunker and stopped as I stepped out. About 40 feet in front of me was a Cobra that was half way into a revetment but was sitting on the ground with its main rotor almost stopped. The other 5 aircraft were still hovering about waiting to enter their revetments. Almost immediately, I noticed that the Cobra in front of me was missing the tail rotor and its gearbox. As I tried to comprehend what had happened, I was suddenly startled and nearly jumped out of my skin as something hit the top of the bunker with a huge "CRASH, THUD!!" a few feet behind me. After I got my heart restarted, I turn and saw the tail rotor and attached gearbox imbedded in the sandbags over the entrance to the bunker, a mere 4 feet from me!! I was too short for this SHIT!!

My initial reaction was to be very pissed off but the pilot of the damaged aircraft came to my bunker to apologize for scaring the crap out of me. I forgave him and asked him what happened. He explained that as he was moving into the revetment, one of the other Cobras was landing behind him and that the down wash blew his tail into the revetment wall. He said that one tail rotor blade was still stuck in the wall while the other blade and gearbox went straight up and, of course, landed next to me. We calculated that with the amount of time that the tail rotor and gearbox were up in the air, they must have attained an altitude of about 500 feet above the ground. The pilot then asked to shake my hand in hopes that some of my "Good Ju-Ju" would rub off on him and he'd be safe for the rest of his tour. Of course, I complied and we went off to the officer's club to have a drink, since we both desperately needed one.

That evening, I did get a chance to say goodbye to all the other pilots as we gathered at the officer's club. They got to tell me of their adventures while at Cu Chi and then we recalled some of the adventures we'd shared over the year. As we started to break up and head off to bed, many of them wanted to rub my head for good luck and to get some of my "Good Ju-Ju" for themselves.

CHAPTER 25

The Final Insult

The next day I caught my flight out of Quan Loi and was on my way to An Khe where I would have to "out-process" from the First Cavalry Division's personnel center. As I handed my orders over to the clerk at An Khe, and he handed me back a raft of forms that would take all afternoon to complete. I'd rather be in combat than be filling out forms. Oh! Well, if this is what I had to do to get home, I'd just have to grin and bear it. As I sat there filling out my ticket home, another pilot walked in to begin the out-processing chore. I was happy to see it was one of my classmates from flight school. We greeted each other with a handshake and nearly simultaneous, "You made it!" as we congratulated each other on having survived the year.

When we finished our paperwork, the clerk told us to head over to the supply room where we could pick up our duffel bags that we had left there a year ago. The bags contained our all-leather jump boots, which had been replaced by our current jungle boots, along with our Khaki dress uniforms. The bags had been stored, along with about 16,000 others in a huge warehouse that had no air conditioning, so, it was not a surprise when we opened them to find all our gear covered with mold and mildew.

We told the supply sergeant about the mold ruining our uniforms and he replied, "Yeah! That's pretty common. Here's a voucher you can use to buy a new uniform at the PX." My classmate and I looked at each other and just shrugged. Quite a system they had here.

After our visit to the PX to get our new uniforms, we decided we should treat ourselves to a steak dinner at the officer's club that evening. We had been put up at the BOQ (Bachelor Officers Quarters) which was actually pretty nice since it had plywood walls, a tin roof and screens on the windows. We were told how to get to the "O" club and set out walking that way.

The route took us across a large open field that had several parallel roads crossing it and each of these roads had about 20 concrete slabs that a tent could be set up on. Additionally, the roads had several standard wooden telephone poles along them, spaced about 50 feet apart. The terrain in the camp was very flat but there was a large, imposing hill just outside the wire perimeter of the camp. This geographical feature was called Hon Cong Mountain and rose about 1000 feet above the otherwise flat countryside. While it was entirely outside the security fence, the very top of the hill was occupied by a U.S. signal unit that maintained its own perimeter security. The unit had also painted a huge First Cavalry Division patch on the side of the mountain in an "In Your Face" statement to the enemy. The patch, with its distinctive bright yellow color, could be seen for miles around the camp.

Anyway, we were walking along one of the parallel roads on our way to the "O" club when, suddenly, we hear a rifle shot and a bullet impacts the dirt about 6 feet to our left. CRAP! Some asshole NVA sniper was shooting at us from Hon Cong Mountain. Without a word, we took off running down the road to the next telephone pole. We pulled up, putting the pole between us and the mountain. As we looked at each other and said, "What now?"

Whap!! Another round hit the telephone pole. We were off and running again to the next pole but this time the sniper fired at us while we were running. The round hit the concrete slab next to us and went ricocheting off, whining very loudly as it passed by. The bad news was that the sniper was getting the range down and had us bracketed but the good news was that our next sprint would take us into an area with building that would provide cover. When the next shot hit the road a few feet from us, we were off and running again. We covered the 40 feet to safety in record time. Now we definitely needed a drink to go with our steak dinner.

When we got to the officer's club, we told the club manager about our experience and he advised us to call the M.P.s (Military Police) and report it. I got on the phone and explained to the M.P. Sergeant what had just happened and he replied, "Yeah! They do that sometimes. You should walk back another way."

"Really? Well, thanks for that advice." Yup! It was quite a system they had here.

We completed our out-processing over the next couple of days and never walked the same way to the "O" club again. Soon, we were on a C-130 Hercules cargo plane headed to Cam Rahn Bay to catch our flight back to the States.

When we checked into the replacement detachment at Cam Rahn, they told us to check the rosters on the bulletin board outside the Orderly Room twice a day. When they got around to scheduling us on a flight home, our names would be listed on the bulletin board along with a time and place to show up. They warned us that there would be a "Ramp Check" of everyone boarding a flight to the States and the M.P.s would be looking for any kind of contraband including weapons, ammunition, hand grenades as well as drugs and drug paraphernalia. This "Ramp Check" would also require us to pee in a bottle and be screened for drug use. Anyone testing positive would be detained and sent to rehabilitation at a facility IN VIETNAM!! This was considered by all the troops as a fate worse than death and totally unfair. The North Vietnamese had flooded the areas around most U.S. bases with very cheap heroin in an attempt to get our soldiers hooked on the stuff so they would be less effective in combat, thereby giving the NVA soldiers the upper hand. Sneaky bastards.

Anyway, over the next two days, as I waited for my name to appear on the "Freedom Flight" list, I found out, through scuttlebutt, that there was a way the druggies devised to avoid testing positive on the pee test. It was explained to us that a drug user could take a packet of powdered vinegar from the mess hall, dissolve the contents in a cup of water and drink the mixture just before the drug testing. Sounds simple enough until you realize that the packet is normally used by the mess hall to make 5 GALLONS of vinegar. We were also told that we would be able to spot the druggies on our flight when they started puking up blood shortly after takeoff. Oh! Great! Now there was something to look forward to.

The next day, March 30th, there was my name on the "Freedom Flight" list. HALLELUIAH! It said my flight would be on the 31st at 4 pm. I was to report to the processing facility at 1pm. I spent the rest of that day and most of that night, celebrating at the "O" club. At one point I began to wonder if alcohol would show up on the pee test, and if so, would I need to start tracking down a packet from the mess hall. Finally, I thought, "Screw it, I'll just take my chances." (That must have been my friend, Jack Daniels, whispering in my ear.)

In the morning, I double checked my new Khaki uniform. I had polished the brass on my collar and belt buckle, shined my silver aviator wings and made sure they were perfectly centered over all my new ribbons representing the medals I'd received over the last year. I had spit shined my new black low quarter shoes and felt I was ready for my trip home. I would proudly wear this uniform on my connecting flights in the U.S. as I made my way home to New York.

I arrived at the appointed place on time and was ushered into a huge, non-air conditioned waiting room that was quickly filling up with hundreds of personnel waiting for flights. I found a spot where I could sit on my duffel bag and rest my back against the wall. As soon as I got settled, there was an announcement on a loudspeaker (that was way too LOUD) saying that flight number so and so was ready to board and everyone on that flight should line up at door number 2 for their

"Ramp Check." I suddenly saw a bunch of guys jump up and line up at the water cooler with packets in their hands.

"Oh! Crap!" I thought, "The whole packet thing was TRUE!"

After they had "quenched" their thirst, they dutifully headed off to door number 2 and their ride home.

Over the next couple of hours, other flights were announced and the process repeated itself. I was getting antsy. It was now 20 minutes prior to our scheduled departure time and there had been no mention of our flight number. I was about to go over to the check in desk and ask about it when the obnoxious loudspeaker came to life and informed us that our flight had been delayed for mechanical reasons and they had no estimate on when it might depart.

Crap! All dressed up and nowhere to go. I settled in for the long haul and started to accept the fact that I might not be leaving today. The hours dragged by with no further news of our flight. We watched others go through door number 2 and heard their aircraft takeoff. The terminal was now deserted, save those scheduled on our flight, and I was expecting an announcement for us to get on the buses to return to the replacement detachment for the night. The loudspeaker came to life about 10:15 pm directing us to line up at door number 2 for our "Ramp Check." Everyone was elated. In fact, some of the druggies actually headed for the door then remembered they needed to hit the water cooler first. That just shows you what drugs can do to you.

By the time everyone had completed their "Ramp Check" and given a urine sample, it was 11:30 pm and we were finally boarding our aircraft. It was a Northwest Airlines 4 engine jet that looked beautiful to all of us. I got an aisle seat near the rear of the aircraft and decided that once we were airborne, I was going to sleep all the way home.

The engines were started and soon we were taxiing toward the end of the runway. We stopped and the Captain came on the PA to welcome us aboard and he thank us for our service. He apologized for the delay but assured us that everything was now working properly. He then said that he had a question for us and we could answer him in unison by saying "Yes" if we agreed or remain quiet if the answer was "No"

His question was, since it was now 11:51 pm on March 31ˢᵗ, if we remained on the ground until after midnight, we would all qualify for another month's "Combat Pay" for April.

"Do you want to wait?" His answer was deafening. Nearly everyone on the plane yelled "Yes!!"

The Captain said, "Okay! Okay! We'll wait, but if we start taking incoming, we're outta here!"

The minutes ticked by quickly and soon the Captain announced, "Congratulations, each of you are now 65 dollars richer and we are OUTTA here!!"

With that we taxied onto the runway and began our takeoff roll.

CHAPTER 26

The Road Home

About 15 minutes after takeoff, the Captain was back on the PA to announce that we were clear of Vietnamese airspace and the combat zone. Another cheer went up and there was an almost palpable, collective sigh of relief. Guys were now chatting and laughing and most had smiles on their faces. But the private that was across the aisle and one row up was sweating profusely and his legs were shaking. Suddenly, he grabbed for the air sickness bag and promptly threw up into it. Unfortunately, the bag was either not positioned properly or not fully open and some of the vomit spew onto his uniform, the seat back in front of him and the floor. The vomit was mostly blood. We had another casualty of the war.

I was amazed at how quickly a flight attendant appeared, holding an array of cleaning products and some more air sick bags. She had obviously been through this drill before. As I looked down the aisle I could see that her coworkers were dealing with similar situations throughout the plane. The packets of powdered vinegar had done their job and the druggies were now paying the price for their freedom.

As dawn broke, the flight attendants began coming around serving breakfast. It was standard airplane food but to us it was like a gourmet meal. As I was chowing down, the Captain was back on the PA to announce that we were going to have to land in Japan to refuel and take care of some of the paperwork that resulted from yesterday's mechanical issues. He told us that it would only take a couple of hours on the ground to sort it all out.

He was true to his word and soon we were airborne again and winging our way over the Pacific. The stop in Japan allowed me to get tickets for civilian flights that I could connect with once we landed at McChord Air Force Base near Seattle. I, and a couple of other Army pilots, had done our research and found that if we got to Seattle-Tacoma Airport by 11:00 pm, we could catch the "red-eye" to Chicago and go on from there to the east coast. The last thing we wanted to do was spend the night in Seattle. Based on our departure time from Japan, we knew that it would be a very close connection.

We were right. We landed at about 8:45 pm. We had to dig through and find our bags when they were unceremoniously dumped in a pile by the Air Force. Once we had all our bags we could proceed to the inspection station where we were required to dump the contents out so the military inspectors could sort through it looking for contraband, once again. (I thought we already did this?) Once we jammed everything back into our bags, we could proceed to the U.S. Customs station where we turned in the forms we filled out on the plane. As the customs officer took my form he asked, "Do you have anything to declare?"

I answered, "I declare I'm glad to be home!!" A very small smile crossed his face as he waved me through. Free at last, free at last...

I joined up again with the other three pilots I'd met on the flight and we all ran outside to find a cab as the clock on the wall approached 10 pm. There was a line of cabs waiting and we grabbed the first one. It was 40 miles to the Seattle airport, so, we told the driver that we had an 11 o'clock flight and we'd double his fare if he got us there by 10:45.

He yelled,"Let's go!!"

We threw our bags in the trunk and the four of us jammed into the cab. Soon, we were flying down the highway at breakneck speeds. The driver was swerving in and out of traffic but otherwise keeping his foot to the floor. We looked at each other and I think each of us realized that we had created some sort of monster. This guy was going to get us to the airport on time, even if it killed us. A vision of tomorrows headlines crossed my mind. "Four Vietnam Veterans Killed in Terrible Taxi Crash!" I don't think I even had that much adrenaline flowing the last time I was shot down.

Miraculously, we pulled up in front of the airport at 10:40 and gladly paid off our driver. We were out of breath when we arrived at the ticket counter where the agents were just finishing closing up for the night. They told us what gate the flight was on and to "Run, you might make it."

As we ran through the terminal, the few people still there looked at us rather strangely. I couldn't quite comprehend the looks until one Hippie looking guy yelled, "You guys looking for some babies to kill?"

What the hell was that about?

As we approached the gate, there was a middle aged woman that I was about to run by that had a very serious scowl on her face. When I was a few feet from her, she suddenly spat on the floor in front of me. As I hopped over the spot I heard her mutter, "Baby killers."

I thought,"What the HELL was going on here?" I was totally baffled.

We couldn't help but notice that the airplane at the gate was being pushed back as we handed our tickets to the agent. The agent said, "Just a minute," as she picked up the phone.

We heard her saying, "I've got four Army guys here that want to get on the Chicago flight. Could you ask the Captain if he'll pull back onto the gate to pick them up? Okay, I'll tell them."

"The Captain said he'd pull back in to get you, so, let me have those tickets."

We thanked her profusely. At least someone was treating us like we were human.

As we boarded the aircraft, the Northwest Airlines Captain was there to greet us. He said, "Welcome aboard guys. Glad I could help out."

We thanked him and headed down the aisle through the First Class section. As we passed, a man seated there looked at us and said, in a very snide way, "I can't believe we came back for the likes of you."

I felt like saying, "And Merry Christmas to you too, ASSHOLE!" but I didn't.

Throughout the remainder of my trip to New York, I continued to get dirty looks and snide comments tossed my way. I was pretty tired of it by the time we landed at JFK but it all faded away as I was able to hold my wife again and my son for the first time. Life was good once more.

CHAPTER 27

Life Between Tours

U pon my return from Vietnam, I was assigned as a Cobra instructor pilot to Hunter Army Airfield at Savannah, Georgia. The Cobra training facility was a former Strategic Air Command bomber alert complex at the southwest corner of the airfield and was segregated from the rest of the buildings, offices and hangars on the airbase. It was called "Cobra Hall" and considered to be a very elite facility, devoted to training pilots in the Army's new attack helicopter gunship, the AH-1G Huey Cobra.

I was very pleased to be selected as an instructor pilot since I felt I had a lot of experience I could pass along to the new pilots that would be on their way to Vietnam once they graduated from Cobra Hall. I got two new students every four weeks and shepherded them through two weeks of transition flight training and two weeks of gunnery flight training prior to their graduation and subsequent deployment.

Our normal routine consisted of a morning briefing, followed by a review of the maneuvers we were going to practice that day as well as a review of emergency procedures. Then, my students and I would walk out to the ramp and conduct a pre-flight inspection of our assigned aircraft. Once the pre-flight was completed, one student would climb into the aircraft with me while the other returned to the briefing room to await our return.

After takeoff, we would proceed southbound at low level (200 to 400 feet above the ground) along Interstate 95, which was still under construction at the time, until we approached the town of Richmond Hill. At that point we were allowed to climb to altitude and enter the traffic pattern at Duc Hoa Stagefield, which was just west of the town. While at Duc Hoa, we would demonstrate and allow the student to practice maneuvers like normal takeoffs and landings, running landings and power off autorotations among others.

Once the training period was over, we would retrace our path to Cobra Hall along the deserted I-95. While much of the roadway was complete, there were two sections of the highway, each about a mile long, that had been completed over the swamp but were not connected since the intervening bridges over the Ogeechee River had not yet been erected. These long stretches of roadway were completely deserted and unoccupied since work on the bridges had not started yet. I don't remember if we had permission or just elected to do it but many of the instructor pilots, myself included, would give their students an emergency situation by unexpectedly rolling off the throttle over these sections of roadway and announcing, "Forced Landing!!" to the student. The student was expected to react appropriately by entering autorotation and selecting a spot to land. Since there was only swamp, the river and the highway to choose from, they would, invariably, choose the highway. While remaining very close to the controls in case a recovery was necessary, we allowed the student to complete the power off landing to the surface of the highway. This gave us a feeling of the student's proficiency in handling the aircraft in an emergency situation, while providing the student with a boost in self confidence.

I, and my two students, shared a briefing table with fellow instructor pilot, CW2 Ed Shanahan and his students. Ed and I got along very well and enjoyed working together. One day, after completing a flight, my student and I walked back into the briefing room and noticed that everyone there had very grim looks on their faces. I asked my flight commander, Captain Dick Lawrence, what was going on and he told me that Ed and his student had crashed a short time ago, into the swamp alongside I-95. The student was injured slightly but Ed was killed in the crash. I was shocked. I had just talked to Ed a few minutes ago, on the radio, while at Duc Hoa. How could he be dead?

The subsequent accident investigation revealed that Ed had given the student a forced landing and that something had gone terribly wrong as they attempted to land on the highway.

To make matters worse, I learned in late August of 1969, that my protege and good friend, Francis "Mac" McDowall, had been killed in action at Quan Loi earlier that month. The details of what had happened were sketchy but nonetheless depressing for me.

Sadly, Ed Shanahan was not the only casualty we had at Cobra Hall while I was there. Another flight instructor and his student were killed a short while later when their tail rotor failed. They crashed just short of the runway at Hunter while making an attempt at an emergency landing. Many of the other instructors and students were witnesses to the crash since they were on the ramp at the time. The Army and the helicopter manufacturer assured us that a fix was on the way and, in the meantime, they would step up inspections on the flawed systems to ensure that it wouldn't happen again. None of that made us feel any better but the war would not wait and we had to keep pushing students through the course so they could be shipped off to Vietnam.

I personally observed another casualty one day as I sat in my aircraft on the ramp at Cobra Hall. I was instructing a new student on how to start and run up the aircraft. I was sitting in the front seat of the Cobra while giving the student in the rear seat instructions over the intercom on how to do some of the run-up checks. As I gazed across the ramp, I noticed that a video camera crew was positioned on a platform next to the open rear door on the right side of a Cobra that was running at idle. I remembered that during our briefing that morning, we had been told that the Audiovisual Aids guys would be on the ramp today, making a video for the classroom on how to do all the cockpit procedures in the Cobra.

As I watched, one of the three men on the platform with the camera, jumped down. Apparently, he needed to say something to the pilot in the front seat of the aircraft, where the door opens to the left, and didn't want to run around the front of the aircraft for fear of being seen in the video. Instead, he took off running to go around behind the aircraft. I screamed, "LOOK OUT!!" but because my door was closed and the distance was too great, he never heard me. Being inexperienced with helicopters and aviation in general, the cameraman turned the corner around the tail of the Cobra too soon and there was a spray of red as he ran into the rapidly spinning, and almost invisible, tail rotor. I watched as he collapsed to the ground. The crew of the aircraft immediately shutdown, as did we. By the time I had climbed out of my Cobra and started running across the ramp, the Medevac helicopter from main post was just landing next to the scene. I ran up and saw that the upper half of the cameraman's body had been virtually cut away. There was no medical emergency here, just the gruesome task of recovering a body. As I walked back to my aircraft, I thought, "This place is more dangerous than a combat zone."

While catastrophic incidents like these did happen occasionally, life in Savannah, for Nancy and I, was great. We enjoyed being a family again, having our own apartment and watching our son grow up. We really loved the town, it's history and all the very nice people we met there. I was enjoying flying 60 to 70 hours per month and got a real sense of accomplishment when my students graduated every few weeks.

My commitment to the Army was for three years after graduating from flight school in January of 1968. It was now the spring of 1970 and I knew that the Army would soon ask me if I intended to remain on active duty or get out once my commitment was complete. Nancy and I discussed the issue at great length while keeping in mind that if I chose to stay, it almost certainly meant another tour of duty in Vietnam. We concluded that it would be best if I got out once my commitment was over.

I started taking flying lessons in civilian fixed wing aircraft to get my commercial airplane rating from the FAA. Having this certificate was a requirement for getting a job as an airline pilot which was my ultimate career goal. While the Veterans Administration did pay about 60% of the cost of the training, it was still a financial burden on our new family.

In March of 1970, the Army announced that since the war was going well, their need for pilots was reduced and as a result, they were offering those with less than a year left on their commitment a 6 month drop. This meant that I could be a civilian again by the end of July. I had a lot to accomplish in a few short months. I immediately increased the number of civilian flight lessons I was taking and began assembling my resume.

I took my check-ride with an FAA Flight Inspector and was awarded my Commercial Pilot's License. I immediately included it in the resumes I was sending out and got a few responses that were promising and asking for interviews.

July arrived and I was released from active duty. Nancy, our son Rob and I "temporarily" moved into Nancy's parents house on Long Island while I searched for a job. The interviews I went on for a pilots job seemed to go well but I didn't get any job offers. I talked this over with some of the other applicants and found that these companies were primarily hiring former Air Force pilots since they had jet fixed wing experience.

I started taking flight lessons at Long Island's MacArthur airport to get my Certified Flight Instructor rating in an attempt to be more marketable in the aviation industry. While talking to my instructor one day, he informed me that the FAA was hiring people to be Air Traffic Controllers. All I needed to do was to go take a written exam at the FAA facility on the other side of the airport and since I was a Veteran, I would also get an additional ten points for preferential hiring from the government. While it wasn't my ideal job, it would be a way to stay in aviation while I worked on my qualifications.

At the FAA facility, I met with one of the supervisors and he looked over my resume. He told me when the next test was and what I could do to prepare for it. He reassured me that I would get the ten preferential hiring points since I was a Veteran.

I felt good about how I had done on the test once I completed it. The supervisor had told me that the list of those that passed the test was ordered from those with the highest scores down to those that had just passed and that they would hire from the top of the list down as positions became available.

Several weeks passed and I heard nothing. One day, while I was at the airport, I decided to stop in and talk with the supervisor to see what was going on with the list and to see if my score had been posted yet.

When he met me, he had a piece of paper in his hand and a grim look on his face. I was worried. How could I have done so poorly on the test that it would warrant this look of disappointment? He ushered me into a conference room and had me sit down.

He started with, "Well, Mr. Hartley, you did very well on the exam, in fact, you scored one of the highest grades we've ever had. With your preferential hiring points you are very near the top of the list. However, I have a bit of bad news for you. If you ever quote me on what I'm about to say, I will deny it and since we are the only two in the room, you'll have no way of proving I said it."

I was not getting a warm and fuzzy feeling about the way this was going.

He continued, "As you may have heard, the government has a relatively new program called 'Affirmative Action' that requires us to hire minorities and now, women. Since the FAA has been lagging behind the other agencies in implementing this program, we have been ordered, by the highest levels, to correct this mistake immediately. Unfortunately for you, you are neither a member of a minority nor a female, so, I have to tell you to not expect an offer of employment any time soon. I'm sorry."

I was caught somewhat flat footed by this and didn't quite know what to say. I managed a "Thanks anyway," and walked out, never to return.

Since the prospects of a job in aviation were growing dim, I was forced to take a job in a department store called "Whites" so we could pay our bills and repay my In-Laws for their hospitality. I started out as the assistant manager in the paint department then was quickly promoted to manager. The pay was meager, the hours long but at least I was able to provide for my family and have a few dollars left to continue taking flight lessons.

In the spring of 1971, I heard from my instructor pilot that an organization called Flight Safety, International was expanding to Farmingdale's Republic Airport and may soon be hiring. Flight Safety was an aviation training company originally based at New York's La Guardia Airport and was well respected in the industry. I went to Farmingdale with my resume in hand and sought out the Chief Pilot. He graciously gave me an impromptu interview and told me to come back on Monday morning. He knew that I was only a few hours short of getting my Certified Flight Instructors license from the FAA and said that he would hire me once I was certified. He asked me if I would be able to go to Florida next week to pick up some new planes and ferry them back to Long Island. He took me out to the flightline to show me the many brand new Cessna 150 aircraft that they already had and told me they had only four more to pick up to complete their fleet. He assured me I would be paid very well for the ferry flights and that they had many new students signing up for flight lessons everyday. I immediately agreed to help him out and told him I would see him bright and early Monday morning with my bags packed.

I was elated! I finally had a job as a pilot. I raced home to tell Nancy. I took her out to dinner to break the news and celebrate. She was very happy for me but asked me not to quit my current job until everything was settled and confirmed with Flight Safety because she had a bit of news of her own. She was pregnant and due with our second child in July. I was elated all over again. Things were falling into place for us.

I told her that to play it safe, I would call in sick next week for my paint department job and play them along until everything was firmly in place. She agreed that that was a good idea.

That Sunday was a beautiful spring day and we decided to take Rob and go to the beach as a way to continue our celebration.

We had just finished our picnic lunch at the beach when I looked back to the northwest and saw that the sky was black with an approaching storm front. I told Nancy that we should head home since the roads would soon be jammed with beachgoers trying to evacuate as the storm hit. She agreed and we left for home. As we were crossing one of the bridges connecting the mainland to the beach, the storm hit. The initial gust front was very strong and had debris flying all about. As we struggled to see through the downpour, I thought of the planes at Farmingdale. I turned the radio on and tuned to the news station as quickly as I could. The reporters were talking of damage reports that were flooding in from around the area. Suddenly, a new voice broke in saying, "We have just received a report that many airplanes at Farmingdale's Republic Airport have been damaged as a result of the storm. There was no report of injuries or how serious the damage may be. More on this as we get additional reports."

My heart sank. I knew it was going to be bad. I just knew.

I took Nancy and Rob home then drove over to the airport to see for myself what had happened. As I drove around the perimeter road on the east side of the airport, I almost cried. ALL of Flight Safety's brand new, bright white and blue airplanes were stacked up in a heap against the fence that separated the road from the parking apron of the airport. The aircraft were all severely damaged and in some cases I could not tell where the parts of one airplane ended and another started. Total devastation! Not just the airplanes but to my spirit as well.

The next morning I dutifully, if not enthusiastically, reported to the Chief Pilot as he surveyed the damage. He thanked me for coming but said that he wouldn't be needing my services for many months to come, at best. He told me to stay in touch and wished me good luck in finding a job.

"Good Luck!" Indeed!

It was at this low point that I decided to try to get back into the Army. I began by calling Warrant Officer Branch in Washington and talking to one of the assignments officers. He told me that they were looking for a few pilots with certain qualifications to bring back to active duty and that I seemed to meet the requirements of what they were looking for. He told me there was a board that met every month to review records of those applying to be recalled and I should fill out the forms he was sending me as quickly as possible so that my application would go before the next board in May. I assured him I would and a few days later the blank forms arrived in the mail.

Now it was time to engage in the hardest combat I would ever experience. I had to convince Nancy that this was the right thing to do. In doing this, I was not only going to be exposed to another combat tour in Vietnam, with its inherent dangers, but I would also be committing, not only myself but both of us to a career of at least 20 years in the Army and the unknowns that it might bring. It was not something to be taken lightly. We discussed it logically and, at times, very emotionally over the next several days. We included Nancy's parents, Alma and Arthur Cliff, in our discussions and I was particularly gratified when her father said he was very proud of me for taking such responsibility, whether I was successful or not. (I was never sure if he just said that to get us out of the house but I appreciated it nonetheless.)

I think it was her Dad's endorsement that eventually tipped the decision in my favor. The next day, I mailed off my application to Washington and began waiting. We waited and waited but heard nothing. I called Warrant Officer Branch again and asked if they had received my paperwork and they assured me they had. They told me that the next board would meet in mid May and that I should hear something after that.

The war was winding down and the Army was actually returning whole divisions to the States. This news was not encouraging since, logically, the Army needed less men for the war effort and the recall board may have been told to curtail the number of people they were rehiring.

I was becoming frantic. Nancy's belly was growing larger by the day (Sorry, Dear!) and we had very poor health insurance at the time. I knew that she would be covered by the military if I was recalled prior to the birth, but otherwise, we would have a nice hospital bill to contend with. I called Warrant Officer Branch again and a secretary gave me the phone number of a clerk that handled all the paperwork for the recall board. When I got him on the line, I explained who I was and what I wanted to know.

He replied, "Oh! Yes, Mr. Hartley. I remember seeing your file before it went in front of the board. Very impressive, Sir. Unfortunately, the board has not published its findings yet and I have nothing I can tell you except that the board was given over 1900 applications to look at of which they seriously considered 200. The good news is that you were one of the 200. Call me back tomorrow and I'll let you know if they have published the results."

It was now June of 1971 and Nancy was a month from her due date. I called the clerk of the board again. When he answered he said, "Oh! Congratulations Mr. Hartley, you have been selected for recall to active duty effective July 1, 1971. You will be attending the Cobra Instructor Pilot course at Hunter Army Airfield in Savannah, Georgia prior to your deployment to Vietnam. By the way, I thought you might like to know that you were one of 19 pilots selected for recall out of the 200 that the board considered. Congratulations once again." He said he would send my orders to me as soon as he got them published.

I received my orders by the middle of June. This meant that the impending birth of our child would be covered by military medical insurance which took a great load off of us.

I flew into Savannah on June 30th and was met at the airport by my high school buddy, Tom Higgins. Tom moved to Savannah with his parents after graduation when his father was transferred there by Grumman Aerospace. I had contacted Tom once I found out I would be going to school in Savannah for six weeks and he told me I could stay with him instead of a small room at the BOQ (Bachelor Officers Quarters). He even provided me with a car to get around while I was there. Thanks, Tom.

I signed in on the 1ˢᵗ of July, a Thursday, and promptly began all the paperwork and other tasks necessary to re-enter the Army. My flight classes would begin on Monday morning and I had to go to supply and get my new flight gear and uniforms, have patches sewn on and complete a flight physical before then. It was a very busy time but I wasn't complaining.

I was ready to go on Monday morning as I reported to Cobra Hall for the first time in almost a year. Many of my old fellow instructor pilots were still there to greet me and I felt at home again. Much to my surprise, CW2 Mike Galloway was there and attending the welcome briefing with me. Mike was a classmate of mine in flight school and had taught as an instructor pilot at Cobra Hall with me until we both left the service last July. When I got a chance to talk with him, Mike confirmed he was one of the 18 other pilots recalled to active duty with me. He'd had a tough time finding an aviation job while he was out, just like me, and applied for recall at the same time I did. We made an unofficial wager on who would score highest overall during our repeat of the Cobra Instructor Pilots Course on this go around. It was a gentleman's bet and the loser would have to buy the winner a six pack of his favorite beer as payment.

My classes and flight training were going very well and I was really enjoying being back in the cockpit flying again. After returning from my flight portion that first Friday, the 9ᵗʰ of July, I was told by the Flight School Commandant that I had gotten an urgent call while flying and I should call back immediately. The number on the piece of paper he handed me was my in-laws home phone number on Long Island. My father-in-law answered the phone and informed me that Nancy had gone into labor and was at the local hospital. I told him I would check back in with him later that afternoon to see how things were progressing.

I called again during my lunch break and found out that I was the father of a new baby girl born that morning. He gave me the phone number for Nancy's room at the hospital and I called her right away. She told me that everything went well and that our new daughter, Kimberly

Ann, was doing fine. Then she asked me if there was any way that I could get home over the weekend to see them. I said that I would have to check and I'd let her know.

I found the Flight School Commandant and asked him if such a thing were permitted and he said, "We don't care what you do over the weekend, as long as you are back here by Monday morning."

"Great" I thought, then I called my buddy and roommate, Tom Higgins, and asked him if he would check on flights for me since I would be in class all afternoon and he assured me he would.

When I met up with him later that afternoon, I asked about the tickets and he said, "I've got an even better deal!"

"Oh! No!" I thought.

Tom was somewhat of a Wheeler/Dealer and I was a bit reluctant to get caught up in one of his schemes right now.

Tom explained that he had a friend that was the manager of a "U-Haul" truck rental business in downtown Savannah and that his friend had three trucks that he needed to reposition to New York City over the weekend. The manager said we would be paid well for this service AND be provided with an airline ticket for the return to Savannah. Tom had a big grin on his face when he announced that he had already signed us up for this "great deal."

It wasn't exactly what I had in mind but it would help Nancy and I save some money that we really couldn't afford to spend right now.

At 5:30 that evening, Tom, the manager and I mounted our trucks, pointed them north on I-95 and headed for New York City. It was difficult staying awake during the drive but an abundance of coffee breaks and pit stops helped. At 9:30 Saturday morning, less than 24 hours after my daughter was born, we pulled into the drop off spot in lower Manhattan. Tom and I were given our paychecks and airline tickets and took a cab to Penn Station to catch a train out to Long Island.

By noon we were standing in Nancy's room and I was holding my daughter, Kim. I spent as much time as I could with Nancy and Kim before Tom and I had to go to the airport on Sunday to get our flight back to Savannah. All in all, it was a great trip.

On Monday morning I was present for duty at Cobra Hall and ready to get on with my training. My thoughts returned to the wager that Mike Galloway and I had made and how the scoring would work.

Scoring for the course was a very elaborate process. The course had 3 separate phases to it. The Transition Phase lasted 2 weeks and taught a new Cobra pilot (and refreshed an old one) on how to fly the aircraft. The second phase was 2 weeks of aerial gunnery, where grading relied heavily on your accuracy with the weapons systems. And, finally, there was the MOI or Methods of Instruction phase for 2 weeks. This phase required you to demonstrate a maneuver while describing in detail what you were doing and how you were manipulating the controls to accomplish the maneuver within acceptable standards thus demonstrating that you could teach a new student how to fly the Cobra. Each day was split into a half day of academic classroom instruction and half a day of flight training. The classroom instruction had a ten question quiz each morning and a 100 question test at the end of each phase. Mike and I did not miss a single question on any of the written tests. We were tied so far.

The scoring on the flight portion was by a check ride at the conclusion of each phase. These check rides were given by Standardization Instructor Pilots (SIP) from the Flight Standards section of Cobra Hall. They were the elite instructor pilots that had an extensive amount of instructor experience in the Cobra and were highly regarded as experts. Each check ride consisted of two scores. The first one was a score that your everyday instructor believed you would score on your end of phase check ride with the SIP and, naturally, the other was the actual score you received from the SIP. These two scores would be averaged to produce your final phase score.

Mike and I were each put up for our first phase check ride with a 100% by our instructors. We each scored 100% on our actual rides.

At the end of the gunnery phase, Mike and I were each put up for our check rides with 100% and we each scored 100% on our actual rides. Still all tied up.

Finally, it was time for our MOI check rides. We knew that our final scores would depend heavily on who we drew as our SIP check pilots. That morning we found out that the random drawing assigned Mike a very well liked and eminently fair SIP while I drew Chief Warrant Officer Jerry Bourquin as mine. Jerry was known as a very strict, by the book, no fooling around kind of guy. He had acquired the nick name of "Butcher" Bourquin because of the number of students he would fail on the check rides he conducted. When he was announced as my check pilot, there was a collective audible groan emitted by those in the room. I could see the pity in their eyes and several of them moved back away from me as if I had caught some highly contagious and deadly disease.

I really wasn't too concerned because I was quite confident in my abilities and knew the standards for each maneuver cold. I knew that Jerry would try to rattle me to see if I could keep it all together but that was his job at this point. Jerry was in the rear seat of the Cobra and I was at the instructor pilots position in the front seat. I would demonstrate a maneuver and then allow my "student." Jerry, to practice it. He would invariably screw it up and I was expected to critique his performance and offer guidance on how he could improve. Finally, Jerry said, "Okay! Let's head back. I have the controls, you take a break." We went through the procedure for positively exchanging who was in control of the aircraft and I relaxed a bit as I relinquished the controls.

As Jerry turned us toward Cobra Hall, he said, "Well, Bob, I have to tell you that I am very impressed. As you know, a lot of people think I'm a hard ass but all I want out of them is to perform like you did today. It was a pleasure flying with you."

Whoa! That was very high praise coming from a man that didn't hand it out very often. I felt very honored. (And pretty confident that I was going to win the bet Mike and I had.)

My hopes were all but dashed when Mike came up to me as I walked out of the Men's room after returning to Cobra Hall. He had a big smile on his face and simply said, "One hundred and one hundred."

I knew that this meant he had been put up for his check ride with a 100% and had been given a grade of 100% on his ride. Damn! The best I could do was a tie. Just then, Jerry came out of the Men's room and took me in tow as we headed for the briefing room.

When we walked back into the briefing room, the other students and their instructors were furtively stealing glances at me as if to determine how badly I was injured. Jerry sensed that this was going on and decided to play a trick on them. Everyone knew that "Satisfactory" grade slips were white in color. The grade slips used by instructors to estimate the grade a student would get on a check ride were green in color. But a "Failing" grade slip was pink in color. As we sat down for the debriefing and critique, Jerry reached into his bag and pulled out a stack of "Pink Slips". As I glanced around the room, I could see that most of those present were wincing and mouthing the words, "I'm sorry!"

I tried very hard not to smile and give away Jerry's secret. He announced in a voice loud enough for all present to hear, "Bob, I'm afraid I'm going to have to give you a.... 100% on your check ride today."

All the instructors and students in the room now had their mouths gaping open and their eyes looked like they were going to pop out of their heads. Jerry and I slowly looked around the room with broad smiles on our faces and those present knew they had been had.

As they recovered from their shock, they started coming by me, slapping me on my back and congratulating me as if I had scored the winning touchdown in the homecoming game. The revery was interrupted by Jerry when he said, "Okay, Okay! Let's get this paperwork done. Let's see what your instructor put you up with for your ride."

My instructor for the MOI portion was CW2 Terry Brooks and he had been impressed with my performance from the start. Terry knew of my "Competition" with Mike Galloway and that, so far, we were tied on our scores. I was sure that Terry had put me up with a 100 for my check ride and with Jerry Bourquin's announcement that he was giving me a 100, Mike and I would be the first pilots to complete the course with perfect scores.

Jerry opened my training records folder and flipped back the green grade slip to see what Terry had put me up with. I watched the smile on his face faded away as he turned the folder around for me to see the score. I looked down and 99% glared back at me!

Jerry said, "I'm sorry, Bob, but you got robbed."

Just then Terry Brooks walked into the room and stopped abruptly as he noticed everyone there scowling at him.

He blurted out, "WHAT????"

"Butcher" Bourquin responded by saying, "I'm sure you had a good reason for putting Bob up for his check ride with a 99 instead of a 100, but what was it?"

Terry answered saying, "Nobody ever makes a 100."

To which Jerry responded, "Bob just did!"

Terry just stood there with his mouth hanging open, looking as if he had just been struck by a bolt of lightning. Finally, I said, "That's okay Terry, the bet was just for a six pack of beer. I'll get over it." But I never did.

At graduation that afternoon, Mike was recognized as the Top Graduate and the first student to attain a "Perfect Score" on the course. I congratulated him and presented him with the six pack of beer to settle our bet.

I flew back to Long Island and Nancy and I got busy getting our family moved into an apartment in the town next to the one her parents lived in. She and the kids would be comfortable there for the next year while I was in Vietnam. I got to spend a few weeks with them in the new place prior to starting my trek back to the War Zone.

CHAPTER 28

Back to Combat

My flight back to Vietnam took off from Travis Air Force Base near San Francisco. I recall being very depressed as I watched the Golden Gate Bridge slide by under us as we headed out over the Pacific. We stopped in Honolulu for refueling and I remembered the good time Nancy and I had there when we met for R&R during my first tour of duty. Maybe we could do that again this time.

Our next fueling stop was at Andersen Air Force Base on Guam. As we sat in the line up for takeoff, I was drawn back into the warrior mode because there was a flight of several B-52 bombers ahead of us waiting to launch. Each of these monsters were bristling with hundreds of bombs hanging on racks under their wings and many more, I was sure, in their bomb bays. These heavily loaded beasts were, no doubt, headed for Vietnam. I could no longer see the B-52s as our aircraft turned onto the taxi way leading to the runway. The three bombers were directly ahead of our aircraft, but I would have a very good view of them as they took off since I was seated at the window on the right side and the 11,000 foot runway stretched out in that direction also.

The first indication we had that one was taking off was a thunderous noise that began shaking our aircraft as the eight engines on the lead bomber went to maximum thrust. I noticed that the left side windows had darkened almost as if it had become night on that side of the plane. This was due to the huge plume of black smoke being emitted by the engines of the bomber. It seemed an incredibly long period of time from when I first hear the rumble of the engines until I could finally see the big black machine slowly rolling into view in my window. He lumbered down the runway, never seeming to gain any speed. Soon the body of the aircraft was no longer visible since the black smoke was obscuring it but I could still make out the wingtips. The plane was nearly two thirds of the way down the runway before the wingtips, and the attached outrigger landing struts, slowly released their hold on the runway and began to arc skyward. As the bomber approached the end of the runway, the wingtips were now bent upward at an impossible angle as they strained to lift the gargantuan load beneath them. The bomber struggled into the air as it crossed the end of the runway and I heaved a sigh of relief. As I continued to watch, I thought my relief may have been premature as the aircraft settled back towards the ground. Suddenly, it disappeared altogether and I waited for the the inevitable fireball to appear.

No fireball!

The next bomber in line was now starting his takeoff roll. Didn't he know that the first guy had obviously crashed? What I didn't know was that the runway ended at the top of a 500 foot cliff on the northeast end of the island and the first aircraft had simply traded altitude for airspeed once clear of the terrain, making it appear as if he had run into the ground. As the second bomber was getting airborne, I could see the black dot that was the first bomber, slowly climbing back into the sky about 5 miles east of the island. I was relieved to know that these guys actually knew what they were doing even though I considered it very dangerous and frightening to watch.

Before I knew it, we were touching down at the airbase at Cam Rahn Bay. We were processed very quickly and got our bunk assignments for the night. The great majority of those on my flight were soldiers and officers on their first trip to Vietnam. When they found out that I was a second tour guy, they bombarded me with questions about all kinds of things. They wanted to know about the best units to be assigned to, the safest places to get assigned to, what it was like being in a fire fight and on and on. I even had one guy ask me what it was like to get shot! I stared at him for a moment before I said, "I've never been shot!!" Immediately he seemed somewhat disappointed. I wasn't.

The following morning, we were all at the admin processing center to fill out the blizzard of paperwork that was thrown at new arrivals. The room had about 20 desks each manned by a clerk that was either an Army Specialist 4th class or an E-5 Sergeant. When my name was called, I sat down at the desk of the of the clerk that had summoned me and handed him my records. He flipped open the folder and immediately said, "Oh! You're a second tour guy and a Cobra instructor pilot. Where do you want to go, Sir?"

Dumbfounded I replied, "What?"

He responded, "What unit would you like to be assigned to?"

"Are you serious? I've never had a choice before," I said.

He clarified things a bit by saying, "You pick a unit you like and if I have an opening there for a Cobra instructor pilot, I'll assign you there. It'll make you happy and make things much easier for me. So, where do you want to go, Sir?"

I immediately answered, "The 2nd of the 20th Aerial Rocket Artillery with the First Cavalry Division." My old unit.

The clerk explained that the First Cavalry had gone back to the States in April of that year, but they left a brigade behind that might have an opening. He checked and said that the 2nd of the 20th had been re-designated and was now F Battery of the 79th Artillery.

The clerk leafed through some more papers and said, "Sorry, I had a slot there but I just filled it yesterday. Maybe you know the guy. It was a CW2 Michael Galloway."

I almost fell out of my chair. It was bad enough that Mike had beaten me going through the Instructor Pilot Course at Hunter but now he had taken my dream job away, to boot. I'd have to get in touch with him to register a formal complaint.

As I was recovering from the news, the clerk was now saying, "I do have an opening in the only other Aerial Rocket Artillery unit, the 4th of the 77th Artillery with the 101st Airborne Division up in I Corps."

"Bingo!" I said. "That's my second favorite place to go."

The Specialist said, "Okay, Sir! Consider it done. I'll have your orders published this afternoon and you can catch a flight out tomorrow morning."

The clerk was true to his word. I got my orders that afternoon and promptly booked myself on a C-130 flight out of Cam Rahn for the next morning.

The C-130 landed at Hue Phu Bai, the airport that serves the Imperial City of Hue. After in-processing at the 101st Airborne Division Headquarters at nearby Camp Eagle, I caught a ride in a jeep that was going back to the airport. My new unit, "A" Battery, 4th Battalion of the 77th Field Artillery, was located there on the north side of the runway.

I reported in to the orderly room and turned in my records for them to process. Next I met the Commanding Officer and some of the other officers that were in a meeting with him. The Commander then introduced me to another second tour guy and said we could bunk together. My new roommate was CW2 Carl Heinze who had been a 101st Airborne Huey lift ship pilot on his first tour of duty but had since been qualified in the Cobra and had graduated from the Aviation Maintenance Officers Course. Carl and I got along very well right from the start. Carl would be the new unit maintenance officer and I was the new unit instructor pilot, and together, we would have a significant impact on how things ran in the unit.

The quarters we shared with all the other officers in the unit was a two story wooden barracks type building. The first floor, which was already totally occupied, had 12 double occupancy rooms with outside entries. The second floor was a completely empty open bay, accessed from the outside by a set of wooden stairs on either end of the building. The commander said we could section off a piece of the bay and enclose it with all the lumber that was readily available in the area. Carl and I set to work and soon had a room that was twice as large as any on the first floor and had far better decor since we had learned during our first tour how to wheel and deal, trade and barter to get what we wanted. We had Air Force beds with real mattresses, comfortable chairs and authentic desks where most of the others were still sleeping on cots and air mattresses and using homemade desks. We had constructed a very nice spot that we could be comfortable in for the next year.

Carl got right to work. He met with the outgoing maintenance officer to get up to speed on the differences specific to the 101st Airborne Division's maintenance procedures. In the meantime, I was waiting for a Cobra Standardization Instructor Pilot (SIP) from division headquarters to come down from Camp Eagle to give me the check ride I needed before I could start to do my job.

Finally, after two weeks, I was notified that the SIP was in operations and ready to give me my ride. I grabbed my helmet and headed for Ops, thinking, "Let's get this over with."

As I walked in, I was somewhat stunned and simultaneously pleased to see that my "Check Pilot" was CW2 Jim Cathy. The last time I had seen Jim was at Cobra Hall over one year ago just before I got out of the Army. Jim broke into a broad grin when he saw me, stretched out his hand to shake mine and said, "I'm really glad you're here!"

At first I just thought he was trying to be funny but he explained, "I'm short, but my boss told me I couldn't go home until I found a replacement and," he paused for effect just before blurting out like it was a game of tag, "YOU'RE IT!!" He then added, "And don't worry, you couldn't fail this check ride if you wanted to. Let's go have some fun."

The author at the controls of an AH-1G Cobra

And we did. We took turns flying the Cobra and doing maneuvers to include a bunch of low level-high speed forced landings where one of us would cut the throttle on the other and then be told what spot on the runway we would have to set the aircraft down on. This maneuver was started by flying at 140 to 150 knots and fifty feet or less in altitude adjacent to the runway. The flying pilot would maneuver the aircraft using turns, climbs and descents to squeeze the last bit of inertia out of the rotor and airspeed, all to touchdown on the exact spot that had been called, without overshooting. We were having such great fun that we didn't notice that we had drawn a crowd. Several of the troops that had been working on the airfield had walked to the edge of the runway to watch us. Some were now clapping while others gave us a thumbs up.

Jim said, "Well I guess your audience approves and so do I. You pass! Let's go back to parking." Jim called the control tower and told them that we would like to return to the Dragon's Den, the name of my unit's parking area on the ramp.

Tower replied, "Roger, you're cleared to the Dragon's Den and thanks, that was a great airshow."

I thought, "Yeah! That was pretty good considering I hadn't flown since mid August and it was now mid October."

As he filled out my grade slip, Jim mentioned that he would be going home near the end of November and that I could expect official orders to Camp Eagle about that time. He said he was going to designate me as an SIP right now so that if he needed help giving check rides in the next month, I'd be available to assist. I told him it didn't matter to me, he'd just have to clear it with my CO.

As it turned out, there would be no scheduling problems at all since there was virtually no combat going on in our area. We did get launched on some missions but it usually turned out to be a small skirmish or a sniper taking potshots at some of our guys on patrol.

All was going well until the CO got up one morning during our daily briefing and said we were tasked to send six Cobras out to the A Shau Valley to provide cover and firepower for a recon operation that was being conducted there. Immediately on hearing those words, I sank into deep despair. I was sure that this trip into the Valley of the Shadow of Death would be my last. I absolutely hated that place.

The author and several crew chiefs and armorers
preparing Cobra for mission to the A Shau

Later that morning we launched the six Cobras and headed west
toward the Valley. We rendezvoused with the scout aircraft near Camp
Eagle and the whole gaggle of helicopters headed up into the mountains.
We passed Fire Support Base Bastogne and continued our climb. We
turned a corner around a low hill and there, stretched out before us,
was the A Shau Valley. The hair on the back of my neck stood up and
I immediately felt that we were being watched by a thousand eyes. The
best term to describe what I was feeling was "spooky."

The scout aircraft began doing their sweeps of the valley floor,
checking the road, which was actually the Ho Chi Minh trail, for
any signs of recent activity. I was expecting all hell to break loose at
any moment. Then it happened....NOTHING!! Absolutely nothing. I
couldn't believe that there was no activity at all. The scouts slowly and
methodically worked their way northward along the road, past A Luoi
airstrip, past what had been Hamburger Hill and past where I had been
shot down with Frank Thornhill and Ben Stevens. They then turned a
slight corner in the road and we flew past LZ Tiger. I had a flashback

to my first combat mission on April 17th 1968 when I watched a Huey with a full load of troops fall to the ground, burst into flames and kill all aboard, except the crew chief, while on approach to this LZ. Then my eyes located it. Unbelievably, the wreckage of that burned out aircraft was still there. Now I was totally creeped out. Luckily, this was where the road crossed back into Laos and our recon was complete. I wanted out of here so badly that I could scream. We all climbed to altitude and proceeded back toward Camp Eagle. The mission was at an end and so were my nerves.

Life at Phu Bai was very sedate and that was just fine by me. I enjoyed conducting classes for our pilots on a range of subjects including preflight inspection criteria, aerodynamics, aerial gunnery and instrument flight procedures to name a few. I made myself available to all the pilots in the unit that wanted to go fly with me so they could practice all the emergency procedures in the Cobra that they were restricted from practicing without an instructor pilot on board. This helped them develop proficiency and build their confidence until they felt that they could handle any emergency situation that might arise. Normally, they only got to practice these maneuver once a year on their annual check ride which, I knew, was not enough. We made it fun by turning each maneuver into a competition like Jim Cathy and I had done.

Actual fire missions were few and far between. The ones that did pop up were minor in nature and almost never required another section to be launched to augment the first one. Additionally, there was almost a total lack of incoming rockets or mortar fire. It was like the enemy had completely moved out of the I Corps area.

During my time off, I usually hung out with Carl while he went about his business as the maintenance officer. As I mentioned, Carl was a wheeler, dealer and he applied his skills to his job as well. When he needed a part for an aircraft and the Army's supply lines couldn't produce it in a reasonable amount of time, he would call other units until he located the part and then "negotiate" with the owner by offering other parts and/ or services to complete the deal.

Carl and I had come to an agreement that one of the things he could offer a reluctant dealer was a ride in a Cobra helicopter. Quite often if the reluctant part supplier was clerk in a warehouse somewhere, he would jump at this opportunity to break out of his boring life and, in turn, we would get our critical part. The payoff often meant that I had to provide the "orientation flight" to the parts supplier since I was an instructor pilot and authorized to conduct "orientation flights" for non pilots with the commander's approval. It might sound a bit shady but was actually quite legal and helped us maintain our aircraft in combat ready condition.

CHAPTER 29

It's a Dangerous World

I was hanging out with Carl one day in the maintenance hangar and he said that he had to walk down the ramp to another unit to get a part that they had and wanted to know if I'd walk with him. I said, "Sure" and we headed out.

It was a beautiful morning and the sun was shining brightly as it climbed into the sky behind us. Our route took us past the aircraft "Hot" refueling pads on the ramp. Though inherently dangerous, if done correctly it was generally a safe procedure.

As we approached the pads, we had to refrain from talking since there was a Cobra on the pad closest to us that was running at flight idle while refueling and the noise of the engine and rotor was too loud to permit conversation. As an instructor pilot, I always looked over such operations to make sure that safety procedures were being followed properly. In this case all seemed to be in order. The rear seat pilot had exited the aircraft and closed his door behind him. He had properly grounded the aircraft with the grounding cables provided at the refuel point to prevent static electricity sparks that might start a fire. He had his helmet on and his visor down and a stable stance as he put the fuel nozzle into the open port on the right side of the aircraft. The open fuel port was only a few feet in front of the right side engine air intake, so, great care had to be exercised to prevent fuel from being splashed into the engine. The front seat pilot had his helmet on, visor down and his door open on the left side of the aircraft to allow him easy egress if there should be an emergency. He had his hands on the controls and seemed prepared to shut the engine down if the need arose. I was satisfied that this crew was properly performing the task.

When Carl and I were about 30 feet from the Cobra we heard a loud "POP." It was not an explosion like an incoming artillery round or a rifle being fired but more like someone had blown up a paper bag and popped it by clapping their hands together, only this POP was about 10 times louder. Carl and I looked at each other in puzzlement, and I noticed that the pilot that was doing the refueling was also looking around, trying to figure out what the noise was. As I looked at him, something was moving behind him and caught my attention. As I refocused on the movement I saw that it was the paint on the engine compartment door. The paint was bubbling! Each bubble was about 5 inches in diameter an once it got about 5 inches high, it would burst open, deflate and the process would start over. There were no flames to be seen, so, I was very puzzled at what was happening. It only took a few seconds but now the paint was finally starting to turn black and was emitting black smoke.

"FIRE!!" Both Carl and I began shouting at the same time. The pilot doing the refueling turned and looked at us as we shouted. I was pointing at the engine compartment while simultaneously drawing the edge of my right hand across my throat in the universally understood sign to shutdown the engine.

The refueling pilot turned around and looked at the engine compartment which was now almost totally black but still showed no sign of flames. He immediately stopped fueling, removed the nozzle and dragged the hose to its full length as he ran from the aircraft.

Meanwhile, the front seat pilot had successfully shutdown the engine and slid out of the aircraft onto the pad. He was now scrambling on all fours to get as far away from the aircraft as possible.

Carl and I took shelter behind a revetment wall about 60 feet from the aircraft and were joined there by the refueling pilot. We asked him if the aircraft had any ammunition on board and he said, "No rockets, just some minigun ammo."

We peeked back out at the scene and saw that the rotor had come to a stop and the aircraft was now totally engulfed in flames, real, visible, yellow and orange flames. As we watched, a firetruck pulled up and began dousing the flames with foam. The flames were extinguished very quickly and we resumed our walk to complete our original mission. Before parting ways with the refueling pilot, I told him who I was and that I had observed he and his copilot properly performing the refueling procedures. If his commanding officer gave him any grief over the loss of the aircraft, he could call me and I would verify that they had done everything correctly. He thanked me and we left him standing there looking at the smoking heap that had been his aircraft.

Carl and I were involved in another incident on the ramp only a few days later. I feel compelled to warn readers that the following story is very gruesome and if you are somewhat squeamish, you may want to skip this section.

Anyway, Carl had asked me to go on a maintenance test flight with him and we were in the unit operations center preparing for the flight. Everyone there was shocked when we heard the unmistakable sound of rockets being launched very close by, on the ramp. We ran out onto the ramp to see what had happened. We immediately noticed two corkscrewing smoke trails that climbed up and away from the section of ramp to our right. Our eyes followed the smoke trails back down to their point of origin, a Cobra in a revetment of the unit next to ours. Strangely, the Cobra was not running and, in fact, the rotor blades were still tied down. As the noise of the rockets faded, we saw a soldier running toward the aircraft. He was taking off his jungle fatigue shirt and rolling it into a ball.

It looked like he might need help, so, Carl and I began running toward the Cobra too. The aircraft was facing to our left as we approached from its left side. The revetment had 3 walls. One in front, one behind and one on the far side of the Cobra. Each of these walls was about 8 feet tall, 3 feet thick and made out of interlocking steel planking. The 3 foot space between planks had been filled with dirt to absorb any shrapnel from incoming rounds.

As we got closer, we could see that there was a person laying on the ground near the rear wall. It turned out that the running soldier was a medic and was taking off his shirt to put under the head of the person on the ground that had obviously been injured. As we came up behind the medic we could hear the injured man on the ground moaning in pain saying, "I can't feel my legs". The medic was cradling his head in his hand as he placed the rolled up shirt under it while saying to him, "You'll be okay, just rest. No! Don't look down there, look at me."

As I came around from behind the medic I could now see why the medic didn't want the injured man to look down. There was a 8 inch diameter hole that began just under the man's ribcage and stretched down to his navel. I could see completely through his body to the ground beneath. The wound had been caused by the exhaust from the departing rocket and, as a result, had been mostly cauterized by the intense heat of the back blast. The medic briefly turned to us to say, "Check on the other guy." as he pointed under the right wing of the Cobra.

Looking in the direction the medic was pointing, we could see another person sprawled on the ground in front of the right wing of the aircraft. We ran up the right side of the aircraft and around the wingtip. The man was laying face down just in front of the rocket pods and there was a considerable amount of blood around his body. Carl got to him first and rolled him onto his back. It was very obvious that the man was dead. Apparently, he had been standing on the steps to the back seat while leaning out to look at the rocket pod when the rockets were fired. The four folding fins on the tail of the rockets snap forward and lock into position, much like a switchblade knife, to stabilize the rocket in flight as it leaves the rocket tube. Each of these thin metal fins are about 8 inches long and two of them hit the man as the rocket went by him. One of the fins had sliced across his neck, nearly severing his head from his body while the other fin had raked across his chest exposing his heart and lungs. By glancing into the cockpit, I could tell that the aircraft's battery was on and the weapons system was in the ARMED position. I ducked under the rocket pods and climbed the steps to the cockpit where I turned off the MASTER ARM switch and the aircraft battery. The aircraft was now safe again.

Since we knew there was nothing that could be done for the man in front of the rocket pods, we walked back toward where the medic was still leaning over the man near the rear wall. As we passed behind the wing of the Cobra, I noticed that there was a rocket system test kit sitting on the ground behind the right inboard rocket pod. Apparently, the two men had been testing the rocket system when the accident happened. The medic turned to us and simply said, "He's gone." Referring to the man he had been assisting.

We told him that the man in front of the rocket pods was dead, too. The three of us just stood there shaking our heads in disbelief and wondering how such a thing could happen.

Other people began to arrive on the scene and we let them take over and handle the situation. Carl and I were asked by the unit's commander to write up a statement on what we observed for the investigation that was sure to follow. We complied and when we turned our statements into that unit's first sergeant the next day, he filled us in on the information they had gathered to that point. He said that the unit's armorer had sent the two victims, who were new to the unit, out to the aircraft with the rocket system test kit and was going to show them how to conduct a test of the system. He stated that he told them, "Don't touch anything until I get there."

Apparently, the victims had decided that since they had done this test in school back in the States, they could show their expertise and initiative by having it completed by the time the armorer arrived at the aircraft. The only difference between the school and the flight line was that this aircraft was loaded with live rockets where the aircraft back at school was not loaded at all. They also didn't know that it was not necessary for the aircraft to be running in order to fire the rockets, just turning on the aircraft's battery would suffice. The man that was standing behind the rocket pod was touching the test kit's wire leads to the firing contact to determine if there was adequate firing voltage to the contact. The other man had turned on the aircraft battery, the armament switches and had his finger on the firing button. He was leaning away from the cockpit to look at his partner for a thumbs up or thumbs down as each tube was tested. They only tested one tube. When the man with his hand on the firing button pressed it, the number one pair of rockets fired. The rocket back blast punched a hole through the man behind the pod and blew him back to the rear revetment wall. The man leaning out of the cockpit was then slashed by the rocket's fins as it passed him. Both rockets went through the front revetment wall and had their fuses jammed by the impact since they had not completed the arming process before hitting the wall. As the rockets passed through the wall, the stabilizing fins were stripped off and the rockets began a wild, corkscrewing flight as they emerged and climbed into the sky over the ramp, then the runway and directly over the control tower. The only good news was that they didn't explode when they landed because their fuzes had been jammed.

Carl and I decided we needed to conduct a class for all the personnel in our unit to review all aspects of safety around our aircraft. Our commander agreed with us and made the class mandatory for everyone under his command. I like to think that our class may have prevented any similar tragedies from occurring in our unit.

CHAPTER 30

Moving On

The week after Thanksgiving, 1971, I was called by our commanding officer and asked to stop by his office, he had something for me. When I arrived, he presented me with a set of orders that reassigned me to 101ˢᵗ Airborne Division's Headquarters at Camp Eagle. I had been designated as the new Cobra Standardization Instructor Pilot (SIP) for the division and was to report for duty the first week of December. Jim Cathy had completed his year and had designated me as his replacement at the Division Flight Standards Office. I had mixed emotions about the assignment. I would miss all the guys I was just getting to know in Alpha Battery, including Carl, and would have to make new friends at my new job. Most regular line pilots in the various aviation units in the division, considered the handful of SIPs at the Flight Standards Office to be elitist snobs. They knew that the SIPs rarely flew on combat missions, so, were reluctant to take advice or constructive criticism from someone that was not flying under the same stressful conditions that they were. Besides, everyone knew that if their unit failed one of the unannounced inspections that the Flight Standards Team was required to conduct, the unit commander could be relieved of his command and the individuals that failed portions of the inspection, like check rides, may get a below average score on their OER and that would threaten their chances of promotion. To give you an idea of how well liked we were, consider this common saying among line pilots. The refrain was, "I'd rather have a sister in a whorehouse than a brother in Flight Standards!" It just gives you a warm, fuzzy feeling about your job, don't you think?

The good news about my assignment was that I would be less exposed to combat, so, I was happy to write to Nancy to tell her of my new job.

I packed my bags and moved up to Camp Eagle the first week of December. I met the other SIPs assigned to Flight Standards, one for each of the different aircraft in the division. There was an SIP for the UH-1 Huey, one for the OH-6 "Loach", one for the CH-47 Chinook, myself for the Cobra and an Instrument Flight Examiner that was qualified in all the aircraft except the Cobra. They were very gracious in welcoming me to the team. The building we slept in was right next to the one that served as our office. It was little more than a tent, like the one I spent my entire first tour living in. It was originally designed to be a G.P. medium tent frame with a wooden floor but at some point, the tent was dispensed with and replaced with plywood walls and a corrugated tin roof.

Our little complex was only about 40 meters from the Division's Headquarters that sat atop a hill in the middle of Camp Eagle. I thought it odd that all of the personnel at Camp Eagle slept in these "up-graded" tents while the rest of the Division, at Phu Bai, resided in the 2 story wooden barracks like the one Carl and I had shared. The living conditions here at Camp Eagle were certainly less comfortable than those at Phu Bai. Even the Division Commander, a two star general, slept in a converted tent.

I settled into my new job and got used to the routine that had us conducting unannounced inspections on different units each week. I would conduct check rides with each unit's instructor pilots, their maintenance officer as well as several randomly selected line pilots. While most were a bit rusty on some of the maneuvers they only got to practice occasionally during the year, almost all were able to complete the maneuvers within acceptable standards. While I was getting quite a bit of flight time, I had to admit to myself that, while it was a relatively safe job, it was also a bit boring. I kept telling myself that I had a family back home that wanted me to be as safe as possible but I couldn't help feeling guilty about this cushy job while the other pilots were facing combat each day.

During the third week of December, it was announced that the Bob Hope USO Christmas Show was coming to Camp Eagle that year. This brightened everyone's spirits significantly over the next few days. When the show finally arrived, I was able to get a seat, even if it was toward the back of the huge audience. Bob was fantastic, as usual, and all the soldiers there went crazy when the bevy of beauties Bob brought with him, showed up on stage. I can't remember if it was Joey Heatherton or Raquel Welch or, perhaps, Anne Margret that accompanied him that year but the troops certainly appreciated the performance. Many of those battle hardened soldiers were moved to tears as Bob lead us all in the singing of "Silent Night" at the end of the show. Quite an experience. Thanks for the memory, Bob.

One of the other forms of entertainment that kept the troops occupied was something they called the "Daily Rat Races." Before I tell this story, I must make it clear that I did NOT participate in this practice nor did I condone it. I am merely reporting what took place. I must also advise you, the reader, that this involves animal cruelty and you may want to skip ahead if are particularly sensitive to it.

My story starts as I was leaving the Flight Standards office at Camp Eagle. I was tagging along with several of the other instructor pilots as they headed for the mess hall for lunch. We were passing the Division's Headquarters and I noticed a crowd of about 60 soldiers standing around on the parade field in front of HQ. The field was about 30 meters by 30 meters in size and had a flag pole in the center flying Old Glory. Arrayed around the parade field were various offices of the Division which included the Division's Command Post and the

Commanding General's personal quarters. The buildings were exactly like our Flight Standards office and our attached living quarters.

I was chatting with the other instructors as we walked but my attention was drawn back to the crowd of soldiers when they suddenly burst into cheers. I asked my companions, "What's going on over there?"

The other three stopped walking and turned to look at me as if I were a complete dunce. Almost simultaneously they said, "The daily rat races." As if I should know what that meant.

The look on my face must have revealed that I still had no idea what they were talking about because one of them said, "The best way to explain this is for you to watch it." And he lead me toward the crowd.

The other two instructors said, "We'll see you at the mess hall. Have fun."

My escort lead me through the crowd until we were standing shoulder to shoulder with the other soldiers. They were forming a circle around the flagpole and were intently watching two men at the base of the pole who were bent over, tending to some sort of apparatus on the ground. I noticed that there were four concentric circles drawn in the dirt with the flagpole as their common center. The first circle was about 5 meters in diameter, the next 10 meters, then 15 and 20 meters, somewhat like a target with the flagpole as the bulls-eye. As I looked around, I noticed that many of the soldiers had money in their hands and seemed to be making bets. I was still confused as the two men near the flagpole stood up and announced, "Ready, Set, Go!"

I could now see that the apparatus on the ground was a "live" rat trap with one of the rodents inside. One of the two men had just doused the critter with a liquid while the other threw a lit match onto the animal while simultaneously opening the trap. The rat took off running while flames engulfed its body. The rat finally expired near the 10 meter ring and some soldiers cheered while others groaned in disappointment. Money changed hands as bets were settled and I turned to my escort and said, "Okay! I've seen enough, let's go." We headed off to the mess hall even though I was no longer hungry.

About a week later I heard that the Commanding General's quarters had burned to the ground. Apparently, those conducting the "Daily Rat Races" had trapped "Super-Rat." When they set him aflame, he made it not only to the 20 meter ring but well passed the circle of soldiers who last saw his flaming ass as he disappeared under the Commanding General's quarters. Those assembled beat a hasty retreat as the C.G.'s quarters burst into flames. As you might imagine, the C.G. was not amused and the "Daily Rat Races" were canceled...permanently!!

The middle of January brought exciting news. The 101st Airborne Division was ordered to "Stand Down" from combat operations and prepare for redeployment to the United States. Rumors ran rampant. Some speculation said that everyone with the division was going home while others said that you had to have 6 months in country to qualify for return to the States. It turned out that the second rumor was correct and since I had less than 4 months in country, I would be reassigned to another unit in Vietnam. Sadly, I wasn't the only one in the Flight Standards Office that this rule applied to. Four of us would be remaining behind and since we had no flight duties to tend to, it was decided that we would be sent back to Hue Phu Bai and given a section of the defensive perimeter to guard while we waited on orders for our new assignments.

Pulling guard duty while everyone else cleaned equipment and packed up to go home was not much fun. We were given a 50 meters section of the wire to guard and a small shack behind it to live in. We split into two teams of two, with one team on duty while the other team relaxed or slept. Since the mess halls were shutting down and packing up, we had nothing to eat but "C" rations. Yum!

At first, it didn't seem too bad but as the weeks went by and there were fewer and fewer U.S. soldiers around, we began getting very nervous and were checking on our orders twice a day. Luckily, the enemy had decided to leave us alone so the division would leave and they could slip into the void after it was gone. I'm sure they considered that if they attacked, the U.S. Army brass may have changed their minds and kept the division in place. We were starting to feel like General Custer at the Little Bighorn when headquarters finally replaced us with ARVN troops that were now arriving to take over defense of the airport. We all heaved a sigh of relief when our orders arrived and we grabbed the first flight out.

My orders were to report to the 5th Aviation Detachment at Vung Tau around the second week of February. I was stunned by my good fortune. The 5th Aviation Detachment was similar to the Flight Standards unit in the 101st Airborne but it's purview included the entire Pacific Theater of Operations to include ALL units in Vietnam. I had been chosen to be one of six Cobra SIPs in charge of standardization training for all Cobra pilots in Vietnam. Our primary job was to train experienced line pilots to be instructor pilots in the Cobra and to administer check rides to current instructor pilots and other standardization instructor pilots. We were considered the ultimate authority on all things about the Cobra. It was quite an honor to be selected.

Once I checked into the unit and met the other Cobra instructors, I kind of knew why I'd been picked. I knew all of them from Cobra Hall back in Savannah but the one that I was sure had a hand in my selection was Jerry "Butcher" Bourquin. I was very glad to see them all again and to celebrate we went out on the town that night. Since Vung Tau was a resort city, the other guys took me under their wing and showed me some of the better restaurants and highlights of the city. They reminded me of the informal coexistence that existed between the U.S. Forces and the enemy troops that were there on secret R&R and that I was not to do anything that would upset that apple cart because, "everyone likes this arrangement." Even though all the others seemed to accept this unwritten peace agreement, I was very uncomfortable with the whole idea. I remained hyper-vigilant whenever we went downtown and always wore my .45 caliber pistol in plain sight. Just call me paranoid but I certainly wasn't going to trust the NVA with my life.

The classes we conducted went very well and I was truly enjoying teaching again. Our typical day was split into two sections. During one half of the day we would take turns presenting classroom instruction on subjects like the hydraulic systems or the rotor system or possibly aerodynamics. During the other half we would take each of our two students up for an hour and a half of flight training. Because of crowding at the airfield, we would often fly out to an old Japanese airstrip from World War II about a five minute flight North of the military base at Vung Tau. The Japanese had used the airstrip for flight training after they invaded and conquered Vietnam early in the war and the strip was still in good shape and required little maintenance. During our training flights, we only carried about 1500 rounds of minigun ammunition for self defense. This reduced ammunition load allowed us to carry a full load of fuel which gave us additional flight time flexibility during training sessions.

I was one of three Cobras at the Japanese strip doing flight training one day and since there was no control tower, we kept each other advised on our position in the traffic pattern and what our next maneuver would be via the radio. There was a small hill just to the west of the strip that rose about 300 feet above the elevation of the strip. As my student and I were taking off on one trip around the pattern, we suddenly started taking automatic weapons fire from the top of the hill. I immediately keyed the radio and yelled, "Snake one five is taking fire from the hill."

I was in the backseat and flying the aircraft at the time, so, I rolled the aircraft to the left, pointed the nose at the spot the fire was coming from and fired a burst of minigun at the interloper. As I watched the stream of tracers hit the ground and ricochet around, I thought, "That's odd, there seems to be a lot of ricochets going in all directions."

It was then that I noticed the other two Cobras were firing their miniguns into the hilltop at the same time. While the bad guy may have fired 20 to 30 rounds at us, the three of us had unloaded about 1200 rounds back at him in about 6 seconds. I'm not sure if we killed the enemy gunner or if his compatriots dealt with him rather severely for violating the "peaceful coexistence agreement" of Vung Tau. We never got shot at near the airstrip again. That was the only "combat" that I saw during my entire time at Vung Tau.

The third week of March, our detachment commander called us all together for an important meeting. He got up in front of all of us and said, "Our detachment just received orders to stand down..." Before he could finish what he was saying, the entire room erupted into joyous hoots and hollers because everyone knew they were going home. As the din continued, the major finally lost his cool and shouted, "AT EASE!!"

The room again became deathly quiet. The major resumed his speech, "As I was saying, our detachment has been ordered to stand down and disband. As most of you know, this unit is a conglomeration of personnel and equipment, drawn from other units to accomplish our mission of training personnel FROM those units, FOR those units. We have accomplished our mission and our services are no longer needed, so, the aircraft and other equipment will go back to the units that lent them to us as will the personnel. I know that most of you thought you were going home but that is not the case. We will all be getting orders in the next few days to return to our old units here in Vietnam or we'll be reassigned to a new one if the old one no longer exists. I'm sorry to be the bearer of bad news."

SCREWED AGAIN!! We had all been hearing about other units that were standing down and being shipped back to the States as the war wound down and we thought it was our turn. After only six weeks in this plush assignment, the rug had been pulled out from under me again. I knew that I'd have to write to my mother-in-law, Alma, and tell her that she could take down her Christmas tree. She had kept it up in hopes that I would be home soon and we all could celebrate a late Yuletide. I was pretty sure there wasn't many needles left on the tree anyway.

Once again, I started packing my bags.

CHAPTER 31

Can Tho

My new orders assigned me to Charlie Troop, 16th Cavalry, 1st Aviation Brigade in Can Tho. Can Tho was centrally located in the Mekong River delta and was a major transportation center for commerce throughout the region. As a result, the town was of significant military importance and needed to be protected from the enemy. The city was about 90 miles southwest of Saigon and was now one of the last U.S. military occupied bases in the entire IV Corps Theater of Operations. The terrain of "The Delta" was much like southern Louisiana and the Mississippi River delta. It was comprised of mostly grasses and bull rushes with many rice paddies throughout. Occasionally, there would be a patch of jungle or forest but generally, it was just wide open plains interrupted by fingers from the Mekong River. This was Vietnam's bread basket (or more correctly, it's rice basket).

When I checked into the unit, I was greeted by many familiar faces. Among the first to greet me was Captain Dick Lawrence who used to be my flight leader back at Cobra Hall prior to my break in service. He would now be my boss again as the leader of the Cobra platoon in Charlie Troop. He told me he was very happy to see me because things were starting to get a bit dicey with the troop reductions that were going on. Then he broke the unpleasant news to me that our unit now had the LAST nine Cobras in all of The Delta, and we were expected, by the U.S. military command in Saigon, to cover this entire huge piece of terrain with one cavalry troop. The area our unit was responsible for ran from just South of Saigon for 180 miles to the Southern tip of the country and from Ha Tien, on the Western border with Cambodia, East for 130 miles to the South China Sea. Indeed, it was a very large piece of real estate to cover with just 9 Cobras. Forget about General Custer, I was now starting to feel like Davy Crockett at the Alamo or maybe a combination of both. I really didn't want to be a footnote in a history book about famous lost battles.

I was still in the "in-processing" mode of turning in all my records to the appropriate offices like operations for my flight records, the orderly room for my personnel file and the medical facility for my medical files. Of course, each of these offices had a flurry of new forms for me to fill out, so, I was busy tending to these tasks throughout my first full day.

Prior to beginning my fun for the day, I was on hand as a "package" of our aircraft prepared to take off for a mission they had been assigned. Since this was a cavalry unit, it was comprised of three different types of aircraft, each with its own purpose. We had UH-1H Hueys that would transport our infantry troops (the Blues), OH-6 light observation aircraft (Loaches) that acted as scouts to find the enemy and AH-1G Cobras to protect the other aircraft and destroy the enemy once they were located. The term "package" meant a team with a mix of these three different types of aircraft that had been put together to accomplish a specific mission. So, I said goodbye to the guys I knew and headed off to do my admin crap.

That day, Fate decided to emphasize how dangerous the situation had become in my new assignment. A Huey had been shot down and our Cobras were providing protection during the attempted recovery of the aircraft. The lead Cobra, piloted by CW2 Joe Hudson and WO1 Robert Stern, was providing suppressive fire on the enemy positions when they were hit by heavy antiaircraft weapons fire. They subsequently crashed and both were killed.

I knew nothing about this as I walked back into the unit area after completing my in-processing that afternoon. It was nearly dark before the "Package" of aircraft returned to Can Tho. I was told the sad news that one of our Cobras had been shot down and the crew was killed. There had been several attempts to get to the crash site to recover the crew but the heavy antiaircraft fire had thwarted all their efforts. There would be an all out assault at first light to get to the crash site and complete the recovery.

Dick Lawrence came to me and told me what had happened. He said he needed as much firepower as he could muster so they could get in to recover the bodies of our dead pilots the next morning. He asked, "Could you fly one of our Cobras and help out with the recovery? I know we are suppose to give you an 'in unit' check ride and an area orientation but we just don't have time for that right now. We are going to be heading out at first light, so, we have no time waste on formalities. Besides, I know you and trust you. What do you say?"

"I just need to know what aircraft I'll be flying and who my copilot will be," was my reply.

I was assigned one of the remaining Cobras and a copilot that I had never met before and we took off with the rest of the "package" as they returned to the crash site early the next morning. The site was along the western edge of the U Minh forest, a particularly hostile bit of terrain near the southwestern edge of the country. The Cobras in the package kept up nearly continuous bombardment of the enemy gun positions as the Hueys inserted the Blues (infantry) to make their way to the downed aircraft. The bodies were recovered and we all returned to Can Tho having fulfilled our solemn promise to leave no one behind. Quite a sobering introduction to my new unit.

A few days later we had a memorial service at the chapel for Warrant Officers Hudson and Stern. Even though I had not met them, the service was a very poignant reminder that the war was not over yet and that my halcyon days in Vung Tau were now very far behind me.

Over the next few days, I went through the formality of completing a check ride and local area checkout and I was now "Officially" ready to go on missions.

Captain Lawrence wasted no time in putting me to work (again). All the Cobra pilots were called together for a briefing on our next operation. Captain Lawrence explained that we had been assigned a mission to support ARVN ground forces that were conducting an incursion into Cambodia to root out the NVA and VC forces that took refugee there. The South Vietnamese government had requested U.S. attack helicopter support for their troops since they did not have any Cobras in their army. We were told that this mission had been approved at the highest levels of government, so, we were committed. Someone brought up the Cambodian incursion back in 1970 and said he thought that because of the political uproar it caused, Congress had passed a law saying we couldn't go into Cambodia or Laos anymore.

Captain Lawrence was ready for that one. He explained that the killing of four students at Kent State University and other protests that arose out of the Cambodian incursion ordered by President Nixon in 1970, made Congress repeal the Gulf of Tonkin Resolution that had allowed LBJ and Nixon to conduct military operations in Southeast Asia for 7 years without a declaration of war. That resolution was replaced by the Cooper-Church Amendment that continued funding for the war but prohibited all U.S. "Ground Troops and Advisers" from participating in military operations in Cambodia or Laos. (I hope you caught the loophole we were about to fly through.)

The rational for our cross border mission was that first, we were not "Ground" troops and secondly, we were not "Advising" anyone. I imagine there was a certain amount of glee in the Pentagon over splitting that hair especially since the politicians they were up against were so good at hair splitting themselves.

With all the legalities resolved to everyone's satisfaction, we were off to the Cambodian border. As I remember it, there were 5, or possibly 6, Cobras involved in this particular operation and one Huey that served as command and control (C&C). The C&C Huey had an ARVN officer on board to serve as a liaison between the ARVN ground forces and us. He had explained that his ground forces were having a tough time moving through an area near the border because of tough resistance coming from an area that surrounded a colonial style French mansion/chateau. As we neared the mansion, we could see that it was two stories tall, made of concrete and stone and had a red barrel tile roof. The mansion had a concrete wall about 5 feet tall that surrounded it. The wall's distance from the house varied from about 50 feet at one point to over 100 feet at another. There were several smaller out buildings within the compound that looked like servants quarters, storage facilities and a garage like structure.

As we got closer to it, we suddenly started taking intense antiaircraft automatic weapons fire. As we turned away to try another approach, I noted the positions of four of the guns that were shooting at us. Two of them were shooting out of the upstairs windows in the mansion, one was near the back wall and the fourth was about 100 meters to the north of the left side of the mansion, in a clump of trees.

We reorganized ourselves and discussed what we had observed. It was decided that these guys were protecting something that was very important inside the mansion since there was so much firepower around it. We decided to attack the mansion but first we would climb to 5000 feet to start our rocket runs since the antiaircraft guns were only effective up to 3000 feet. We set up a daisy chain so that each aircraft had another covering him as he pulled out of his dive. This resulted in a continuous rain of rockets on the mansion and, hopefully, caused the enemy gunners to flinch and miss as they fired at us. While most of the rockets were hitting the mansion and blowing out roof tiles and chunks of concrete, they were not causing any serious damage to the interior of the building.

We were starting our fourth or fifth rocket run and I decided I would shoot at a garage sized out building tucked into the corner of the wall. I fired three or four pair of rockets at the "garage"and began to pull out of my dive. Suddenly, there was a bright flash followed closely by a huge BOOM!! I quickly rolled the aircraft back around so

I could see the mansion again. I was amazed. There was a huge black mushroom cloud rising from the compound area and climbing past me at 3,500 feet. The radios erupted with hoots and hollers by the other pilots saying, "Holy Crap!! What did you hit? You blew the whole frigging place up."

Indeed, I had blown the "whole frigging place up." The smoke was clearing in the compound and we could see that, not only had I leveled the "garage" but half of the concrete mansion as well. Several sections of the wall around the compound were also blown flat and one of those flat sections was where the gun by the wall had been located. I had taken out 3 antiaircraft guns with a few pair of rockets. Just pure dumb luck...or was it?

Later, we surmised that the "garage" had been their ammo dump and I had just gotten in a lucky shot. I did not argue the point.

When we got back to Can Tho that night, some of the other pilots bought me a congratulatory drink at the Officer's Club as the story was told and retold, again and again. Thanks guys! Glad to be of assistance.

CHAPTER 32

Roommates

My roommates Hugh Mills (L) and
Rod Willis next to "Miss Clawd IV" (Hugh's OH-6A)
Photo courtesy of Hugh Mills

W hen I had arrived at Can Tho, most of the rooms in the
officers barracks were already occupied. The building was
a two story wooden barracks with 24 total rooms, each
with an outside entry door. When I initially checked in with my old

boss and the current Guns Platoon leader, Dick Lawrence, he said he knew where there was an opening but we'd have to check with the guys that were currently occupying it to see if they'd let me bunk there. Dick explained to me that both of the occupants were Captains, both scout pilots and one was the Scout Platoon leader, so, he wasn't sure they would be okay with a Warrant Officer Cobra pilot bunking with them. The room was on the West end of the second floor and Dick knocked very loudly as he stood to one side of the door. There was a shout from inside saying, "Come in" and Dick gingerly pushed open the door while still standing to one side. This whole process was making me nervous and I wasn't sure I even wanted to meet who or what was behind the door, let alone bunk with them. Dick slowly stuck his head inside and once he was sure the coast was clear, pushed the door all the way open so we could enter.

The room was only about 10 feet by 10 feet and nearly a third of it was occupied by a set of bunk beds to our right as we entered. There was no one in the room but the back wall had a hole, similar to a doorway, cut through it and connected with the room on the other side of the building. As I followed Dick into the room, I could feel that it was air conditioned. Quite a luxury in Vietnam.

Dick led me through the makeshift doorway into the room beyond. He had already started the introduction before I could get through the doorway saying, "Rod, this is our new Cobra IP, Bob Hartley. Bob, this is Captain Rod Willis."

I said, "Glad to meet you," while reaching out to shake his hand. Captain Willis was holding a large knife in his right hand and quickly switched it to his left, just before clasping my out stretched hand. He said, "Me too. Just call me Rod."

As we were gripping and grinning, I noticed that there was another doorway to my left that lead to a third room in this L shaped suite. Someone in there was walking into our room and I heard him exclaim, "Bob! What the heck are you doing here?"

I turned and saw Hugh Mills, a Captain that I had met while going through the Cobra IP course at Cobra Hall just before I came back to

Vietnam. Hugh told me that he had flown Cobras for awhile but just felt more comfortable flying scouts. Hugh had quite a reputation. He was one of the most highly decorated scout pilots, ever, and had written a book about his adventures during his first tour of duty called "Low Level Hell."

Dick explained to Rod and Hugh, that I was in need of a place to bunk and he wondered if they would put me up in their complex. Both of them said, "Sure, you bet. You can take one of those bunk beds in there." Indicating the room we entered through. "Let us know if you need any help."

I said, "Thanks a lot, I really appreciate it. I'll go get my stuff."

Dick and I turned to go out the door we had come in and I noticed that there was a silhouette of a man drawn on it and the plywood of the inside of the door was all splintered and torn up. As we walked away, I asked Dick about the door and his cautious entry. He explained that Rod liked to practice throwing his knife from his room, through the makeshift doorway and into the silhouette on the back of the entry door to what was now my room, some 15 to 20 feet. Dick suggested that I be very cautious about opening the door to my room just in case Rod was practicing. That sounded like very good advice and it seemed a small price to pay for a great room with air conditioning. We all got along very well and I enjoyed having them both as roommates.

One day, I had gotten done flying early in the afternoon and decided to take a nap. I climbed into my bunk and pulled the blanket up while the air conditioner hummed. A short while later I was suddenly startled awake by a very loud "KA-CHUNK" sound. I sat bolt upright in bed and saw a Bowie knife sticking into the back of my door, just 3 feet away from my head. I yelled, "Rod!"

He was just entering my room as he went to retrieve his knife and said, "Oh! Geez, sorry. I didn't see you when I peeked in before. I guess you were under the blanket."

My thoughts went back to the time I fired my .45 pistol next to Steve Woods' head to kill a rat. Steve had been under his blanket and I didn't know he was there either. I said, "Please, next time come in and check to make sure I'm not here. Okay?"

We came to a mutual understanding and I never had another "knife" problem.

I feel compelled to take a moment and talk about scout pilots at this point. They're a different breed. While I had worked with scout pilots from other units at various times before, I developed a new appreciation for their skills once I worked with the scouts on a daily basis at Charlie Troop. My initial impression of the other scout pilots had been that they were simply suicidal maniacs, hellbent on self destruction. But I learned, very quickly, that their true drive was more on the order of the idea that the best defense is a good offense. These individuals were aggressive in everything they did, both in the cockpit and outside of it. I have seen a single OH-6 scout aircraft charge a group of about 20 NVA soldiers preparing an ambush and the soldiers scattered and ran in different directions while wildly firing their weapons over their shoulders, at the pursuing aircraft.

Our scout aircraft typically had a crew of two. The pilot in the right front seat and the crew chief/gunner in the backseat behind the pilot. The gunner had an M-60 machine gun and would use it to protect the right side of the aircraft while the pilot had control of a minigun that was mounted on the left side of the aircraft.

There was much said about the life expectancy of a scout pilot. Anyone with more than 2 months as a scout pilot was considered an "Old Timer" since the greatest majority of them had been either killed or severely wounded by that point. I knew of several units that would reassign a scout pilot to other duties if he made it to the 6 month benchmark of flying scouts. I guess they thought it was the humanitarian thing to do. One telling statistic was when I was in the First Cavalry Division and our sister unit, the 1st of the 9th Cav Squadron, had the dubious distinction of never having one of their new OH-6's make it to the first 100 hour maintenance inspection without having been shot up or totally destroyed. This provided the scout pilots there, with a continuous supply of brand new OH-6 aircraft and the maintenance folks got a break from their regular work of changing oil even though they were kept busy patching bullet holes.

That's why Hugh and Rod were anomalies. They both loved flying scouts and were very, very good at it. They had been doing it for years now and though they'd been shot down many times, they had honed their skills to a razors edge. Working with them reminded me of how the Indian scouts in the old time westerns could tell volumes of information about the people or animals they were tracking, simply by looking at a bent blade of grass. I was sure that it was an outrageous exaggeration when Tonto looked at that blade of grass and told the Lone Ranger something like, "Hmmm, Kemosabe! The five bad guys went this way fourteen and a half minutes ago and were riding three horses, a mule and a camel that has a sprained left rear leg. The leader of them weights 187 pounds and has a patch over his right eye."

I simply knew it was not possible to derive that much information from a bent blade of grass. I now stand corrected. Hugh and Rod had that kind of power of observation and I got to see it in action, so, I know it's true. They also had done a great job of educating the other scout pilots in the unit by passing along some of the tips they had learned the hard way, giving us some of the best scout pilots I ever had the pleasure of serving with.

Most cavalry units in Vietnam would conduct routine recons using a "Pink" team that consisted of one OH-6 scout down at treetop level looking for signs of enemy movements and a single Cobra flying above and behind the scout to provide covering fire should the scout run into the enemy forces and be shot at. Once clear, the "Pink" team would then report the enemy's location and additional forces like artillery, airstrikes or even a combat assault with infantry would be allocated to deal with the threat. But times had changed and, with the reduction in U.S. forces that was taking place, especially in The Delta, there were fewer and fewer airstrikes, artillery bases and infantry to deal with these targets of opportunity. As a result, our unit had gone to using "Heavy" teams to do recons. A "Heavy" team consisted of two OH-6s down low, covered by two Cobras flying above and behind them. The pilot in the lead scout would do all the talking once they got into the recon area. He usually used the FM radio to transmit a continuous stream of information on what he was seeing and his impressions of what the enemy was up to. This information was copied down by the pilot in the front seat of the lead Cobra who also noted the map coordinates of the information being reported. Since the scout pilot was continuously transmitting on the FM radio, he could not receive a transmission on it, so, we would talk to him on either the VHF radio or UHF radio which he was listening in on.

To illustrate, I was the lead Cobra in a "Heavy" team one day and the scout lead was saying that he thought the enemy had recently gone through the grassy area he was currently over. He said, "It looks like about 5 to 7 soldiers went through here less than 10 minutes ago because water is still seeping into their footprints. Two of them were carrying something heavy."

I could see from my higher vantage point that the disturbed grass left a trail from his current position toward a treeline that was about 200 meters to his right front. There was a separate treeline about 300 meters to his left front but no disturbed grass went in that direction. The scout pilot, whose voice was now higher in pitch, was saying, "They started running right about here. They must have heard us coming. I think they are setting up a heavy machine gun in that treeline at my 12 o'...." He never finished his sentence because the treeline he indicated came alive with muzzle flashes and tracers aimed at the Loach. I was already into a dive and firing rockets at the muzzle flashes as the scout pilot was screaming on the radio, "TAKING FIRE! TAKING FIRE! BREAKING LEFT."

As I pulled out of my gun run, my wingman was firing a bunch of rockets under me and into the enemy's location with great accuracy. The scouts had gotten away without being hit and we rendezvoused with them at a safe distance from the enemy. I told the scouts that we would fire about a half a load of rockets into the treeline and then they could probe it to see if we'd gotten the bad guys. After we'd fired, the lead scout approached the area from over the trees and reported that there were 5 dead bad guys and their 12.7mm heavy machine gun was destroyed. That day our system and tactics had worked perfectly.

Our tactics were proven to produce results while minimizing danger as much as possible but, occasionally, the nutty scout pilots went outside approved tactics and did some crazy and dangerous things in their zeal to wreak havoc upon the enemy. I need to reemphasize that these guys were all incredibly brave and very skilled at their job but, sometimes, their judgment was a bit lacking.

One crazy idea they had was to make "Bombs" that could be tossed out of a scout to blast the enemy. Sounds like something that makes military sense but let me explain. Someone had the "great" idea to take a normal fragmentation hand grenade, remove the time delay fuse and replace it with an instantaneous fuse. Then, while FIRMLY holding the safety spoon down, the grenade pin was pulled and the grenade was, ever so gently, put into a Mason jar (like grandma used for canning). The glass of the jar would hold the spoon down, preventing detonation, and the jar was then filled with jet fuel and the lid secured. When dropped or thrown out of the helicopter, the jar would shatter when it hit the ground, releasing the safety spoon, thereby causing the fuse to detonate the grenade instantaneously which then ignited the surrounding pint of fuel.

They worked very well but I think you might be able to detect some flaws in the design. For instance, if during the loading of the grenade, the safety spoon was momentarily allowed to move, BOOM! The normal five second delay had been removed.

OR, if the Mason jar was inadvertently dropped as it was loaded into the aircraft, BOOM!

OR, if the jar was fumbled while being grabbed to be tossed out of the helicopter, BOOM!

OR, if enemy bullets fired at the helicopter (which was a regular occurrence) penetrated one of the jars, BOOM!

You might say that the plan had a few flaws and you would be right. The practice came to a screeching halt one day when a "Bomb" that was being loaded aboard one of our parked Loaches, fell out of the far side door as more ammo and equipment was loaded aboard the aircraft by the crew chief on the opposite side. The crew chief was injured and the aircraft destroyed by the blast. Good idea but...

Another questionable practice that I observed was when an OH-6 conducting a recon would hover over a hootch and lift up the corner of the thatched roof with the tip of his skid to peer inside for enemy soldiers. What could go wrong? Well,

A. There could BE enemy soldiers inside pointing there guns at the new skylight.

B. The "Bomb" that was going to be thrown into the hootch could blow the roof up into the rotor.

And

C. The skid could get tangled in the thatch preventing a getaway.

I'm sure there were many more problems with this idea, so, you're welcome to think up as many as you'd like.

One final example of questionable practices and I think you'll see what I mean about nutty scout pilots. I was covering two of our scouts one day on a recon when the lead scout said he could see footprints going up a trail into a wooded area. He told the other scout to wait out in the open while he followed the trail INTO the woods.

I immediately protested saying, "I can't cover you if I can't see you!! You won't have any room to maneuver in there and you might hit a limb of a tree and crash. Don't do it!"

The scout pilot said, "Well I'm not letting these assholes get away!" And with that he disappeared up the trail and into the forest.

When he got inside, he said, "It's pretty dark in here, I can't see their footprints anymore."

Snidely I responded, "Don't worry, you'll see them when they start shooting at you."

With that, he thought better of his idea of going for a walk in the woods and made his way back out into the sunlight. Scout pilots, ya gotta love em!

While we're talking about scout pilots, I'd like to mention the machine that they flew. The Hughes OH-6A was an outstanding aircraft that was perfectly suited for the scout mission. It was light, agile and extremely maneuverable. It had an engine, about the size of a Thanksgiving turkey, that produced 317 horsepower, more than enough for any job. It was also a very tough machine. It could take a licking but keep on ticking. But perhaps its greatest attribute was that it crashed very well. It was designed somewhat like an egg. When it crashed, it would roll, like an egg, while shedding parts and eventually come to a stop and the crew would emerge virtually unscathed.

I had witnessed this phenomenon during my first tour of duty while flying in the mountains near Camp Evans. A scout was trying to show us where the enemy position was and started taking fire. He quickly banked the aircraft to evade the bullets but drove right into the side of the mountain at 80 knots. The rotor blades immediately separated from the craft and it began rolling down the mountainside. The tailboom separated as did the skids and the odd shaped ball that was left, accelerated as it headed downhill. After rolling end over end for about 100 meters, the wreckage came to an abrupt stop as it hit a rocky outcropping. We were still cringing at the violence of the crash as we saw the two crew members release their seat belts and climb out of the the pile of trash that used to be their aircraft. They dusted themselves off and then gave us a thumbs up to signal that they were OK. Unbelievable!

CHAPTER 33

Things Heat Up

Beginning in April of 1972, Jeane Dixon's prognostication of a huge battle for the An Loc and Quan Loi area finally became a reality. North Vietnamese forces began pouring over the border from Cambodia and were initially confronted and stopped by the defending ARVN forces in the town of Loc Ninh, just a few miles north of An Loc. The invading enemy troops were accompanied by tanks and other armored vehicles which were protected by heavy air defense artillery. The ARVN forces were assisted by U.S. military advisers who were now trapped in the surrounded town. There were many heroic attempts by U.S. Army helicopter pilots to extract the advisers and some were successful but not all. After a couple of days of battle, Loc Ninh was overrun and the NVA charged down Highway 13 towards An Loc. Soon, the invading army was on the outskirts of An Loc and a fierce battle ensued. If the enemy overran An Loc, they would have a clear shot down Highway 13, straight into the heart of Saigon.

The First Cavalry Division had been redeployed back to the States in April of 1971 leaving behind its 3rd brigade to cover the division's entire area of operations. There were few U.S. ground forces left to battle the invaders. When the First Cav left, it was decided that the 1st of the 9th Cav and 2nd of the 20th Blue Max (my old unit) would be part of a task force to assist the ARVN units in defending the area. These units were re-designated as "F" Troop of the 9th Cav and "F" Battery of the 79th Aerial Field Artillery (AFA). The courageous pilots of these units helped turn the tide of the battle and enabled the ARVN forces to prevent An Loc from being overrun. The victory was not without heavy losses. Because of the intense antiaircraft fire, many of those brave pilots were shot down and killed. The town of An Loc was reduced to rubble and thousands of soldiers and civilians lost their lives during the two month long battle.

During the battle, the Cobra pilots of F/9th and F/79th found that they could destroy a tank with rockets, something that the U.S. experts on armor warfare said was impossible. The only problem was that the enemy had a lot of antiaircraft weaponry that they brought with them to defend their troops and tanks. While helicopter pilots were somewhat used to dealing with the heavy machine guns used against them, the enemy was now using hand held, shoulder fired SA-7 heat seeking missiles they had recently acquired from the Russians. The missiles proved to be highly effective and many of our Cobra pilots fell victim to them.

Meanwhile, in Can Tho, we were all well aware of what was going on in An Loc and were wondering when the deadly SA-7 missiles would show up in our neighborhood. We had already heard that an entire ARVN division had been pulled out of The Delta and sent north to An Loc to help in the battle. With few U.S. ground forces left in The Delta and now, an entire ARVN division pulled out and sent north, I was again picturing myself as a modern day Davy Crockett or, perhaps, Jim Bowie as Santa Anna and the Mexican Army closed in.

In an attempt to allay our fears, we were told there would be a "SECRET" briefing in the mess hall to tell us about new methods and equipment that would prevent us from being shot down by one of these missiles. On the way to the meeting, we were all talking about how relieved we were that the research and development guys had come up with a missile defensive measure so quickly. The mess hall was surrounded by armed guards and we had to show our IDs and be checked off against a roster as we entered. Pretty super-secret stuff.

We took seats down front so we wouldn't miss a word during this critical briefing. The briefing officer was a major that had flown in from Saigon to pass along this highly classified information. He began by telling us everything that was known about the SA-7 missile. He said it had a maximum altitude of 10,000 feet (much higher than we'd go), and flew at 900 miles per hour (a bit faster than a helicopter). He explained that the infrared seeker head, homed in on the hot gas plume emitted by our engines or could possibly catch the reflection of the sun off of a windshield. So far, this guy was just full of cheery information.

But he did go on to say that the "Good News" was that we could see them coming!

Oh! Great! I felt so much better now.

He continued, saying, "The missile leaves a very distinct corkscrew pattern of white smoke during its launch sequence and you should be able to see it quite easily. The first pilot to see it should transmit the phrase, 'MISSILE, MISSILE, MISSILE' immediately. Those hearing this transmission should immediately scan the ground around them to locate the white smoke trail and then turn and point your nose at the spot." (All this while a 900 MPH missile streaked across the 4 or 5 miles separating us from the shooter.)

He continued, "This procedure masks the hot gas plume from the engine and should alter any sun reflections off your glass. The missile will lose its lock on you and fly harmlessly by." Sounded like all smoke and mirrors to me.

The briefer went on saying, "Well, that's the tactics we have developed and here is the hardware that we've come up with to defeat these missiles!"

I thought, "Well, it's about time! Let's see this new fangled gizmo the R&D guys developed for us." The briefer threw back a piece of canvas that was covering an object on the table next to him, picked up the object and held it high so everyone could see it. It was a Very pistol! You know, a flare gun from a boat.

I quickly looked around to see if anyone else was about to burst out laughing but they all seemed more confused than amused.

The briefer explained that if you heard the transmission of "Missile, Missile, Missile" and turned toward the smoke trail, then all you had to do to ensure you weren't hit was to shoot the flare at the missile. The missile would "see" the flare and track it instead of you. Problem solved. He went on to say that every Huey, Loach, Chinook and Flying Crane would have one of these on board before the day was out.

All the Cobra pilots had the same thought and our hands went up simultaneously. The briefer pointed at one and said, "Yes?"

Our Cobra pilot asked, "What about those of us flying Cobras?"

The briefer said, "Well, because of your canopy, we haven't figured that out yet." Oh! Well, back to the drawing board.

CHAPTER 34

B-52s Strikes

The North Vietnamese government had been engaged in peace talks with the U.S. but now that their "Spring Offensive" was rolling toward Saigon, they abruptly walked out of the talks in Paris. President Nixon decided to "Bomb" them back to the talks and launched round the clock bombing of North Vietnam and any imaginable target in South Vietnam. During the battle of An Loc, B-52 bombers were putting in "Arc Light" strikes around the city every hour of the day and night. Once the enemy attack on An Loc had been repulsed, the B-52s were redirected to take out any area that authorities even suspected the NVA might be using to build up troops, supplies or equipment.

As the only Cavalry unit left in the Delta, we were tasked to conduct Bomb Damage Assessments (BDA) on as many of the bomber strikes in the region as possible to quantify their success. During our daily briefing, we would be given a list of the coordinates for the 10 or 12 most promising strikes planned for that day. Our "package" was usually 2 scouts, 2 Cobras and one UH-1 that would act as command and control (C&C).

The package would arrive near the coordinates of a planned strike a few minutes before it was scheduled to happen. We would hold several kilometers away, ready to go into the strike zone right after the last bombs exploded. Paddy Radar would broadcast its "Heavy Artillery" warning on Guard frequency and we'd look for the inbound bombers. Since the weather in the Delta was usually pretty good, we could normally see the contrails of the inbound bombers as they cruised at 30,000 feet. Invariably, there were 3 bombers that produced 3 distinct strings of bombs that landed right next to each other and wound up obliterating an area 1000 meters wide by 1000 meters long. (Think ten football fields by ten football fields.)

After the bombs stopped falling and Paddy Radar gave us clearance into the strike zone, the scouts would go in low, looking for any evidence of damage to the enemy. They may see destroyed equipment, blown up food storage areas and, of course, bodies (or parts there of). They would count up the legs and arms they saw, divide by four and the resulting number would be the body count reported for the strike. Sometimes (but not often), there would be a survivor wandering around, dazed and confused and the lead scout would cautiously approach him to see if he wanted to surrender. If he raised a weapon, he was added to the body count. If not, he was picked up, tied up, had his wounds tended to and then he was turned over to the intell guys to be interrogated.

BDAs had become part of our life. While I am reluctant to say it, they had become routine and a bit boring. Many of the strikes produced little more than blown up trees and craters in rice paddies. After a while, they all started to blend together and I couldn't remember one from the other, with the exception of a few that stand out.

The first strike that is now permanently burned into my memory, started out like all the others. We were all holding a few kilometers away from the strike zone, waiting for the bombers to arrive. It was a clear day and we could see the contrails as the bombers closed in on our position. Paddy Radar had already broadcast its "Heavy Artillery" warning and we waited for the explosions to start. The lead bomber's contrail showed that he was in a turn and would soon be headed back the way he had come. The turn indicated that he had completed dropping his bombs. I could see that the second bomber was just beginning his turn too.

The light was just right that day and I was able see the bombs as they streaked through the sky on their way to the target. They looked like a bunch of black gnats, in trail formation, going much faster laterally than dropping vertically. The explosions from the first bomber began. The bomb bursts overlapped each other as they marched onward for 1000 meters. Mixed in with the standard 500 and 750 pound bombs was an occasional 2000 pound bomb that really lit up the area. Just as the first string of bombs finished exploding, the second string began to detonate adjacent to the first string's starting point. These explosions also marched for 1000 meters alongside the first string.

As the second string ended, we looked back to the starting point to watch the third string go in. We waited. And we waited but no third string! What the Hell was going on? Normally, when one string ended the next one started without any pause. Something was wrong.

We listened in as the C&C Huey called Paddy Radar on guard frequency to ask about the third string and if we were cleared into the area yet. Paddy's response was that the third bomber had a malfunction and was returning to base and that we were cleared into the area to conduct our BDA.

The lead scout that day was Lieutenant King, an excellent pilot. As soon as he heard that we were cleared into the area, he was diving down to treetop level and headed for the still smoking bomb craters. His fellow scout was right on his heels as King began talking a mile a minute about everything he was seeing. My wingman and I followed them into the area at about 1500 feet above the ground. We were keeping a lookout for any bad guys that might pop up to threaten the scouts when, suddenly, out of the corner of my eye, I caught the movement of something that horrified me. I turned my head quickly enough to see the second bomb explode. The third string of bombs was inexplicably pounding the strike zone with us in it. I immediately started screaming on the radio "GET OUT, MORE BOMBS!!"

I turned my aircraft 90 degrees to the axis of the bomb strike and pulled all the power I had to exit the area as quickly as possible. My wingman had been behind me but was now alongside as we got away. I looked back and saw that the second scout was right behind us at low altitude but where was Lt. King?

Over the commotion, I heard his voice on the radio droning on with his observations. I scanned the area and spotted him still in the strike zone as the bombs closed in from behind. The blasts went directly over his position and threw a curtain of black mud, trees and boulders up to my altitude. As I turned back toward the strike, I saw a full size palm tree directly in front of me tumbling end over end as it fell back to earth right where I had last seen Lt. King's aircraft.

As the last bomb in the string exploded and the black curtain of mud rained back down, what to my wondering eyes should appear but an OH-6 Loach clawing its way out of that curtain of muck and debris. The flight of the aircraft reminded me of a fly that had been swatted but not quite killed. It buzzed and jerked and fluttered but it was still flying. As I looked closer, I could see that there was no plexiglass left in any of the windows, there were no skids and the tailboom was bent at a 30 degree angle but it was still flying. The crew would not or could not respond to us as we called them on the radio over and over again.

Lt. King flew the valiant little craft about 300 meters clear of the strike zone and set it down in about a foot of water in a rice paddy. The aircraft leaned to one side but remained upright as it was shutdown. Immediately, the C&C Huey was setting down next to the stricken craft and it's crew were scrambling out to assist Lt. King and his crew chief. They had had their eardrums broken by the blasts and mud and dirt was packed into every orifice of their bodies but they were alive.

The investigation into what caused this screw up began the next day. There were Colonels and Generals from the Army and Air Force, a lot of finger pointing and loud voices but in the end an agreement was reached on how to preclude such a thing from happening again. Previously, the Strategic Air Command (SAC), for operational security purposes, would only let bomber crews take orders from SAC headquarters for fear that some sneaky Russians or other bad guys would be able to trick the crews into bombing the wrong target or not dropping their bombs at all (think nuclear weapons). It was decided that the bomber crews could monitor the frequency of the unit conducting the BDA so that if they detected that something had gone awry, the bomber crew could immediately check with the targeting radar facility (Paddy Radar in this case) to get a thumbs up or be told to abort.

This arrangement was satisfactory to all concerned and the bomber pilots really liked it because they could get real time feedback on what they had accomplished. Before this, they would fly for four and a half hours from Guam, drop their bombs and fly four and a half hours back. The next day they might get a piece of paper with a single line of information on it saying what they hit and what kind of damage they inflicted on the enemy, if any. Not very exciting stuff. But now they could listen in as the lead scout described, in gory detail, what they had achieved.

Another strike that was very memorable was in an area between two branches of the Mekong River about 25 miles southwest of Can Tho. The area had been targeted because some local farmers had reported that there was an NVA headquarters along the canal that joined the two branches of the river. The canal was about 2000 meters long and about 30 feet wide and straight as an arrow.

Because of the policy of gradually turning over control of the war to the South Vietnamese, we were required to have a local South Vietnamese province chief aboard the C&C Huey and he had to approve of everything we did or were about to do. Not all, but some of these province chiefs let their new found powers go to their head and I believe some of them were actually working for the enemy and did all they could to thwart our operations. It was at this point in the war that I was required to get approval from my entire chain of command before I could shoot at anyone, even if he was already shooting AT ME. The political situation now dictated that the local province chief be included in this "Chain of Command." In theory, I was to write down the initials, in grease pencil on my canopy glass, of each person in the chain of command as they granted their approval for me to shoot back at the enemy. Normally, we didn't worry about this rule very much but when the province chief was aboard the C&C Huey, we had no choice.

On this particular day, we arrived near the planned strike zone and held about 5 kilometers to the north while waiting for the bombers to arrive. As we surveyed the planned strike zone, all looked peaceful and quite. We did not see anyone moving around and there were no sampans on the canal or the adjoining river branches. In fact, it was too quiet.

I was startled when guard frequency on the UHF radio came to life saying, "This is Paddy Radar on guard with a heavy artillery warning on the one nine five degree radial of Tan Son Nhut TACAN for one hundred and seventeen miles. All aircraft should avoid this area for the next 15 minutes. Paddy Radar, out."

Suddenly, the area alongside the canal came alive with hundreds of people coming out of the jungle and tossing camouflage covers off of hidden sampans on the bank of the canal. It looked like someone had stomped an ant hill and the ants were now flooding out to defend their lair. There were now at least 50 sampans heading down the canal in both directions in an attempt to flee the area before the strike. Apparently, these guys had been monitoring guard frequency and knew that the heavy artillery warning was for their area, so, they were trying to get gone as fast as possible.

Upon seeing this mass evacuation, we immediately requested permission to fire on the fleeing sampans but the province chief in the C&C Huey denied our request. We watched helplessly as the lead sampans were nearing the river and safety. Just as we had given up hope, the first bombs began to explode. By pure luck, the first string of 100 bombs were impacting right along the bank of the canal. Almost all of the sampans were blown out of the water and into the trees on the far side of the canal. The second and third strings of bombs devastated the area of jungle that the fleeing NVA had come from.

We received confirmation from Paddy Radar that the strike was completed and were cleared into the area to do our BDA. The scouts immediately headed for the canal. As they approached, the few sampans that had escaped, began firing at them. I'm sure you have heard the phrase, "...like shooting fish in a barrel." That's the best way to sum up what happened at that point.

Once that situation had been dealt with, the scouts headed down the canal and began reporting the carnage they were observing. There were many bodies and sampans blown up into the trees and the lead scout made the comment that it looked like some sort of bizarre Christmas tree that was decorated with bodies and sampans instead of ornaments. He continued the analogy by saying that even the colors were appropriate since the mashed up green of the palm tree leaves were sprayed with the red of the blood from the bodies. How festive!

Because of the incident where Lt. King had been bombed, the B-52s were listening in on our frequency so they could monitor what we were doing in hopes of preventing a repeat of that terrible day. As the lead scout continued to enumerate the body count, there was suddenly a new, strange sounding voice on the frequency. It sounded like someone with an oxygen mask covering his face and he was very giddy as he asked, "Was that the strike that just went in at grid coordinates Whiskey Romeo 123456?"

The C&C Huey replied, "Yes it is, who is this?"

The phantom voice answered saying, "Oh! It's just a bunch of very happy dump truck drivers. Thanks a bunch guys, you've made our day. The long ride home won't be so bad this time. Good luck!"

I glanced up and could still see the contrails of the bombers heading southeast towards Guam. My guess was that there would be a few rounds of celebratory beers at the Andersen AFB Officers Club tonight.

Another strike that sticks with me was one that should never have happened. Our package arrived in the vicinity of this planned strike and began orbiting a few kilometers away from the designated grid coordinates. As was our normal routine, we got out our maps and began comparing the outlined strike box on the map with the actual terrain on the ground. It didn't take any of us very long to determine that this strike was planned on what was nothing but a very large field with a couple of rice paddies along the edge. The only thing of note in the field was what appeared to be a John Deere tractor that was currently plowing the very center of the designated strike box. While we couldn't confirm it was a John Deere tractor from where we were, it was painted the appropriate shades of green and yellow. We immediately began to protest this strike with those aboard the C&C ship but were quickly told that the province chief would not allow us to stop the strike. One of the scout pilots said he was going in to pick up the farmer and get him out of there but the C&C ordered him to stay put.

The heavy artillery warning was issued by Paddy Radar and the bombs began falling. It was like watching a train wreck, I couldn't look away. I saw the tractor take a direct hit and yellow and green parts went flying. As the dust settled we were cleared into the strike zone. The lead scout headed directly for the remains of the tractor in hopes of finding the farmer alive but that was not the case. The BDA report officially showed one field used by the NVA to produce food was heavily cratered, one NVA tractor was destroyed and one enemy sympathizer was KIA.

We protested to our HQ when we got back to Can Tho but they weren't interested. They said that the province chief himself had requested this mission and since he knew the area better than we did, it was approved. The only thing I could think of was that the farmer had somehow pissed off the province chief and paid for it with his life. Perhaps the farmer was richer than the province chief or maybe the farmer was having an affair with the province chief's wife or daughter, it didn't matter. The strike was just plain wrong and besides killing a farmer, it wasted hundreds of thousands of dollars to accomplish nothing. I was getting pretty tired of this war.

This next story takes place while we were conducting a BDA on a B-52 strike but has less to do with the strike than with one particular scout pilot involved in the mission. I shall call this scout pilot "Tee" instead of using his real name and you'll understand why, shortly.

Tee was a very likable guy and had a good sense of humor but he did have one major flaw. As I've mentioned, being a scout pilot was a very dangerous job and many pilots that tried it, sought to get out of the job as quickly as they could because their nerves just wouldn't or couldn't deal with the pressure. This wasn't the case with Tee because he had found a solution to the nerve problem. He found he could calm his nerves with an elixir called beer. In the morning, before heading out to his aircraft to go on these dangerous missions, Tee would stop by our little lounge and slam down a six pack then head for his aircraft with another six pack tucked under his arm. I know that you are all horrified by the thought of this, and so was I, but I have to tell you that Tee was an outstanding scout as long as he had his nerve medicine.

He flew his aircraft with exceptional skill, was able to communicate like a seasoned news anchor, was as accurate with his minigun as Wyatt Earp was with a six gun and had the analytical skills and deductive powers of a Sherlock Holmes. In short, a great scout pilot.

While covering Tee, I had to be a bit careful because while covering other scouts, one of the clues a Cobra pilot looked for was when the scout pilot suddenly dropped a smoke grenade out of his door. This usually meant he had spotted a target and was marking it for the Cobra to shoot at. Quite often this would happen a few milliseconds before the scout called, "TAKING FIRE! TAKING FIRE!" Which was my cue to start shooting rockets under the scout's tailboom to aid in his escape. In Tee's case, I had to pause a moment when I saw him toss a canister out the door, just to make sure it wasn't an empty beer can.

None of the other pilots or even Tee's crew chief complained about Tee's drinking because he did such a great job but someone eventually spilled the beans and our Commanding Officer found out. Tee was chewed out by the CO and ordered not to drink before or while on a mission.

To Tee's credit, he did as he was told but the results were a total disaster. Tee's flying skills were now nonexistent. Everyone headed for cover as he picked his aircraft up to a hover in the revetment. Really scary to watch. He now sounded like he had a speech impediment when he talked on the radio. The best that could be said about his accuracy with the minigun was that he could usually hit the ground. And his analytical skills and powers of deductive reasoning were akin to those of the Three Stooges. It was like the difference between day and night.

The following incident occurred during Tee's "Sober" phase. It had been decided that the safest missions to send him on was BDAs on B-52 strikes since most of the enemy we might encounter were either already dead or knocked so silly that they didn't even know their own name. Tee was down in the strike zone and was attempting to tell us what he was seeing but most of what he was saying was simply gibberish. My front seat pilot, whose job it was to write down Tee's observations, said to me, "I can't understand anything he's saying. Can you?"

I told him, "No, I can't either but don't worry about it."

At some point Tee managed to make it clear to us that his minigun was jammed and he needed to exit the strike zone so he could clear the jam.

The strike zone was near a branch of the Mekong River that was about a mile wide at that point, so, I told Tee that I would follow him out to the river and he could clear his gun there without worrying about any bad guys getting the drop on him. He agreed and we headed for the river. Once there I suggested that he come up to altitude and we could cruise down the middle of the river while his crew chief worked on clearing the gun. Tee said, "No, I'll stay down here over the water." It was odd but many scout pilots seemed to have a fear of heights.

I dropped back a distance and followed Tee as he flew up the center of the mile wide river. I was not really concerned about Tee's safety because we were far enough offshore to preclude any enemy fire and there were no sampans around that could be a threat.

As we flew along, I was watching the shoreline to my right when something caught my attention near Tee's aircraft. I quickly looked at his aircraft and saw an ever widening circle of waves behind him that looked like something large had fallen overboard and made a big splash. I immediately called Tee and asked, "Did you guys drop something into the water?"

Tee responded saying, "No. No. Everything is all right, don't worry about it."

I began to worry about it. I decided to keep a closer eye on what Tee was doing. His flight pattern was a little erratic but not too bad and I could see that he would occasionally turn around in his seat to see how the crew chief was doing with his repairs. Everything seemed okay but I kept a close eye on him anyway.

Then it happened. As I watched, the OH-6 nosed over and plunged into the water. The body of the aircraft was totally submerged as a huge wave flowed up and over the windshield and streamed back, obscuring the rest of the machine. The only recognizable part sticking out of the water was the rotor system. It is a true testament to the skill of the designers and builders of the Hughes OH-6A that Tee was able to pull the aircraft (or watercraft) clear of the river and resume flying instead of sailing the machine.

I was stunned to say the least. I noticed that the aircraft did not have any skids left but that seemed to be the only damage. I wasn't sure that his radios still worked but I called Tee and said, "What the Hell happened?"

He responded by saying, "I hit the water but we're okay."

I snapped back, "You didn't just hit the water, you went UNDER the water! And in case you haven't noticed, you don't have any skids left."

At this point I could see him lean out of his door and look down. His reaction was priceless. He rolled his head back and began shaking it from side to side. I began to worry that he might go in for another dip so I said, "Let's call it a day and head home. The maintenance folks have some work to do on your aircraft."

He climbed to altitude and we headed for Can Tho and were joined by the other aircraft in our package. As we cruised back, I asked Tee what had happened and he said that when he would turn around to see how his crew chief was coming along with the gun, he would inadvertently push the cyclic stick forward causing the nose to go down. The first time they just kind of bounced off of the water but the second time they really hit.

When we got back to Can Tho, the maintenance folks were ready for Tee. They had stacked up some old mattresses and had Tee set the aircraft down on them as gently as possible. Once they had placed more mattresses around to stabilize it, they had Tee shut down the engine. The aircraft settled in and remained upright. Soon, the skids were replaced and the aircraft was back in service but we still weren't too sure about Tee. He took a lot of ribbing about "Tee and his O.D. Green submarine."

CHAPTER 35

Missions Other Than BDAs

While BDAs on B-52 strikes were the majority of our missions, we did have other operations we were involved in. One day we had a big combat assault in which a battalion of ARVN troops were to be airlifted into an LZ southwest of the town of Vi Thanh. The ARVN had requested that the U.S. Forces supply some scouts and Cobras to assist with LZ preparation since the VNAF (Vietnamese Air Force) did not have any.

I was tasked to be the Cobra section lead and Hugh Mills would lead the scout section. When we arrived at the air strip at Vi Thanh, it was already crowded with about 400 ARVN troops waiting for the VNAF Hueys to come in and pick them up. The troops were all milling around as we landed and pulled into the refueling point. When they were done with refueling, Hugh and the other scout repositioned to the middle of the field and shutdown so that Hugh could coordinated with the ARVN battalion commander on the details of the combat assault.

Once my section was done refueling, we repositioned next to the scouts and shutdown to await Hugh's briefing. During this time, we were surrounded by a flood of ARVN troops who were taking a close-up look at our Cobras and wandering around by the scout aircraft, as well.

Soon we saw Hugh heading our way and we grabbed our maps to mark them with the info from the briefing. Hugh stopped at his aircraft first then walked over to us. He spread out his map on my ammo bay door and proceeded to pass along the info we would need for the mission. Once he was done with the briefing, he turned to us and said there was another matter that he had to deal with. He explained that while he was with the battalion commander, someone had stolen his expensive 35mm SLR camera out of his aircraft and he was going back to the battalion commander to demand that the commander get it back from whichever one of his troops that took it. Hugh said, "Bob I need you and your wingman to takeoff and fly overhead in as threatening a manner as you can so that the battalion commander gets my message. Okay?"

"I've got you covered," was my reply.

As we took off, I saw Hugh talking with the ARVN commander. He had his hands on his hips and seemed to be giving Hugh a hard time. We climbed to about 1500 feet and I told my wingman that we would do some "practice" dry gun runs on the assembled crowd below. He rogered me and I rolled into a dive directly towards where Hugh and the commander were standing. I pulled out of my dive at about 30 feet over their heads and was going at maximum speed as I did so. The noise on the ground must have been deafening since everyone stopped talking and turned to watch me. As I began to zoom back to altitude I watched my wingman repeat the maneuver over the crowd.

The battalion commander had now climbed into the bed of a truck so he could be seen by all of his troops. I could see him gesturing wildly and then started stabbing his index finger and arm down towards the ground in front of him. Less than a minute had elapsed when I noticed a group of about six soldiers surrounding a seventh man and moving him towards where the battalion commander stood. The battalion commander jumped down off of the truck and walked over to the man. The man reached into his gear and pulled out a camera that was dangling from a strap and handed it to his commander. The commander took it, turned and handed it to Hugh who began to walk towards his aircraft. The commander then turned back to the man and slapped him so hard that the man's helmet flew off. He then said something to the six men around the thief who then grabbed him and began to drag him away. Though I did not see it, I suspect that the thief became another casualty of the war.

Just as Hugh was taking off, the VNAF Hueys began arriving to pick up their first sortie of troops. Hugh told us that since time was short, we would split up into two pink teams to do the recon of the LZ before the VNAF lift ships arrived. Hugh and I would do the east side of the LZ and my wingman and the other scout would do the west side.

Hugh dropped in and began reconning our sector as I assumed my protective position above and behind him. We had cleared almost half of our assigned area when we came upon an area that had been clear cut of all its trees. The area was about 100 meters wide and 200 meters long with some scrub trees starting to grow in it. Hugh dropped down into the area and was skimming over the brush in search of signs of enemy activity.

He interrupted his normal litany of reporting what he was observing by pausing briefly, then saying, "I think we have about 20 to 30 NVA walking along the treeline at my 12 o'clock, moving from left to right towards the LZ."

With his expertise and vast experience, when Hugh made a statement that started with "I think..." or "There could be..." it was not his way of voicing a suspicion as much as it was a statement of fact. As a result, I was already in a dive towards the treeline as Hugh called, "I'M TAKING FIRE, I'M TAKING HITS, I'M HIT!!"

The treeline was lit up with the twinkling of muzzle flashes as Hugh broke left, away from it. About the time he started transmitting that he was taking fire, I was already punching off rockets at the treeline. The enemy switched their aim from Hugh to me as I closed in on them. We could now hear the unpleasant sound of popcorn popping all around us as I continued to unload rockets into the treeline.

As much as I would have liked to continue hammering the bad guys, I had to break it off and rejoin Hugh. He said he thought that he could make it back to the airstrip at Vi Thanh but that he had been hit in the leg and didn't know if he could work the pedals for a landing. He told me his entire leg was numb and he was afraid to look at it in case it was really bad.

When we arrived at Vi Thanh, Hugh told me he was going to do a short running landing since that would preclude the need for any large pedal movements. The maneuver was a success and the aircraft came to a stop on the runway. I landed next to him, rolled my throttle to idle and jumped out with my aircraft's first aid kit. As I ran up to his aircraft I saw that Hugh's crew chief was helping him out of his seat. Hugh stood there on one leg and held the injured leg just off the ground. I was expecting to see a lot of blood but there was none. The heel of his jump boot was missing but I saw no other damage. While looking away, Hugh asked, "How's it look?"

The crew chief and I exchanged glances and I said, "Not too bad. Let me take a closer look." I came up next to him and lifted his leg like a blacksmith shoeing a horse and saw that the only "damage" detectable was the missing boot heel. I had Hugh take off his boot and we inspected his foot and leg but there were no bullet holes anywhere. He apologized for the drama and said that the feeling was starting to return to his leg. It was then that he became very irate at the enemy for "ruining a brand new pair of jump boots." I was sure the bad guys would pay dearly for this insult at some future date.

It wasn't long after Hugh's "wounded boot" incident that we received a mission to provide cover for one of the CH-47 Chinooks that were based at Can Tho with us. They had been tasked with moving some artillery pieces around for the ARVN and requested that "Charlie," 16th Cav provide a section of Cobras to protect them as they flew this mission. I was selected to lead our section of Cobras on the mission and we joined up with the Chinook after he completed picking up the 105mm howitzer he was to deliver to the ARVN compound at Ca Mau, a town about 70 miles south of Can Tho, near the southern tip of the country. The flight down to Ca Mau was uneventful but as the Chinook, with its howitzer hanging under it on a sling load, began its turn for final approach to the artillery compound, it started taking fire.

Apparently, the local NVA troops were thinking, "We don't want no stinkin' howitzers around here," and unloaded on the heavily laden ship.

The Chinook pilot immediately started screaming, "WE'RE TAKING FIRE, WE'RE TAKING HITS!!"

I rolled into a dive towards a clump of trees that I saw a few muzzle flashes come from, and fired a couple of pairs of rockets at it but was distracted by the Chinook. He had rolled into a near 90 degree bank in order to turn around quickly to get away from where the enemy gunners were. As he was in this bank, the sling that the howitzer was suspended on was nearly parallel to the horizon. It was at this point that the pilot decided to lighten his load to get better maneuverability out of his aircraft. He punched off his sling load and the howitzer went flying off, tumbling end over end as it headed earthward. The oddest thing was that it was headed straight for the clump of trees that I saw the muzzle flashes coming from. I had to stop shooting just to watch what was about to happen. The Chinook was passing by my right side heading in the opposite direction for the safety of the artillery compound, while I watched the howitzer continue on its ballistic trajectory toward the clump of trees. I imagined that right about now there were some enemy gunners that were pooping in their pants as that huge hunk of metal soared towards them.

The cannon hit the ground about 30 meters in front of the enemy position, threw up a huge geyser of black mud and then bounced back into the air. It then plowed its way through the treetops directly over the enemy position, shattering branches and obliterating leaves. It hit the ground again just behind the clump of trees, sending up another geyser of mud. It tumbled end over end a few more times and came to rest in the middle of the field. I thought, "Hey! This could be a new Olympic sport, Bowling with Cannons!"

I fired a few more rockets into the clump of trees and my wingman followed suite. We then headed for the artillery compound to see how the Chinook had fared. As we were landing, the Chinook pilot told us that his copilot had been hit in the foot by one of the rounds and needed to be medevaced. He said his aircraft was not flyable due to the

the number of hits it had taken. Then he asked if one of us could fly the injured man back to Can Tho since there was no medical facility here and his copilot was in considerable pain. I said, "You bet."

I told my copilot that he would have to wait here while I flew the injured man back to Can Tho but that I would notify operations as soon as we got within radio range and they would send a Huey down to get him. He wasn't thrilled with the idea but understood. I told my wingman to remain behind and provide as much cover for the compound as he could, just in case the bad guys decided to try something else.

They had removed the man's boot and applied a temporary dressing to the wound and then loaded him into my front seat. I could tell he was in significant pain by the grimace on his face as they helped him into position. They plugged in his helmet, fastened his seat belt and closed the canopy and we were off. I pulled in maximum power and coaxed as much airspeed out of my machine as I could. We were averaging between 145 to 150 knots as we headed north. Even at that speed, it was going to take nearly 30 minutes to make the trip. I felt sorry for the guy as I heard him groaning in the front seat over the noise of the aircraft.

I called ahead and told operations what had happened and asked them to notify the hospital that I was inbound. They said they would and that they would coordinate with the Chinook unit to send a recovery team to Ca Mau.

As I got close to Can Tho, I called the tower and told them I was about 5 minutes to the south. They already knew I was coming and cleared me to land on the big red cross of the Medevac pad. As I set down on the pad, about 8 medical personnel came running up to the aircraft, extracted my passenger, laid him on a gurney and wheeled him toward the hospital. He was in good hands now and would get something for his pain very soon. I repositioned my aircraft back across the runway to our revetments and called it a day.

CHAPTER 36

The Moc Hoa Operation

W e were all called into a major briefing one day in June and told we would be conducting a large operation, involving a lot of our aircraft and crews and this mission might extend for several days depending on the resistance we found in the targeted area. Our operations officer explained that the area of concern was near the town of Moc Hoa, which was about 50 miles north of Can Tho and 50 miles west of Saigon. It was near a bend in the Cambodian border called "The Parrot's Beak" because of the way the border looked on a map. Intelligence reports said that the NVA were coming across the border there and infiltrating the town in preparation for an assault on Saigon. The airstrip just outside the town was still held by a small contingent of ARVN forces and we would be using it to stage our operation.

The next morning, we took off for Moc Hoa with a package that contained six Cobras, four scouts and six Hueys with their "Blues" infantry platoon on board. One of the Hueys was also the Command and Control aircraft and the Air Mission Commander (AMC) aboard it was none other than my roommate, Rod Willis.

As the flight turned final for the airstrip, I called Rod and said that I would keep my section airborne while the rest of them landed and refueled. This would provide some security while they were on the ground and vulnerable. He agreed with me and my wingman and I broke off to circle the airstrip and keep an eye out for trouble.

After the others had landed and moved into the refueling points, I was coming around the airstrip's south side and watching the activity on the ground when something caught my attention further up to the north. As I focused on the movement, I saw the distinctive trail of smoke from enemy 122mm rockets being launched from the vicinity of a French style villa about six miles to the north and just across the Cambodian border.

I immediately broadcast a warning to all those on the ground to take cover because of the incoming rounds. At the same time, I pulled in maximum power and headed toward the launch site. As I passed the strip, I saw the rockets impact around the airfield but luckily, none of them hit near any of our aircraft. I could have fired on the villa but I couldn't be sure if the launch site was the villa or somewhere beyond it. The villa was situated in a relatively wide open area, surrounded by fields and a few clumps of trees. I thought that the launch site may have been a clump of trees about 100 meters north of the villa so I held my fire until I could positively identify the target.

It took us about 2 minutes to cover the distance to the villa. During that time no other rockets had been launched but I was prepared to fire on the site if they began firing again. We circled the villa once and did not see any activity, so, I flew to the clump of trees to the north to check it out. Still nothing.

We returned to the villa and I told my wingman to stay at 1500 feet while I dropped down to check out the villa more closely. We had become a pink team and I was now the scout. As I circled the compound a second time, I saw that there were black streaks on the ground in the courtyard that I was sure were made by enemy rockets. As I climbed back to altitude, I decided that the villa was in serious need of being blown up.

As I was briefing my wingman on my attack plan, several of the scouts and other Cobras, accompanied by Rod in the C&C Huey, arrived. Rod had overheard my plan and said to hold off, he was sending in the scouts to check it out. He told me to head back to the airstrip to get refueled in case this turned into an extensive operation. He said he couldn't bring the other Hueys with the Blues platoon because "ground forces" weren't allowed in Cambodia. I rogered him and headed for the Moc Hoa airstrip.

I was about halfway done hot refueling my aircraft when I looked to the north and saw the entire flight of Cobras, scouts and the lone Huey heading my way. All the other aircraft seemed to be following a lone scout that was leading the group. As they got closer, I could see that the leader was having difficulty flying the aircraft and his flight path was getting more erratic as he got closer. He was about 150 feet short of my position as he attempted to set the Loach down on the runway. It was then that I noticed several large bullet holes in his windshield just before he crashed. He hit very hard and the rotor blades flexed downward and cut off the tailboom sending it skidding to the edge of the runway. The rotor blades were broken and flopping around wildly since the engine was still running. I dropped the fueling hose and started running toward the stricken craft but stopped abruptly as I saw Rod jump out of his Huey that he had landed next to the Loach. He ducked under the swirling blades, got to the pilot and started to assist him out of the aircraft. The crew chief was okay and had managed to get clear of the aircraft on his own. As Rod began to drag the pilot clear of the wreckage, a rotor blade snapped in half, dropped down and hit Rod right across the middle of his back, sending him flying across the pavement.

I started running again but by the time I got there, others were tending to Rod and the scout pilot, who had managed to crawled clear of the wreckage. Rod was alive but in serious pain. The scout pilot's face was all cut up by flying plexiglass but he would survive. I turned to someone and asked, "What happened?"

The other pilot replied, "He started taking heavy antiaircraft machine gun fire from the villa, just after you guys left. We all escorted him back here when he was hit."

I asked, "Did the Cobras take out the villa?"

He answered, "No, they fired a few rounds to break contact then flew back here with us."

I quickly decided that I was taking all the Cobras back to the villa to level the place. I rounded them up and we all took off within a couple of minutes. We climbed to a safe altitude and began taking turns on dumping every rocket we had into the villa. It was soon reduced to rubble and several fires were burning. As we flew back to Moc Hoa, I wondered why the enemy gunner had not shot at me while I was low and slow during my initial recon. Oh! Well, I guess he won't make that mistake again.

Rod and the scout pilot were flown back to the hospital and we continued our original mission. Our operations officer assumed Rod's position and we began searching for the NVA that were reported to be in the area. Some of the local people our scouts talked to said that the bad guys were hold up in a community south of town and the airstrip. I had noted this little, square village on our way into Moc Hoa and thought that it looked strangely out of place. It was in the middle of a forested area but was, itself, treeless. The 40, or so, hooches were all lined up in rows with a space between them large enough for another hooche. There were several rows of these thatched roof huts, making the whole community look something like a checkerboard.

The scouts started at one end of the village, checking out the hooches to see if there was any evidence of bad guys in the area. Some of them would use the tip of their skid to lift the corner of the roof on a hut to look inside. It did not take long before they started to take fire from inside the hooches. (Imagine that!) The scouts would scatter, we would roll in and shoot at the hooche and the bad guys inside would vacate the premises, split up, then run into another hooche. It became like a game of concentration. We had to try to remember which hooches the bad guys ran into so we could shoot them on our next pass. Actually, the process was more like the popular arcade game, Whack-a-Mole. The bad guys would shoot at us from one hooche, we'd shoot back, they'd run to another, we'd shoot that one, they'd run again, sometimes back to the first hooche, and on and on and on. This was getting us nowhere.

I finally recommended to our new C&C that we start at one corner of the village and destroy each hooche and work our way to the other corner. Quick math told me we had over 400 rockets between the six Cobras and could accomplish the task before we needed to rearm or refuel, IF we did it methodically.

He vetoed the idea because, "There might be civilians in some of those hooches."

I thought, "And the moon might be made of green cheese, but I doubt it."

I flew over 10 hours that day and other than blowing up the French villa that morning, I felt we accomplished little or nothing. We returned to Can Tho that night and prepared to do the whole thing again the next day.

It proved to be a repeat of the Whack-a-Mole game we had already played. When my section got low on ammo, I told the C&C we were heading to Dong Tam to rearm and refuel since Moc Hoa was getting low on rockets. Dong Tam was an old U.S. Army airfield to our south, that was now being maintained by ARVN forces, and had plenty of fuel and rockets. We climbed to 3000 feet as we headed for it, just to be on the safe side, since there were so many bad guys in the area. 3000 feet put us above the effective range of all small arms weapons and even many of the heavy antiaircraft machine guns we'd been encountering lately.

It took about ten minutes to get there and as we lined up on final and prior to starting our descent, I prepared to make an advisory call about our intentions to land. This was a required call to warn other aircraft, since there was no longer a manned control tower at the airfield. As I keyed the mike and began to talk, BANG!

It sounded like my copilot, in the front seat, had dropped a hammer on the floor. I looked into the small mirror that was mounted to his right, and saw his wide eyes looking back, and asked, "Did you drop something?"

He said, "No! I was hoping you did."

Right about that time, I began hearing a low whining sound that quickly increased in intensity until it was almost deafening. Suddenly, the noise stopped and the MASTER CAUTION light illuminated, accompanied by a segment light on the warning panel. The segment light announced that our #2 HYD SYS (number 2 hydraulic system) had failed. I knew that this meant we had to land as quickly as possible, just in case the # 1 system also failed, since that would likely be disastrous.

I was pretty sure we had been hit by ground fire and wondered what else the bullet might have damaged besides the hydraulics. I keyed the mike again but changed my planned call a bit by saying, "This is Darkhorse 38, a flight of two Cobras, two miles west of Dong Tam, declaring an emergency, landing at Dong Tam."

I did a running landing just in case the other hydraulic system failed. Had I tried hovering and the other system failed, we would have crashed. I shut down the aircraft on the runway but knew this would not be a problem since there were no other aircraft in the area. My wingman landed next to me and we determined that I had, indeed, taken a .30 caliber bullet just under the forward fuel tank. While we were not leaking any fuel (self sealing tanks) we were still leaking bright red hydraulic fluid. I asked my wingman to takeoff, climb to altitude over the airfield and call our operations office at Can Tho to tell them what had happened and request maintenance come up to fix my bird. I said, "While you're up there, you'd better call the C&C ship at Moc Hoa and let them know we won't be back up there today."

When he landed again, he said that maintenance was on the way and would be here shortly with some new hydraulic lines and fluid. Then he broke the news that our operations officer in the C&C at Moc Hoa had requested that we return as soon as possible because things were getting out of hand up there and they needed all the help they could get. I was very disappointed to hear that. Especially since I knew that without any large numbers of friendly ground forces, we had little or no chance of stopping the flow of enemy forces and equipment across the border. The whole operation was simply a waste of time.

About 20 minutes later, a Cobra came in, landed and hovered over to us. It was the maintenance officer and a mechanic. The maintenance officer said that I was to take his Cobra, rearm and refuel, then go back to Moc Hoa and rejoin the others up there.

We refueled and were in the process of loading rockets into the empty tubes as the maintenance officer walked up and handed me something. It was the AK-47 round that had hit us. He said that they traced the path of the bullet to see what else it had hit. The round had entered the bottom of the aircraft, severed the # 2 hydraulic line, entered the bottom of the forward fuel tank, angled forward and exited the tank about halfway up, went through the floor of the cockpit between my legs and hit the bottom of my armor plated seat. He found the round resting on the floor under the seat. He added that the round was so spent when it got to my seat, that it barely put a dent in it. I sure am glad that we decided to fly at 3000 feet on our way to Dong Tam.

CHAPTER 37

Time Out!

N ear the end of June, I got a letter from my wife, Nancy, and when I opened it I noticed that a picture was enclosed. Before reading the letter I glanced at the picture and saw my mother-in-law, Alma, seated on the left. In the middle was Nancy's sister-in-law, Louise Cliff, who was holding my 1 year old daughter, Kimberly. On the right side was a woman I did not know and thought it must be one of Nancy's friends. There was nothing on the back of the photo but the date. I began reading the letter and abruptly looked back at the photo because the letter said it was a picture of, "Mom, Louise and me with Kim."

The person on the right in the photo looked very little like the wife I had left behind. The person in the photo was much thinner than my wife, her face was drawn and my initial impression was of a POW from WWII. (I'll pay for this later, believe me!) I couldn't even schedule a M.A.R.S. call to talk to her since there wasn't a station left at Can Tho and the turn around time on mail was nearly two weeks. Something was wrong and I had to get home.

I went to my commanding officer and explained my situation. I took the photo with me and another earlier photo for comparison purposes. He looked them over and said, "You have to go home!"

Because of all my moving around during this tour of duty, I had not taken an R&R or any leave time and was overdue for a break. The CO said he would approve a two week leave and I could go as soon as I made my travel plans.

I found out that Pan American Airways was flying the relatively new jumbo jet, the Boeing 747, on it's globe circling routes and these flights flew through Saigon every day. I booked myself on Clipper Flight #2, the eastbound flight, and got one of our Hueys to drop me off at Tan Son Nhut International Airport in Saigon. I was on my way home after 9 months in country. Because of all the abuse soldiers had been taking from our fellow citizens while traveling in uniform (some were actually shot and killed), the military said it was okay to travel in civilian clothes now. I quickly changed into "Civies" just before boarding my flight. At least I wouldn't be spit on or shot while flying home. Who needed the NVA or other terrorists, we had our fellow citizens to worry about!

When I got to Los Angeles, I surprised my wife by calling her to say I was on my way home and gave her the flight info for my arrival at JFK. I landed at Kennedy a few hours later and seeing her in person confirmed my suspicions. She was much thinner and the stress of raising two kids alone was taking its toll. We scheduled some doctor visits and they did some lab tests but the results would not be back before I was scheduled to return to Vietnam. I called Warrant Officer Branch in Washington and explained my situation and they approved a two week extension of my leave. They said they would let my commander know.

After several weeks of good food and some help in taking care of the kids, Nancy was looking better and seemed to be in much better spirits. While she was sad that I had to go back, I reminded her that I only had two months left on my tour of duty and I would be back, for good, in just 60 days. She said she'd be okay and she was sure she could make it another 60 days, so, I was off on Clipper Flight #1, westbound, back to Saigon.

My flight landed at Tan Son Nhut just after noon. I changed back into my uniform and walked across the street to Hotel 3, the American helipad next to the airport. I tried to contact my unit on the land line (military phone system) but I couldn't get through. I told the duty officer that my unit did not know I was coming back and I needed to try to call one of our aircraft to see if they could come by and pick me up.

He said, "Sure, let's give it a try. Come with me." He lead me up the stairs into the control tower where they had a bunch of radios set up. He turned and asked me, "What's the frequency?"

I told him, he dialed it in and handed me the microphone saying, "It's all yours."

I made a blanket call on our unit's frequency saying, "Any Darkhorse aircraft, this is Darkhorse 38, do you read me?"

Almost immediately a response came back saying, "Darkhorse 38??? Where are you?"

It was the voice of one of our other Air Mission Commanders. I answered him by saying, "I'm in Saigon at Hotel 3 and I need a ride home. I just got back in country a few minutes ago."

Somewhat shocked, he replied, "Well, I'll be..., we didn't think you were coming back. Yeah, no problem. We're working out near Moc Hoa and I'll have one of our aircraft come by and pick you up when we're done here. It'll be a couple of hours though. See you at the club tonight and you can tell us all about it. Good to have you back!"

I said, "Okay! I'll see you at the club. Darkhorse 38, out"

The duty officer told me I could hang out in the lounge downstairs until my ride showed up. He said one of the tower controllers would let me know when a Darkhorse aircraft showed up.

I was napping in the lounge when one of the controller shook me awake saying, "Sir, there is a Darkhorse Loach landing on the 'Hot Spot' to pick you up." I thanked him, gathered my gear and walked out just as the Loach was landing.

It was Tee and I immediately became concerned. His crew chief had caught a ride home with one of the other aircraft to make room for me and my luggage. I was hoping that he had gone back to staying hydrated with a couple of beers each day and started looking for empty cans as I threw my gear into the back seat. No cans here. I climbed into the left front seat and strapped in and pulled my harness a little tighter than normal, just in case. I pulled on the helmet I found there, plugged in and said, "Hi!" to Tee on the intercom. He said, "Hi!" And asked if I was ready to go. I paused for a second, since I wasn't quite sure of the answer, but eventually said, "Yeah!"

Tee took off and headed south towards Can Tho. So far, he seemed okay and we began catching up on what had been going on. I told him that everything was okay with my wife and he started telling me about the missions we were still doing in Moc Hoa.

As we flew along, I started to become concerned again. Tee was flying at about 800 to 1000 feet above the ground. This was an altitude commonly called "The Dead Man's Zone" since it was well within the range and accuracy of most enemy weapons. The best altitudes to fly at were either above 1500 feet or on the treetops but not where we were. My guess was that Tee was still on the wagon.

I said, "Hey! Tee, why don't we go up above 1500 feet, just to be safe?"

His reply was, "Nah. We're okay right here. Besides, you know us scout pilots, we don't like getting too high."

This time I said, "Well, let's go down to the treetops so we can see things up close."

He persisted, "Nah. That's too much work." I tried again but he blew it off and went back to telling me about the missions at Moc Hoa.

The 30 minute flight to Can Tho was starting to feel longer than my flight from JFK. I couldn't wait for it to be over. About halfway back, I had settled in, accepted my fate and started watching the country go by. I looked up ahead and saw a man step out from under a corrugated tin roof shed. He held a long tool in his hands that was currently pointed down on a 45 degree angle towards the ground. We were about 1000 meters from his position and would fly almost directly over him. He slowly turned to face us and began raising the "tool" to his shoulder. As the angle of light changed on the "Tool", I could now make out that it was really a Rocket Propelled Grenade Launcher and he was aiming it at us.

I know I lost my cool but I started yelling at Tee, "HE'S GOING TO SHOOT AT US, DO SOMETHING!"

Tee's reply was a chuckle followed by, "Yeah. He's shootin' at us." But he took NO evasive action!

I was about to grab the controls in an attempt at self preservation but I saw the back blast of the launcher as the grenade streaked toward us. I didn't know whether to continue to get on the controls or cover my eyes with my hands and, actually, did neither.

Luckily, the round exploded just below our aircraft causing us to go over the largest speed bump I have ever experienced. As we settled back into our unwavering flightpath, Tee keyed the intercom and said, simply, "He missed."

I was about to go nuts and strangle the life out of my fellow pilot when I noticed that the man on the ground was rapidly reloading his launcher. We were just about to pass over the man as I saw him raise the weapon to his shoulder and take aim at us again. Was this really happening or was it some sort of very bizarre dream I was having in the lounge at Hotel 3 during my nap?

I leaned out my door and looked back at the man as he fired his second round. NOPE! It was REALLY HAPPENING! It was kind of like when people say they couldn't look away from a train wreck that was about to happen. I couldn't take my eyes off of the inbound grenade.

It looked like it was coming straight for us but at the last second it streaked past my door, across the windshield and exploded about 30 feet above us.

I was so shocked at our close call that I couldn't say a word. But Tee managed a few words of wisdom.

"He missed, AGAIN!" Was his brilliant observation.

I didn't think there was enough bourbon in the world to make me forget about my trip back to Can Tho, but I was going to get started that night in an attempt to find out.

CHAPTER 38

The Cement Plant

The next day, I officially checked back into the unit while I nursed my hangover. The CO welcomed me back and said he was glad I was here because we were losing a lot of our experienced pilots. They were all coming up on their DEROS dates and going home and we weren't getting any replacements. Hell of a way to run a war, I thought.

He explained that the majority of our missions were still BDAs on B-52 strikes and our continuing mission to stem the flow of bad guys and equipment coming across the border near Moc Hoa. He added that on top of everything else, we were expected, by our higher headquarters, to have a "Ready Reaction" team on standby, 24 hours a day, to react to any big flare ups that might occur throughout IV Corps (The Delta, a very big area). I couldn't help but think that those guys in the Head Shed were as nuts as my taxi driver, Tee. It must be in the water, I thought. I made a mental note to stick to the bourbon.

Over the next few days, I flew several BDAs on the B-52 strikes that continued to hammer The Delta. Almost all produced nothing worth noting. I did get tasked to go back to Moc Hoa on one mission, but nothing had changed there. We were still playing Whack-A-Mole with little change in the outcome. A very addictive game, apparently.

One day, my section was tasked to be the Cobra section on the Ready Reaction team. I thought, "Just like when I was with Blue Max on my first tour but we weren't required to be off the ground in under two minutes. A piece of cake!"

The commitment time ran from 6am one day, till 6 am the next. I guess that meant no bourbon tonight. We had gotten through the entire day and I'd gone to bed that night without any alerts. At 3 am, someone was rudely shaking my shoulder, trying to wake me up. It was the duty sergeant and he was saying, "Mr. Hartley, you have to wake up. We have an emergency and you need to launch your section."

I rolled over and was promptly blinded by the sergeant's flashlight as I asked, "Is this some kind of trick one of the practical jokers put you up to?"

The sergeant said, "Oh! No, Sir. I would never do that. They really need you."

I said, "Okay, okay. I'm coming." I rolled to an upright position and began pulling on my boots, a luxury during sleeping I didn't have in my Blue Max days.

I was close behind the sergeant as he headed back towards operations. When I walked into ops, Captain Ken Hibl was there, reviewing some maps. He had been designated as the Air Mission Commander for our Ready Reaction Team that day and would be in charge of whatever we were required to do. My wingman for the day, Warrant Officer Danny Wright showed up, still wiping sleep out of his eyes.

When Ken saw me, he immediately began to brief me on our mission.

He said, "Bob, we have to fly to Ha Tien to extract a U.S. Army Major that is an adviser to a battalion of ARVN soldiers that have managed to get themselves surrounded by a regiment, or more, of NVA."

I thought, "Oh! Is that all? Three helicopters against 800 to 1000 NVA soldiers, no problem, we should be home in time for breakfast."

In actuality, I said, "What? Are you frigging kidding me!!??" Was this the start of the invasion to overthrow the the country? I felt like the little dutch boy, putting his finger in the dike to stop the invading ocean. This could be IT! With resolve I thought, "Theirs is not to reason why, Theirs is but to do and..." I couldn't finish the Tennyson quote, especially since our 3 helicopters weren't exactly a light brigade.

Ken and I decided that since Ha Tien was over 100 miles away, we would have to stop at the small ARVN airfield at Rach Gia to refuel before continuing on to Ha Tien. Ken explained that the Major and the ARVN battalion were holed up in a cement plant near the city. He planned on me providing cover while he swooped in and landed on the roof of the plant, picked up the major and hauled ass out of there. He explained that higher, higher headquarters were only interested in saving the Major's life and didn't really care what happened to the ARVN forces afterward. I thought, "Okay! It's finally coming down to the brass tacks in this war."

Ken asked, "Any questions?"

I replied, "Nope. Let's go." And we headed out the door to our aircraft.

We landed at Rach Gia as planned, got fuel and were off the ground and heading for Ha Tien again within 15 minutes. Dawn was just starting to break as we arrived over the cement plant. It was a large building that covered an area equivalent to a football field and we could see the exchange of tracers that was taking place, quite a distance away.

Ken called the Major and got an almost immediate reply. He explained the plan for the extraction and asked the Major what area on the roof would be best for him to land on.

The Major responded with, "They may let you come in and land but they will never let you leave. There are at least four 12.7mm heavy machine guns situated around the plant and besides that, they have been firing RPGs into here since this thing started. It would be suicide for me to crawl into your aircraft."

Ken asked him, "Okay, sir, what do you want me to do? My orders are to get you out of here."

"I would like to put your Cobras to work and maybe we can blow a hole in their lines and all of us can get out of here," he replied.

Ken asked me what I thought, on a separate radio, and I told him we would give it a try. He called the Major back and said, "They are all yours. My lead Cobra is Darkhorse Three Eight and he is monitoring this frequency."

The Major said, "Hey, Darkhorse 38, I think the best place to start is about halfway up the southern most marble to our west. You may be able to make out a small cave there, and the NVA have a 12.7mm machine gun in the entrance that has been giving us a real hard time. If you can take him out it will really help."

About 200 meters to the west of the plant were two limestone mountains, actually, they were more like pillars similar to Devil's Tower in Wyoming. They were being used to mine the limestone used in making the cement at the plant and were commonly referred to as "marbles." Each of the towers were about 300 to 400 feet tall and about 100 feet in diameter. They were sparsely covered with some brush type vegetation and rocks and boulders were scattered around their bases. Much of the tracer fire that was going into the plant was coming from behind these boulders. By dawn's early light, I could see the cave quite plainly and saw some movement there. I stood off about 4 kilometers to stay out of range of the gun, lined up on the cave and fired 3 pairs of rockets, aiming them just over the entrance. They hit exactly where I had intended and the entire cave collapsed. That gun would no longer be a problem. I called the Major and said, "Okay! What's next?"

He said, "Whoa! That was great. Nice shooting. Well, the next big problem we have is the hundreds of troops they have that are scattered around the base of the marbles. The bad guys are hiding behind the boulders and we can't get a clear shot at them. Any ideas?"

I told him that we would go around behind them and attack from west to east, forcing the bad guys to move around the boulders for protection. That would give the ARVN forces in the plant a clear shot at the enemy's backside and, quite literally, put them between a rock and a hard place. The Major liked the plan and said he would brief the

ARVN on it. The Major then told us that he knew of three additional 12.7mm machine guns in the area but he was not able to pinpoint their locations. He knew two were to the east of the plant and one was to the north, so, we should be careful in those areas.

I said, "Thanks for the info, we'll deal with them later. We are planning to break right from our dives, so, that should keep us away from those guns since we'll be heading out over the Gulf of Thailand. Let me know when your guys are ready."

"We're ready when you are," he answered.

I rolled into a dive and began shooting rockets, scattering them around the area, in an attempt to get as many of the bad guys to move around the boulders as possible. As I was firing, I could see the muzzle flashes and tracers coming out of the cement plant and they were hitting in the same area as my rockets. I knew the NVA soldiers were now having a very bad day. My wingman, Danny, and I took turns dumping rockets on the area and the ARVN kept up their barrage from the plant.

Soon, we were low on rockets and fuel and I told the Major we would have to break station and go reload. I told him we would be gone for about 30 minutes and asked if he thought they'd be okay for that long. He told me they'd be fine but were starting to get low on ammunition, so, please hurry. Ken said he still had plenty of fuel left, so, he'd stay in the area. Danny and I headed off to a small, ARVN run, resupply point about 10 minutes away. After refueling, we hovered over to some CONEX containers that had rockets stored in them. I landed next to one and immediately began loading up the 10 pound HE rockets we found inside. Meanwhile, Danny had landed next to a container further down the line, pulled open the doors and started yelling at me with obvious joy in his voice. I couldn't understand what he was saying over the noise of my still running aircraft, so, I yelled back, "WHAT?"

He decided to show me instead of shouting. He reached into the container and pulled out a rocket with a Flechette warhead on it, held it up for me to see, smiled, then mouthed the word, "NAILS."

"YES!!" I thought, just what we needed. I motioned back for him to load his inboard pods with a full complement of Nails and he gave me a thumbs up and got to work. A few minutes later we both took off with our inboard rocket pods full of Nails and our outboards full of 10 pound high explosive rounds. On our way back to the cement plant, I told Danny that we were going to dispense with standard tactics and would split up. One of us would roll in from the east and the other from the west firing the Nails we had just acquired between the two marbles from opposite directions. This way, I said, the bad guys would have nowhere to hide and we could cover the entire area in one pass. Danny agreed.

When we arrived back at the cement plant, I checked in with the Major and asked if anything had changed. He informed me that we must have hurt them with our two pronged attack last time because they seemed to be bringing up reinforcements.

"Ah! Perfect," I thought. I told the Major our plan and said that he needed to make sure all his people were under cover and kept their heads down as we fired the Nails. He assured me they would.

As we were flying in from the east, I told Danny to hang back and when I got past the marbles, I would roll in from the west and he could roll in from the east at the same time. I said, "You break right when you pull out and so will I, that way we won't have to worry about running into each other."

"Sounds good to me." said Danny.

I rolled into my dive and saw Danny do the same off to the east. We each fired about half of our Nails and broke to the right. We joined back up and I called the Major to see if everyone in the plant was okay. He replied, "Yup. Everyone in here is okay, but it sounds kind of quiet outside. We are going to do some 'recon by fire' to see if they'll shoot back."

I rogered his transmission and saw the tracers emerge from the plant and start ricocheting off of the boulders but saw no return fire. They waited a few minutes and tried it again with the same result. The Major called and said they were sending out a patrol to check it out. "Please keep them covered in case they start taking fire," he requested. I told him we had their backs.

We saw the patrol of about 12 men leave the building and immediately take cover behind some equipment next to the plant. Groups of three men would sprint from one object that provided cover to another and they gradually moved up into the rocky area between the marbles. They were now just walking upright and not bothering to seek shelter. I called the Major to see if he had heard from them and he replied, "I'm out here with them and I have to tell you guys that you did an awesome job. There are bodies everywhere. We're trying to come up with a body count right now. There is no one left alive."

Ken and I weren't very happy that the Major went on the patrol without telling us but we were pleased with the damage that Danny and I had done to the enemy. The Major called us back and said, "Well, a preliminary count shows you guys killed over 500 NVA and it's pretty appalling down here. Because of political considerations, I'm going to give you a body count of 245 KIA and my ARVN counterparts a total of 255 kills, but I'm telling you that almost all of these are yours. I didn't know those Nails were so lethal. It's kind of scary."

Ken called the Major and asked if he wanted to be extracted from the area now since it was safe enough to land but the Major said, "No, I think I'll stay here. We are going to kick ass on what's left of this regiment. I just found out from my counterpart that additional ARVN forces are going to start arriving by helicopter at any moment."

We were told by our command that we were to stay around and help as much as possible as the new ARVN troops began arriving in the area. We did manage to locate and destroy two of the three remaining 12.7 machine guns in the area and the new ARVN troops together with the ones from the cement plant were routing the remnants of the NVA regiment.

Late that afternoon, we were released to return to Can Tho. Several Chinooks from our neighbor unit at Can Tho had been involved with flying in some of the additional ARVN troops and they had been released also. As we tried to catch up with them to fly back home together, one of them called to say his copilot had just been shot in the head. Apparently, the one 12.7 machine gun that we couldn't find, had gotten in a lucky (or unlucky) shot, just as we were at the extreme eastern edge of his range. I still kick myself for not finding that gun.

Several months after I got home to the States, I got an envelop in the mail from Warrant Officer branch in Washington. It contained orders awarding me the Vietnamese Cross of Gallantry for our actions at the cement plant. I would much rather have had a live Chinook pilot around to enjoy a beer with.

A few days after the cement plant action, my commanding officer called me into his office at Can Tho and said, "I have something for you. Congratulations." And handed me some papers. I looked at them and it was my DEROS orders. The CO then said, "They are curtailing everyone's tour of duty and you got a six week drop. Now you can go home and take care of your wife and kids. Thanks for all your help."

It was over! I was on my way home for good. While I would certainly miss most of the people I had been stationed with, I wouldn't miss this place. Goodbye Vietnam!

EPILOGUE

After returning from Vietnam the second time, I was assigned to Ft. Rucker, Alabama, the home of Army Aviation and affectionately known as "Mother Rucker" by all who serve there. I was ordered there to attend the Aviation Warrant Officer Intermediate Course which was a career development program. Strangely enough, Nancy was pregnant again and our third child was due in August of 1973. While I had completed my course in July, Nancy's doctors decided she was too far along to travel to our next assignment, so, we waited.

My buddy and former roommate, Carl Heinze and his wife Kathy were also stuck at Mother Rucker at this time. Carl and I had attended the Intermediate Course together and he was now waiting for a follow on course to start while I was waiting for a child. Since the Army wouldn't let us just stay home and do nothing, we were assigned as duty officers and we alternated nights being on one and off the next. The job involved sitting in for the commander during the overnight hours and making any "command" decisions that arose during that time. We would annotate all incidents in the official duty log and brief the commander in the morning. It wasn't a tough job, just boring.

About 9 pm on the 5th of August, I was on duty and got a phone call from Nancy saying it was time to go. I called Carl and he came in to take my duty while Kathy went to our house to watch Rob and Kim. I drove Nancy to Lyster Army Hospital where she was admitted and set up in the labor room. Her doctor arrived a short while later and, after checking on Nancy, he asked if I would like to be in the delivery room for the birth. Since I had not been present for the births of my other two children and since I had just been through two combat tours, I thought, "How bad could it be?" and promptly said, "Yes" to the doctor.

When it was time, the doctor had me gown up and we all went into the delivery room together. I sat next to Nancy, holding her right hand with my left. After several very strong contractions, the doctor said, "I can see the head. One more good push should do it." At this point, Nancy blurted out several profanities about the doctor's questionable lineage, screamed, took a deep breath and began to push. As she bear down, she wanted me to share in the joy of birth and pulled my hand toward her mouth and promptly bit it. It was not a little nibble, it was what "Jaws" did to her prey. I opened my mouth to scream but just a gurgle came out. The doctor and the nurse stopped what they were doing and stared at Nancy with their eyes bulging out. I'm sure their mouths were hanging open beneath their surgical masks as well. As if on cue, our daughter Kris popped into the world at that very moment, simultaneously relieving Nancy's pain and mine as well.

The doctor handed Kris to the nurse and asked if I would like to cut the cord. I think he did this so I would have an excuse for removing my hand from Nancy's so I wouldn't be subjected to another round with the wood chipper. After I cut the cord, the doctor looked over my hand and declared I would be fine though a bit sore for a few days. I thought that this was appropriate since I knew Nancy would be sore for a few days as well. And so, began the life of Kristen Marie Hartley.

After a week or so, the doctor declared mother and daughter fit for travel and we headed for our next duty station, Fort Knox, Kentucky. I was assigned to a newly formed attack helicopter company that was being created to deploy to West Germany in three years. Currently the unit had 21 AH-1G Cobra helicopters but would be outfitted with 21 AH-1Q Cobras prior to deployment. The AH-1Q was a heavily modified Cobra that now was equipped with the TOW missile system. TOW stood for Tube launched, Optically tracked, Wire guided missile.

The TOW missile was capable of destroying any known armor vehicle in the world. All the gunner needed to do was to hold the cross hairs, in his gyro stabilized 13 power sight, on the target until the missile hit it. The advent of this system would have a dramatic effect on the "Cold War" in Europe since it gave the U.S. and our allies a rapid response capability to thwart any large Russian armored invasion of the West.

For three years at Fort Knox we trained, developed tactics and were very heavily scrutinized by those in Washington. We must have done well because in early 1976 our helicopters were loaded aboard seagoing barges and shipped to Germany with all of the rest of us going on military contract flights to Frankfurt.

We were assigned to the 3rd Infantry Division in Wurzburg just northwest of Nuremberg. Division headquarters had us set up shop at an old Nazi airbase near the town of Geibelstadt. This airbase had been used by the first jet powered fighter-interceptor, the Me-262, developed by the Nazis toward the end of WWII. It was also renown as the base that Francis Gary Powers flew his U-2 spy plane from prior to being shot down over the Soviet Union in 1960. A lot of history here.

After we had settled in and gotten all our aircraft flying again, it was time to go to the aerial gunnery range and check out our weapons systems to make sure they were in proper working order. We were sent to Grafenwoehr training area near the Czech border. Each pilot in the unit was required to shoot a TOW missile and hit a target to be certified as "Current" in the weapon system. As we were conducting this range operation, we were notified that a VIP would be joining us to observe. I was told that the VIP would ride in my front seat to observe the firing of a missile from one of our other Cobras. They said the VIP was General George Patton, the son of the famous WWII General of the same name.

With the General on board, I hovered next to a Cobra that fired a TOW at a decommissioned tank that was one of the targets on the range. To add insult to injury, the target tank was an M-46 "Patton" tank. The gunners had been using the white star on the side of the turret as an aiming point and this missile hit it dead center from more than 2 miles away. Afterward, I flew the General down to the target tank so he could view the damage. The turret was covered with holds punched through it by the missiles. He said to me on the intercom, "Okay! I've seen enough, we can go back now."

After we landed and shutdown, the General came up to me and said, "I think that what I have seen today signals the end of the dominance of armor on the modern battlefield. I think that you and your fellow pilots are the wave of the future. Thank you for enlightening me."

I replied, "Well Sir, as you know, it takes a combined arms team to be successful in battle. The infantry can't do it alone, neither can armor or artillery assets. Our helicopters are just one more tool for a commander to use to achieve success."

He thought for a moment then said, "Well, thank you for that, son. I appreciate it." We exchanged salutes and he walked away.

After I completed those three years in Germany, I was assigned to Fort Hood, Texas and the 6ᵗʰ Cavalry Brigade. While there, our unit participated in some classified testing on the Tonopah test ranges near Area 51 and Nellis Air Force Base in Nevada. Very interesting stuff.

In 1981 I was promoted to CW4, the highest rank, at that time, for a warrant officer. I was also selected to attend the Warrant Officer Senior Course at Fort Rucker, Alabama. The Warrant Officer branch assignments officer called me to ask what I wanted to do after the Senior Course. He said I could have a transition course to the AH-64 Apache, the new attack helicopter, or he could send me to the fixed wing qualification course to learn to fly airplanes. I chose airplanes since I had already spent 15 years in attack helicopters and I still had a dream of being an airline pilot someday.

Upon completion of my courses, I was assigned to the 207ᵗʰ Aviation Company at Heidelberg, Germany. The unit's mission was to provide aviation transportation to the four star general that was Commander in Chief, United States Army, Europe (CINC, USAREUR), his staff and visiting dignitaries. Our area of operations was throughout Europe, North Africa and the Middle East. To accomplish this task, we were provided with a fleet of UH-1H Hueys, UH-60 Blackhawk helicopters and Beechcraft C-12 executive turboprop airplanes.

A year after arriving in the unit, I was appointed as one of the CINC's pilots-in-command of the C-12 airplane and flew the general regularly throughout our area of operations. In May of 1984, I and the rest of my crew of the C-12, were assigned to support the White House Flight Detachment during President Reagan's trip to Europe for the G-8 conference in London and the 40th anniversary ceremonies commemorating D-Day at the American Cemetery overlooking the beaches of Normandy.

During this assignment I reported directly to the Chief of White House Flight Support, a full colonel. I was tasked to fly Secret Service personnel along with White House communications specialists between London, Shannon, Ireland and Cherbourg, France. On the 5th of June, the colonel told me that due to security requirements, the President needed to be able to board Air Force One within a very limited amount of time if a crisis arose. He continued, saying that because the helicopters that were flying him to Normandy from London could not return him to Air Force One in the required amount of time, I would have to sit standby as "Army One" at Deauville airport in Normandy because my aircraft could cover the distance in the required time frame. Even though the events of the day did not require me to actually fly the president, I was honored, just the same.

After completing my tour of duty in Germany I was reassigned to Fort Hood, Texas. There, I was appointed as pilot-in-command of the commanding general's C-12 airplane and flew him throughout the United States and even to Guantanamo Bay, Cuba. As I was preparing to retire, Warrant Officer Branch called me and said, "If you stay in the Army we will promote you to the newly authorized rank of Master Warrant Officer (MWO-5)." I asked them what commitment I would have to give them for the "honor" and they said another two years. Since I already had been offered a pilot's job at Pan Am, I declined the nomination.

After 22 years of flying for the Army, I retired in February of 1989 and was hired by Pan American World Airways. Pan Am at that time was splitting its new hires into two groups. One group was trained as flight engineers on the Boeing 727 (which was a non flying position) while the other group was sent to Pan Am's regional airline, Pan Am Express. At Express, the deal was that after four years you would go directly to the right (Copilot's) seat of a Boeing 727 jetliner, skipping the flight engineer position altogether. I was in the group sent to Express and was trained on the De Havilland Dash-7 short takeoff and landing (STOL), 50 passenger, four engine turboprop airplane. We flew out of JFK airport in New York as far north as Maine, as far south as Richmond, Virginia and as far west as Columbus, Ohio.

A year after being hired, I was certified by the FAA as a Captain on the Dash-7. This checkout allowed me to boast that I was a Captain on one of Pan Am's last four engine propeller driven airplanes. Unfortunately, two years after that, Pan Am went out of business and our Express operation was bought by the corporate raider, Carl Icahn of TWA. Many of us began seeking employment elsewhere and I was lucky enough to be hired by Northwest Airlines. I flew as copilot on the Douglas DC-9 for five years and then in the same position on the Airbus A-320 until I retired in 2002.

During my aviation career, I was privileged to fly over our nation many times and observe her beauty from above. I still remember scenes like the New York City skyline, the snow capped Rocky Mountains, the Grand Canyon and the azure blue waters of the Florida peninsula. Quite often we would be cruising along, looking out our cockpit windows and admiring the awesome view when I would begin to chuckle. My fellow pilot would invariably ask me, "What's so funny?" while looking at me a bit strangely. I would then explain that while looking at the scenery, the words of my high school Latin teacher came to mind. When Ms. Davis caught me staring out the window on a beautiful spring day she said, "Mr. Hartley, no one will ever pay you to look out a window!!" She was wrong. Actually, they paid me quite well to do exactly that.

Life is good!!

GLOSSARY

Agent Orange: A herbicide sprayed by aircraft on the jungles of Vietnam to defoliate the trees so enemy activity could better be observed. Years later it was discovered to cause severe health problems and birth defects in humans exposed to it.

Aircraft Commander: A crewmember designated on orders and responsible for all decisions while airborne. He may be out ranked by other crew members on board the aircraft but ultimately is in charge.

AK-47: Soviet or Chinese made semi-automatic and fully automatic assault rifle carried by most North Vietnamese and Viet Cong soldiers.

ARVN: Pronounced Are-vin. The Army of the Republic of Vietnam. South Vietnamese soldiers allied with U.S. Forces to defeat the communist North Vietnamese.

Autorotation: A state of flight in a helicopter that allows the rotors to continue turning even though the engine has failed. It is similar to an airplane gliding and upon reaching the ground the helicopter can be smoothly landed by using the inertia in the rotor to cushion the landing. A hovering autorotation uses the remaining energy in the rotor to "cushion" a landing if the engine fails at a hover.

Base Camp: A semi-permanent base of operations for large tactical units like brigades and divisions.

Battery: An artillery unit consisting of approximately 100 personnel.

Bingo Fuel: The minimum amount of fuel required for an aircraft or helicopter to safely return to its base of operations.

Blivet: A rubber bladder used to store fuel at temporary locations and refueling points.

Chicken Plate: Slang for the body armor worn by aircrew members. It consisted of a metal plate that had a frangible ceramic plate bonded to it and covered with a fiberglass skin. The whole thing was then inserted into a cloth vest that was secured to the wearer by Velcro straps. Pilots worn a single plate over their upper torso since they sat in an armor plated seat. Crew chiefs and door gunners wore two plates, one in front and one covering their back. A single plate weighed about 30 pounds and would stop a .30 caliber bullet.

CO: The commanding officer.

Collective: The collective pitch control. It is the lever in the pilot's left hand and controls the amount of pitch applied simultaneously to all blades in the rotor system of a helicopter. By pulling up on it the helicopter will rise off the ground to a hover.

Concertina wire: A type of barbed wire or razor wire that comes in large rolls and is used for security on the perimeters of base camps and fire bases.

Conex Container: A large corrugated metal shipping or storage container.

Crash Crew: Fire trucks and firemen specifically trained in aircraft firefighting and crew rescue.

CS Gas: Military grade riot gas that is much stronger than Mace or pepper spray.

Cyclic Stick: The helicopter control stick mounted to the floor between the pilot's legs. It works like the stick in an airplane. Left and right to turn, forward to move forward or dive and aft to raise the nose or slowdown and pull out of a dive.

Effective Translational Lift: The extra lift provided to a helicopter's rotor system because of forward movement from a hover. This phenomenon occurs at about 16 to 24 knots and dramatically reduces the amount of power needed to fly.

EOD: Explosive Ordnance Disposal. Teams of personnel specifically trained on the safe handling and disposal of all types of unexploded ordnance.

FAC: Forward Air Controller. An Air Force pilot flying a slow single engine O-1 Bird Dog or a twin engine O-2 Skymaster or OV-10 Bronco that would mark targets for the high performance fighter-bomber jets.

Fire Base: Normally a small cleared area with a concertina wire security fence around it that contained a field artillery unit. It could vary in size from 20 meters in diameter to several hundred meters depending on the size of the unit occupying it.

Fire Mission: A preparatory alert order for a firing artillery battery. Once received from higher headquarters, the firing battery would man its weapons and prepare to fire them in support of friendly ground forces.

Flak: Antiaircraft artillery shells set to explode at varying altitudes.

Ho Chi Minh Trail: A network of roads and trails running from North Vietnam through Laos and Cambodia and into South Vietnam to provide personnel and materials to the communist insurgents trying to overthrow the South Vietnamese government.

Howitzer: An artillery piece that typically fires at a high angle and is used in indirect fires.

IMC: Instrument Meteorological Conditions. The condition where visual reference to the ground or horizon is lost due to intervening clouds, fog, heavy rain, snow or smoke. This condition forces the pilot to fly the aircraft using only the instruments in the cockpit.

LRRPS: Pronounced Lerps. Long Range Reconnaissance Patrols. Teams of usually five specially trained infantrymen that patrol the jungle looking for enemy units. Once the enemy is located, the team follows them for days, reporting on their activities and other information.

LZ: Landing Zone. Normally a small clearing large enough to land at least one helicopter. Sometimes large enough to land many helicopters at once. Occasionally, they become secured areas and may become base camps as more units are brought in.

Marking Pair: A single pair of rockets fired to mark a target. The supported ground unit then issues adjustments to the firing aircraft to move the impact of the next rounds onto the enemy position. A single pair is fired to limit casualties to friendly units in case the firing aircraft has misidentified the target.

Monkey Strap: A safety cord worn by a crewmember in the cargo compartment of an aircraft to prevent an inadvertent fall overboard while moving about the compartment.

Monsoons: A seasonal wind that brings weather changes. The northeast monsoon during the winter months brings low clouds, cool temperatures and heavy rains to the northern sections of South Vietnam. The southwest monsoon brings fair weather with heavy afternoon and evening thunderstorms during the summer months.

NVA: The North Vietnamese Army. Communist insurgents attempting to overthrow the South Vietnamese government.

Pop Smoke: A command to a ground unit to throw out a smoke grenade for identification purposes.

Running Landing: A helicopter maneuver that simulates an airplane landing but at a much slower speed. It is used in emergency situations to preclude the large control movements and power changes necessary to bring a helicopter to a hover.

Salvo: In attack helicopters it means to fire all remaining rockets in a ripple fire with about two tenths of a second between subsequent launches of each rocket. An entire 19 shot rocket pod can be emptied in about three seconds.

Section Leader: The pilot in charge of a section of two attack helicopters on a combat mission. The section leader is responsible for all aspects of the tactical employment of the section.

Target Fixation: A phenomenon where a pilot of an attacking aircraft becomes so mesmerized and fixated on destroying the target that he flies right into it.

Triple Canopy Jungle: Mostly found in the mountains of Vietnam, the first set of shorter trees have their canopy at between 40 and 60 feet above the ground. The next set of somewhat taller trees have their canopy at about 100 feet above the ground and the tallest trees have their canopy at about 150 feet above the ground. The foliage can be so dense that it is like night on the ground below these trees during midday.

UHF, VHF and FM Radios: The three different radios used to communicate in our helicopters. UHF radios were used to communicate with the Air Force and certain control towers, the VHF radios were used to communicate between our aircraft and the FM radios were used to communicate with the ground troops.

VNAF: The Vietnamese Air Force. (South Vietnam)

Warrant Officer: Highly skilled technical experts in their field. They are ranked above all enlisted men but below regular officers like lieutenants, captains, majors, etc. Their ranks include Warrant Officer (WO1), Chief Warrant Officer (CW2, 3, and 4) and Master Warrant Officer (MWO-5).

XO: Executive Officer. The second highest ranking officer in a unit after the Commanding Officer.

ABOUT THE AUTHOR

Robert F. Hartley

Photo Courtesy of Tom Cerzan at Cerzan Studios

Robert F. Hartley retired from the United States Army at the rank of CW4 after 22 years of service and two combat tours of duty in Vietnam as an attack helicopter pilot. Bob's military awards and decorations include the Distinguished Flying Cross, two Bronze Star Medals, two Meritorious Service Medals, 38 Air Medals, an Army Commendation Medal for Valor, the Vietnamese Cross of Gallantry as well as Master Army Aviator Wings.

Mr. Hartley is a graduate of Embry-Riddle Aeronautical University with a Bachelor of Science degree in Professional Aeronautics. He holds an Airline Transport Pilot's Certificate from the Federal Aviation

Administration and is Type Certified in the DeHavilland Dash 7, the ATR 42/72, and the British Aerospace Jetstream 3100. He is also qualified on the Douglas DC-9 and Airbus A-319/320 commercial jet aircraft.

He was hired by Pan Am World Airways and served as an airline captain for their Express operation. After Pan Am went out of business, he flew for Northwest Airlines for seven years before he retired. While at Northwest, he was awarded the Northwest Airlines Medal of Honor for Heroism for saving the lives of the passengers and crew of a severely crippled DC-9 jetliner during an in-flight emergency.

Bob has accumulated over 14,000 hours of flight time during his aviation career and now lives near Orlando, Florida with his wife of 47 years, Nancy. They have three children and four grandchildren.